# Table of Contents

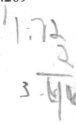

# Introduction  *

Serial killers; they cross the bounds of darkest evil. They murder at random without logic or reason other than the one twisting in their sick and evil minds. They are diabolical vile creatures devoid of morality or pity. You will meet a chosen few of them in these pages. We will see that serial killers are roaming among us all, from small towns to big cities. They are not limited to a particular place, gene pool, culture, social class or religion. They are not restricted to any particular demographic, political propensity and they can be of any gender.

We have adopted in this anthology the FBI-NCAVC 2005 San Antonio Symposium definition of serial killer as an individual who has murdered two or more people on separate occasions with a cooling off period between murders (this cooling off period varies with each serial killer). They kill for many different reasons, from sexual gratification to profit, anger, hate and thrills. Despite this new lower two-victim threshold for serial killers, it is not an exaggeration to claim that the handful of few serial killers chosen for this anthology collectively amassed at least five hundred victims and probably more.

As you will read in this anthology, serial killers commit grotesque acts of murder and mutilation but they are not insane; they coldly know what they do and go to any ends to cover their tracks. Serial killers are popularly thought to be of high intelligence, but studies reveal the opposite. While they score low to middle on Intelligence Quotient (IQ) tests, many are possessed of an animal cunning and charisma which makes them seem super intelligent.

Some of the serial killers chosen for this first annual Serial Killers True Crime Anthology you might have heard of and we present their tales in new ways. Others have not graced every newspaper, tabloid or television screen and represent tales of true crime horror told in detail for the first time in these pages. Five of true crime's most prolific authors have come together in these pages to present their most compelling cases of serial homicide, famous and not so famous.

Along the male serial monsters described here, you will also discover serial killers who were historically expected to be nurturers in our society: women to whom children looked to for assurance, comfort and security and instead found death and torture. One in nearly every six serial killers is a woman. Celebrated British author Sylvia Perrini has penned some of the most cutting-edge books on female serial killers and she delves here into the murderous exploits of Martha Wise whose preferred method of choice was arsenic poisoning, and Mary Bell who killed her first victim when little Mary was eleven-years-old, perhaps the youngest serial killer ever on record.

The history of serial killers goes back to the dawn of time when humans first walked the earth. Criminal justice historian and bestselling author Peter Vronsky compares the serial killer brain to a fictional zombie's brain to explain why human serial killers exist while describing his brief encounter with serial killer Richard Cottingham, "The Torso Killer," in his article "Serial Killer Zombie Apocalypse and the Dawn of the Less Dead: An Introduction to Sexual Serial Murder Today."

Bestselling master true crime author Michael Newton brings us the story of the Blood Countess Elizabeth Bathory, a Hungarian aristocrat who bathed in the blood of virgin peasant girls because she thought it preserved her beauty; Bathory perhaps is the most ruthless female serial killer to have ever lived. Michael Newton also tells the tales of former Sweetwater, Florida, Police Officer Manuel Pardo, a rare serial killer cop and the story of death row's "Nazi Transvestite," Frank Spisak.

Taking a step back in time, serial killers have plagued the United States since its founding in 1776. Notable author Dane Ladwig reveals an engaging and fascinating view into a pioneering family of serial killers as he excavates and probes the Midwest of America's heartland and retraces the steps of the "first-family" of serial killing, the Bloody Benders. He also reveals the mind of a serial killer in an up-close and personal interview with convicted rapist and serial killer, Timothy "TK" Wayne Krajcir.

Award winning bestseller true crime author and indie publisher RJ Parker examines and searches through the convoluted minds of serial killers such as the Bible-quoting pig farmer Robert Pickton and the recent case of Anthony Sowell the "Cleveland Strangler," two of the most notorious recent fiends to plague our communities in search of victims to prey upon.

Our collaboration to present accounts of some of the most malicious inhuman predators and the stories of their innocent tragic victims marks the first of a proposed annual Serial Killer True Crime Anthology. We look forward to bringing you the next volume in this series. Please visit the authors websites listed in their "Bio" where you can gain a broader view of their past and current projects.

Our most sincere gratitude, Sylvia Perrini, Peter Vronsky, Michael Newton, Dane Ladwig, RJ Parker.

# Prologue

*Serial Killer Zombie Apocalypse and the Dawn of the Less Dead:*

*An Introduction to Sexual Serial Murder Today*
**by Peter Vronsky**

\*\*\*

I am an American and I killed Americans.
I am a human being, and I killed human beings;
and I did it in *my* society.
**Edmund Kemper**[1]

In the beginning was the Word...
**The Gospel of John, 1:1**

\*\*\*

Some serial killers are like drooling zombies with bared teeth driven by primitive hunger to attack, bite, rape, kill, rape again, mutilate, dismember, harvest or eat body parts from the corpses of their victims in a weirdly ritualistic and compulsive instinctual frenzy. I believe that zombie stories today are about serial killing in the same way as in the past tales of vampires, werewolves, demons, and ghouls were often really about unidentified human monsters roaming among us: serial killers, lust murderers and necrophiles.[2] They were monsters for us because the term "serial killer" and "serial murder" and its cultural construct were not in popular usage until a mere thirty years ago when the *New York Times* first began using it in the spring of 1981 to describe the crimes of Wayne Williams in Atlanta.[3] Until then it was a term occasionally raised in crime literature or proposed by a pioneering few in the close-knit law enforcement and criminal justice communities of California and Pacific Northwest awash at the time in unsolved sequential homicides that seemed similar to each other but could not be linked together.[4]

Slowly shuffling up on us in the 1950s and 1960s, serial killers were overrunning us in what seemed like zombie waves by the 1970s and 1980s. By the mid-1980s Congress declared war on a "serial killer epidemic" in response to claims that there might be hundreds of unidentified serial killers murdering as many as 4,000 victims a year.[5] The FBI received funding to beef-up its Behavioral Science Unit (BSU) and to build a massive data collection and analysis system: Violent Criminal Apprehension Program (ViCAP). In the end the claims of thousands of serial killer victims annually turned out to be an exaggerated misinterpretation of homicide statistics. These claims and reports, nevertheless, left a deep impression on our paranoid public psyche and fear-selling media. With 'ordinary' homicide rates escalating an astounding 300% in the twenty year period between 1970 and 1990, there was an accompanying peak of unsolved motiveless stranger-on-stranger killings; it certainly *felt* like there was an epidemic of thousands of serial killings all around us; Americans were dying in plague of unsolved homicides. As for actual serial killing cases, they were and remain so today, statistically an extremely rare phenomenon. A recent study identified 63 serial killer apprehensions in the US in 1997-2007, confirming some later updated 'post-epidemic' annual victim rates reported by the FBI in the next decade of the 1990s. Collectively these offenders were responsible for a yearly average of 75 serial killing victims a year, hardly thousands, but still an unsettling number of victims. (Of the 63 serial killers, 19 had been killing for over ten years and 8 for over 15 years prior to being apprehended.)[6] But we are not out of the woods yet.

While some sources argue that serial murder has been declining since the 1990s, along with the dramatic drop in general of murder in the USA, from a historic high of 24,760 homicides in 1993 down to 14,612 by 2011, other sources contend that the rate of serial killings might actually be increasing.[7] According to serial

8

homicide expert Eric Hickey "we have more cases of serial killers in eleven years [2000-2011] than we did in the previous 25 [1975-2000]."[8] Hickey is also concerned by the continued rising rate of unsolved stranger-on-stranger homicides, some linked to recent unidentified serial perpetrators on the loose like the "Long Island Killer" suspected in as many as thirteen recent murders, the "Bone Collector" linked to thirteen murders in New Mexico, or the "February 9 Killer" who has killed at least two women in Salt Lake City on the same date in different years.[9] The ditches and roadsides of the American interstate freeway system alone are the scene of so many unsolved homicides over the last thirty years-- almost 500--that the FBI in 2009-2011 launched a special Highway Serial Killings Initiative (HSKI) targeting serial killers suspected to be working as truckers.[10] At least twenty-five truckers in the past have been convicted in serial homicide cases while the HSKI is investigating a suspect list with over 275 names currently on it, almost all long-haul truckers.[11]    With the trucking industry's adoption of GPS tracking and logbook data keeping, the FBI is reconstructing the past movements of suspected truckers by linking their trucking data to unsolved homicide occurrences and their locations in the hope of identifying some of the killers.

The result is that while serial killers are indeed still rare, their rate of increase might be escalating upwards toward some kind of critical mass still awaiting us in the future; hopefully in the *near* future, before it reaches the apocalyptic epidemic proportions algorithmically guaranteed if the current claimed rate of increase does not abate.

This rise of serial killing since the 1950s is awe inspiring in its scope and virality. Of all the known identified male serial killers in the United States since 1800, a period of two hundred years, 84% appeared in the last fifty-four years in 1950-2004.[12]    It is no coincidence that the movie that gave rise to our current apocalyptic zombie genre, George A. Romero's *Night of the Living Dead,* was made in 1968, a particularly weird and nasty year in that rising wave of violence in America in all of its many mutating forms and colors, from serial killing to mass murder, assassination, riot, race and sex crimes and military atrocities overseas in Vietnam, all televised, live SNUFF TV on the news in our living rooms. And 1968 was just the beginning! There was still Charlie Manson to come in the summer of 1969 and forthcoming 1970s were going to make *Night of the Living Dead* look downright sweet and utopian in the face of the serial killer zombie apocalypse to come.

\*\*\*

### The biogenics of the serial killer zombie brain

Today almost fifty years after *The Night of the Living Dead,* we understand that if you take away the supernatural qualities of zombies--the idea that the dead can be undead--zombie and serial killer behaviour is physiologically and biogenically rooted in the same anatomical place. Zombie hunger and serial killer sexual cannibalism is imbedded in the most primitive part of the human brain, the unthinking part, a small knot at the base of our brain, the 'basal ganglia' (or 'basal nuclei')--also called the 'R-complex' or the "reptilian brain."[13]

Like a prehistoric archeological ruin, the lobes of our brain consist of three temporal layers, like three separate brains from different eras, stacked and wired together in a loop, each layer more ancient and primitive than the next. They call it the 'triune brain'. From lizards, snakes and birds to cats and dogs and lions and apes and humanoids like us, the primordial R-complex is the part of the brain that drives a set of instinctual self-preserving and reproductive behaviors essential to the survival of any species: running away, killing, eating and having sex. Until relatively recently in evolution, the human reptilian brain did not 'choose' these behaviors but was instinctually driven to perform them mindlessly. Pioneering Yale neuroscientist Paul D. Maclean described the functioning of the R-complex as a "primitive interplay of oral, aggressive and sexual behavior."[14] Since no species can survive without the functioning of these instincts they are very deeply "hardwired" into the core of our mind and brain, into our "souls" if you like, driving us like a hidden coiled spring to run away, fight, bite, eat or mate and reproduce.

This 'zombie' R-complex reptilian brain interacts with a newer, more evolutionary advanced and complex 'limbic system' part of the brain, a part that hosts emotions, long term memory and sensory and motor functions. It is the part of our brain that sees, hears, tastes and smells things, and feels raw emotions like anger, pride, humiliation, desire, sadness, love, hate, loneliness, compassion, etc. The limbic system is wired down to our R-complex and sends sensory and emotional signals which trigger in the reptilian cells of a healthy human brain the appropriate '4F survival response': Flee, Fight, Feast or Fuck.

Making things more complex for humans, however, is even a newer, more developed third layer to our brain, a uniquely mammalian 'neocortex' that can overdrive both the lower R-complex and the limbic system. Our ultra-high intellectual abilities like language, logic, reasoning, the artistic and creative impulse, abstract thinking, rationalization, imagination and fantasy, are all rooted in the neocortex. Unlike animals, humans have a highly evolved neocortex capability of making philosophical-spiritual, cultural and psychological interconnections to the limbic system emotions and the lower R-complex reptilian impulses; it is why the concept "good and evil" is non-existent in the animal world driven by hunger and instinct alone.

This capacity to reason, deduct, deduce, abstract, project, imagine and fantasize, produces a layer of conceptual 'rational' (or sick 'irrational') modulators of how limbic system functions might be interpreted or neurotransmitted to the reptilian brain and to which part of it, the run, kill, eat or sex part. Our three brain layers are constantly input-outputting between each other, triggering reptilian instincts through the emotional, memorial and sensory circuits of the limbic system while moderating and analysing them--rationalizing them (or conversely distorting them--irrationalizing) through conceptual capacitors of the neocortex. The triune brain is a type of triangular cerebral slave trade loop. In other words, there is a lot of wiring that can go wrong between these three diverse systems working with each other, each one more archaic and simplistic than the other. One short circuit and the whole thing can go spinning homicidally out of control, especially in the old reptilian part that should have been upgraded in male humans long ago.

In a serial killer's brain if the higher limbic system 'misfires' or gets distorted or damaged by lack of infantile bonding, formative childhood trauma, sexual or physical abuse, by unbearably bad memories, rejection, abandonment, lack of familial stability or maybe by physical blows to the head or exposure to violent media and pornography or substance abuse or some organic brain disorder or chromosome abnormality or blood or urine chemistry, allergy, (etc., etc.)--the result often is sex and aggression linking and merging. Nobody knows for sure how and why. We have some good ideas how, but *exactly* how is unsettled as experts battle out how to interpret the data and *which* data. Today we still do not understand completely how sex and aggression fuse and intertwine with death, torture and cannibalism. In his 1886 book *Psychopathia Sexualis,* published two years before the "Jack the Ripper" Whitechapel murders in London, the pioneer of forensic psychiatry Richard Kraft-Ebbing named this fusing process "paraesthesia" describing it as "abnormal emotional coloring of the sexual impulse." It was Kraft-Ebbing who coined the term "sadism" to describe the paraesthesia between aggression and the sexual reproductive instinct.

As forensic psychiatrist James Money more recently explains, "The limbic region of the brain is responsible...for predation and attack in defense of both the self and the species. In the disease of sexual sadism, the brain becomes pathologically activated to transmit messages of attack simultaneously with messages of sexual arousal and mating behavior."[15] Another sums it up more simply, "The predatory serial killer is literally a limbically kindled 'engine of destruction'. He won't stop and he doesn't want to because nothing in life could possibly replace the thrill of dominating and destroying..."[16]

We depend on the limbic system and the neo-cortex to keep the instincts apart but the system keeps crashing. In California, after killing his fraternal grandparents in 1964 at the age of fifteen on an impulse ("I just wondered how it would feel to shoot grandma") and a five year confinement in a psychiatric facility, after his "cure" and release, Edmund Kemper in 1972-1973 killed, dismembered, beheaded and raped (in precisely that order) six hitchhiking college coeds. He ended his series of murders after killing, dismembering and raping his mother and her friend who dropped in for a visit and then surrendering to police. In a prison interview Kemper described how his dual reptilian brain operated when it came to women he found attractive, "One side of me says, 'Wow, what a pretty chick, I'd like to talk to her, date her.' The other side of me says, 'I wonder how her head would look like on a stick.'"[17]

***

*"I am an American and I killed Americans. I am a human being and I killed human beings..." Edmund Kemper after his surrender to police in the murder and dismemberment in Santa Cruz, California, of six female hitchhikers, his mother and her female acquaintance.*

*A serial killer's lust bite on the back of the leg behind the knee of child victim murdered in Toronto, Canada, 1956.*

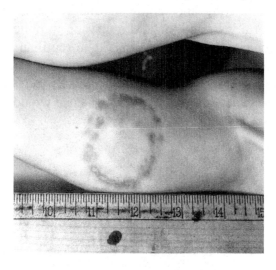

*Lust torso cleaving, organ harvesting and disembowelment of a female victim with raw [uncooked] cannibalism perpetrated by Andrei Chikatilo in Russia, circa 1980s.*

\*\*\*

The problem is that (notwithstanding the claims of 'creationists') human beings emerged from an evolutionary line of prehistoric humanoid species which had to constantly run and fight and bite and kill and eat and chew and rape like zombie apes to survive for over two million years. We were lean and mean and in a perpetual mindless state of anger, fear, hunger and arousal. It was only a 100,000 years ago that we finally successfully killed, ate and fucked our way to the top of the animal food chain, emerging as the aristocrat *Homo sapien* species which dominate the planet today. We did this by killing and/or raping in a prehistoric act of genocide a co-existing rival humanoid species, the *Homo Neanderthals* (Neanderthal Man), the DNA traces of which have been recently discovered in humans.[18] This genocidal episode is probably transmitted from our primordial memories to us today in the form of the biblical passages about Cain murdering Abel in *Genesis 4*.

One theory of why *Homo sapiens* evolved to survive out of all the other perished erect-walking humanoid species that roamed the planet for two million years, is that around a 100,000 years ago we developed *necrophobia*--a fear and aversion to death and the dead within our own species—the opposite pole to *necrophilia*. As an evolutionary device *necrophobia* functioned as an inhibitor of intraspecies aggression and cannibalism and behaviourally gave rise to emotional and social constructs like mourning our deceased, compassion for our weak, ill and aged, and an aversion to, repulsion and fear of corpses. [19] Rather than looking at the weak and the dead as a source of food and a subject for forced sex, we instead developed notions of familial love, charity, kindness, empathy and respect for the aged and other positive social constructs towards members of our families, tribes, and species (and a genocidal hate and fear of anything that wasn't ours.) We developed a value system where except for certain specific circumstances, killing within our own species became "murder." In other words, the reason other humanoid species did not survive, is because they serial killed each other out of existence. Serial killing became "bad" or "evil" for *Homo sapiens* because it was anti-evolutionary. (It can be argued that the current rise of serial killers can be perhaps attributed to a new evolutionary prerogative for the demise of our species; Mother Nature's little way of saying, in among several other ways, that there might be too many humans on the planet.)

To put things into chronological perspective, after two million years it is only in the last 40,000 years that we started to do something strange that no other living things on the planet did or do today; we started to store information outside of our brain in the form of cave drawings and later written language. We developed the imaginative capacities of our neocortex and simultaneously began to draw together our families, clans and tribes into highly organized societies. Only in the last 10,000 years have we became broadly "civilized" as a species and started to build cities, write, count, plant food and domesticate animals instead of exerting huge energy and time to gathering and hunting for food.

In this new civilized world killing became strictly confined within political, legalistic and moral-religious parameters, as was sex, while intraspecies feeding became "cannibalism" and was highly discouraged and taboo. Over the last 3,000 years, in the Mediterranean region we codified these values in the form of Judeo-Christian ethics that prevail in post-industrial Western civilization today while other civilizations in their own regions, the Islamic, Eastern, Buddhist, Hindu, Animist, Confucian, (and even agnostic-atheist culture), all developed very similar universal ethical precepts unanimously proscribing murder, rape and cannibalism. And only 500 years ago with the Guttenberg press that humans have been able to share and distribute knowledge and ideas on a mass scale in the form of printed text, as you are currently reading it here; and only 300 years ago with the Enlightenment have we affirmed that each human is equal in their fundamental right to life, liberty and the pursuit of happiness and that the most noble exercise of power was for the strong to protect the weak, rather than dominate, exploit, destroy, rape or eat them. Humans began to routinely fly 100 years ago and a mere 40 years ago our evolutionary intelligence transformed us into an extra-terrestrial species with brief primitive visits to the Moon; and finally, only about 30 years ago, we found a word for something monstrous that had always been there with us from the beginning, gave the word meaning, and transformed it into a totem in public consciousness, discourse and collective psyche; and the word was "serial killer."

When you stack two million years of reptilian brain-driven killing, eating and raping against thirty years of our forensic concept of 'serial killer,' we are going to be falling behind for some time to come before we understand this phenomenon, let alone figure out how to deal with this thing that is increasingly circling us, snatching from our midst the lost, the weak, the unlucky and the less dead when dead.

***

## Making the Word

While serial killing had been around for aeons, even before the Bible, and the term "serial killer" had been occasionally used in law enforcement and in a few literary sources in the 20th century, for the average person the word only began to enter into popular usage in 1981 when the 'serial killer' construct first appeared in the pages of the *New York Times* to describe Wayne Williams, suspected in the murders of 31 children in Atlanta in 1979-1981.[20] If the *New York Times* is America's national paper of record then Wayne Williams is our first 'serial killer of record' even though in the end he was convicted of murdering only two adult victims (until recently, unless he killed a minimum three, he was not even 'officially' a convicted serial killer.) But before the word in 1981, there was not the thing, and until we had the word for it, serial killers were perceived as simply something insane or supernatural, akin to evil, unimaginable, indescribable, inexplicable, uncontrollable, namelessly "monstrous" like the supernaturally invincible slasher Jason. In fact, the first *Friday The 13th* movie came out in 'pre-serial killer era' 1980.)

It means that if you are over the age of thirty-five, the way I am, you might remember a world without serial killers, a world when they were rare Hitchcock movie madmen and fiendish ghouls with no explanation. That's how it was for me when in December 1979, before the Word, I was briefly 'bumped' by a monster by the name of Richard Cottingham in the lobby of a New York City hotel I was checking into, as he was fleeing the scene of

17

his crime upstairs, an episode I described in my first book on serial killers, *Serial Killers: The Method and Madness of Monsters.*[21]

Cottingham was a Manhattan insurance company computer data technician by day, the "Times Square Ripper" and "Torso Killer" by night. He drugged women's drinks in bars or picked up street prostitutes, playing the dumb john, buying them dinner which he would lace with date rape drugs when they weren't looking. He would then walk the groggy women to his car and drive out to seedy hotels and motels in New York and New Jersey and 'help' his staggering victims up to a room, close the door and viciously rape and torture them to death. Cottingham was a particularly rare ultra-vicious category of serial killer--'anger-excitation or sadistic-lust type'--which comprises only a small seven percent of both serial and single sexual murderers.[22] For Cottingham it wasn't about the killing at all but everything about the torture and control. He did not care if his victims lived or died, and therefore some of Cottingham stronger victims survived. Once Cottingham was spent he would leave his victims like garbage to him on the floor of the hotel room or dumped in parking lots or on roadsides where they would regain consciousness. Others simply died from the torture. Towards the end he began to mutilate the corpses of those that died, as an act of final disdain for the victims he felt were not "strong enough" to take the punishment he meted out.

When I encountered him in the elevator doors of the hotel lobby on a Sunday morning in early December, he was all glassy eyed and sweaty leaving the scene of a double murder on the fourth floor. He smelt of something like BBQ lighter fluid fumes. He had lured two Times Square street sex workers up to his room, probably one at a time, raped and tortured them to death, sawed off their hands and heads which he took away with him while laying out their torsos on the twin beds and setting them on fire. In the smoke of the room a responding FDNY fireman attempted to give a victim mouth-to-mouth resuscitation only to find a bloody gapping neck stump where her head once was. He required treatment for post-traumatic shock afterwards.

\*\*\*

*Richard Cottingham, the "Times Square Ripper" during his trial for some of the six homicides he will be convicted of.*

*In December 1979 Cottingham raped and tortured to death two of his victims in this W 42nd Street hotel.*

*Cottingham crime scene photos of the decapitated victims in the hotel room show severe signs of torture prior to his cutting off their heads and hands and setting their torsos on fire. The body parts were never recovered and one of the victims remains unidentified to this day.*

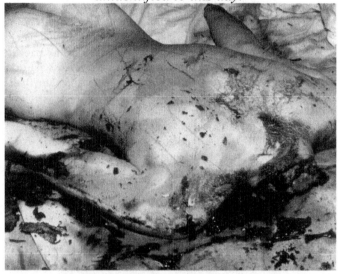

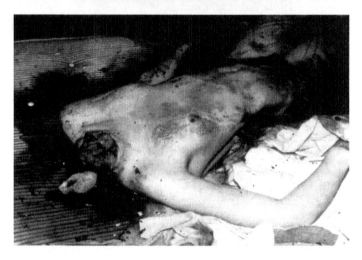

\*\*\*

Shortly after the torso double murder, Cottingham killed a prostitute in another Manhattan hotel and left her severed breasts posed on the bed headboard. He left the battered and handcuffed corpse of a victim in a New Jersey hotel room jammed under the bed to be discovered by the housekeeper in the morning. Cottingham was so invisible that he returned only weeks later to the very same hotel with a second victim and was not recognized. Arrested in 1980 when that victim's screams alerted hotel staff to call the police, Cottingham was convicted in the torture-rape murders of five women 1977-1980 and recently (in 2010) he confessed and pled guilty to killing another victim earlier in New Jersey in 1967 and hints that he killed others.

In a 2009 interview with journalist Nadia Fezzani, Cottingham told her, "I wanted to be the best at whatever I did. And I wanted to be the best serial killer, yes. I've probably done anything a man would want to do with a woman. Obviously I must be sick somehow. Normal people don't do what I did. I could put myself into a zone to do something like that. It would be like remote control."[23]

While it is unclear exactly how many victims he killed and when, Cottingham is believed to have begun his last primary killing cycle of his five victims in December 1977 when New York was experiencing a string of bizarre serial killer cases. Cottingham was following in the footsteps of the six '.44 Caliber' serial killings in 1976-1977 in the Bronx, Queens and Brooklyn by David Berkowitz the "Son of Sam" who used to sneak up on dating couples with a .44 Bulldog revolver and open up on them. Berkowitz was arrested in August 1977, the "Summer of Sam", after a search of parking violations linked his car to the murder scenes. The Son of Sam killings were following in the wake of yet an earlier case of nine necrophile rape murders in 1973-1974 in New York by Calvin Jackson.

Eight of Jackson's elderly female victims lived in a long-term hotel for welfare indigents on the Upper West Side at 50 W 77th Street called the "Park Plaza" (not to be confused with the posh "Plaza" on Fifth Avenue and Central Park South.) The ninth victim was murdered nearby. Jackson had been employed as a hotel caretaker and porter and found easy pickings. He would gain access to the rooms, strangle or suffocate his elderly victims and rape and mutilate their corpses. He would make sandwiches from food he found in the victims' fridges and linger over the corpses as he ate. With access to the victims' rooms, he probably returned to have sex with the corpses for another few days before the fly larvae eggs in their nostrils and dead eyes began to hatch maggots and neighbors would begin complaining of the smell. By then the bodies of the solitary semi-homeless victims were so badly decomposed, that police did not recognize them as homicides and wrote off the deaths of the decayed lonely elderly women as a result of alcoholism or natural causes. Jackson was arrested after he was seen carrying a television set belonging to the ninth victim down a fire escape and eventually confessed to all the murders. Just to show how naive the world was to serial killing even as late as 1975, Calvin Jackson's primary motive was attributed to theft of property in support a drug habit while the murders and necrophiliac rapes were seen as secondary factors. The prosecutors could not understand why Jackson "had to" kill his victims and violate their corpses while committing the thefts! Jackson's response was, "I guess I kind of broke wild there, you know?" Today we understand it was never about the thefts but always about the necrophiliac rape from the beginning. The TVs were the serial killer's trophies, entirely secondary to the commission of the post-mortem rapes.

In the meantime Rodney Alcala, who wasn't convicted until 2011, in 1971 posing as an amiable artist photographer, raped and murdered in her East Side apartment Cornelia Michel Crilley, a Trans World Airlines flight attendant, and in the summer of 1977 lured Ellen Jane Hover, an aspiring orchestra conductor to her death. Her remains were found nearly a year later in Westchester County. These kinds of Hitchcock movie-like murders of women were on the rise since the appearance in early 1960s of the Boston Strangler, who mostly targeted elderly victims in their apartments in the afternoons or early evenings.

My brief 'close encounter' with Richard Cottingham in 1979, a monster in a wave of recent monsters terrorizing New

York, left me puzzled as to what kind of dark hole these creatures were crawling out of and why did it seem like there was a rising tide of them, to the extent that I had actually bumped into one "in the wild", however briefly and randomly. I did not have the term 'serial killer' to comfort me with its explanation of what I had encountered. It all appeared as monstrous as *Tales From the Crypt* comics I had read as a kid. A year later after Cottingham had been arrested and identified, I read my first book on the subject of serial murder, *The Stranger Beside Me,* Ann Rule's seminal 1980 account of the iconic post-modern serial killer Ted Bundy; but the word "serial killer" did not appear in the pages of her book when it was first published.

Just how viral reports of serial killing became once the word was coined in the *New York Times* for public consumption is dizzying. In the decade between its first use in 1981 and 1989, the term "serial killer" appeared 253 times in the paper; ten years later, in the 1990s it appeared 2,514 times.[24]

Several years after my encounter with Cottingham I went to work for CNN in the mid-1980s. In its early days CNN had hired many of its staff from the newsrooms of local television stations in Atlanta. Almost everybody had a story to tell of their brief 'close encounters' with the Atlanta serial killer Wayne Williams who used to 'string' or freelance as a cameraman for local news and whose father was an Atlanta press photographer. Then in October 1990 while working on a documentary film in Moscow, I was approached for an interview (on an unrelated subject) by the notorious serial killer Andrei "The Red Ripper" Chikatilo, a month before he returned to his Rostov home to kill his 51st, 52nd, and 53rd victims and then was arrested. This time there was a weird conversation, but again, I did not know at the moment I was conversing with a serial killer. I found out only much later about the monster I had been conversing with.

My random encounters with *two* serial killers was looking like weird math but still, I also as a kid bumped into Robert Kennedy in Montreal in the summer of 1967 just as randomly, Andy Warhol in a bar doorway one day in New York, Elton John and Peter O'Toole on hotel elevators in Toronto, Sammy Davis Jr.

in a cigar store in London and Bryan Adams in an airport waiting
for a flight to Moscow we were both on, without trying to seek out
any one of them. It 'just happened' and maybe the math was not
really all that weird when you are travelling, as I was when I
encountered on these voyages 'unordinary' people, including serial
killers. Still, while anything can happen *once*, to randomly
encounter serial killers *twice* was a little too much for me and
that's how I ended up writing my first book, a history of them. I
really should not have been all that surprised by the 'six degrees of
separation' from roaming serial killers. By then a White House
First Lady, Rosalynn Carter had met a serial killer when John
Wayne Gacy hosted her in Chicago as the director of the city's
annual Polish Constitution Day Parade in May 1978. The White
House released an official photo of Jimmy Carter's wife posing
with Gacy.[25] Six months later police would find 27 corpses of
young men in the crawl space of Gacy's home. He was convicted
of murdering a total of 33 victims.

***

*White House press photo of serial killer John Wayne Gacy posing
with President Jimmy Carter's wife Rosalynn on a visit to Chicago
six month before his arrest in the murder of 33 victims*

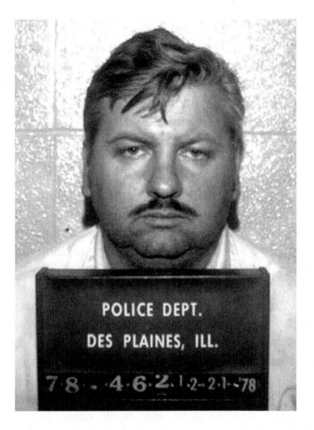

POLICE DEPT.
DES PLAINES, ILL.
78 - 462. 12-2-1-78

\*\*\*

In the meantime, on the eve of his first of seventeen future serial murders, the teenage Jeffrey Dahmer on a school trip to Washington D.C. as a "prank" arranged a spontaneous visit for himself and some classmates with Carter's Vice President Walter Mondale in his office.[26] If there were serial killers getting into the White House (aside from the ones sometimes occupying its offices) my own little brief encounters with them were beginning to look pretty lame. Roger Alcala convicted in the murder of seven women and suspected in as many as 130 was reportedly taking filmmaking lessons in the extension school of Colombia University from Roman Polanski and was about to become a contestant on *The Dating Game* TV show. By now accused

Chicago satanic cult serial killer Robin Gecht, later linked to the gang rape cannibal murders of 17 female victims, was employed as a laborer by serial killer John Gacy, neither aware of each other's serial killing. There was even a case of one serial killer killing another serial killer when Wayne Henley shot Dean Corll in 1973, after the two had tortured, raped and murdered 28 teenage male victims. Corll threatened to make Henley his 29th victim; Henley struck first.

By the 1990s everybody was familiar with the term serial killer and many had encountered one for themselves, however randomly. In the meantime, upon having met two, (and recently realizing as I was writing this, it was actually three --the third a serial killer in between his first and second murders, when he wasn't yet a serial killer) I began to wonder how many serial killers we might have stood in line behind at McDonalds, or sat down next to on a train, in a food mall, parked our car near to or just passed by randomly in the street, without knowing? That's how I ended up writing about serial killers, just trying to figure out where they had come from. After my book was published, I later found out that one of the first people to buy it was a serial killer. Dennis Rader, the BTK Killer had it in his possession when he was arrested several months after my book came out.[27] While I appreciate the "professional" endorsement, all this shivered me out just the same.

***

## Redefining the Word

Making matters complicated is that over the last thirty years everybody had a different definition of what a serial killer was and how many victims defined serial murder. Experts argued whether serial killers are defined by the compulsive sexual character of their crimes and whether they were exclusively male. (Statistically almost one in every six serial killers is a female, 53% of whom killed at least one child or female victim.)[28] They debated whether the perpetrator and victims were always strangers. At one time, serial killing was called "stranger-on-stranger murder", "thrill killing", "multicide" or confusingly "mass murder" which today we define as a single rampage episode of multiple murders. Can organized crime 'hit men' contract killers and genocidal war criminals be considered serial killers since they are killing strangers? Or does a serial killer need to choose his own victim and what constitutes "choice"? Is serial killing a symptom of parallel classes of behavioral disorders and do we classify them as 'psychopathy' or 'sociopathy' or as addictive paraphilia? Many of these important debates are still ongoing today in conferences and in the pages of academic justice and forensic literature.

Until recently the FBI's definition from the 1980s was the basis of the traditional definition of what constitutes a serial killer as somebody who kills *three* victims on separate occasions with a "cooling off" period in between, a definition still mistakenly attributed to the FBI today which has changed it since 2005. The 'three victims' definition presented all sorts of problems, as it excluded murderers who have a serial killer psychopathology but are apprehended after their first or second murder before they can commit the prerequisite third. It also technically excluded historical killers like Albert Fish, Ed Gein and Wayne Williams who each had been convicted in court of "only" two homicides or less, notwithstanding suspicions of more.

Since a gathering of experts in 2005 at the San Antonio Serial Murder Symposium sponsored by the FBI's National Center for the Analysis of Violent Crime (NCAVC) Behavioral Science Unit (BSU), the FBI now defines serial murder as "The unlawful killing of *two or more* victims by the same offender(s) in separate events" for *any reason* including "anger, thrill, financial gain, and attention seeking."[29] [My emphasis.]

It makes sense; if you are going to kill once, go away and think about it, and then kill again, a second time, you *are* a serial killer, for whatever reason; period. (At least in my and my tribe's book. Serial killing is not like baseball, you don't get three tries at it.) Most experts today simply define serial killing as the murder of two or more victims for any motive on separate occasions with a 'cooling off' period in between.[30]

It also means that if we 'open the books' on what makes a serial killer, to include those with two victims, profit killers, health care killers, female Munchausen by proxy syndrome killers, black widows, war criminals, genocidal murderers and contract killers, who we find often have behavioral psychopathologies similar to 'traditional' serial killers, we are going to have statistically more serial killers from the past than we had a decade ago, and a lot more coming at us in the future under the new definition. (The redefinition of the term 'serial killer' is *one* of the several factors that Hickey attributes to the continued statistical rise of serial killing today, despite the overall drop in US murder rates.)[31] But this is how 'history' works: we are constantly changing the past as historians discover new things about it and rethink what *really* happened in the past. The past is always in the present; it always *is* and never *was*.

Once we had the word and its concept and definition, the question that remained is *why* do sexual serial killers do what they do? How does their mind work? Why do they kill serially, rape, mutilate, cannibalize? In trying to answer that question over the last thirty years, we ended up with a new word today.

***

### The new Word: "serial erotophonophilia."

Despite the fact that there are legions of forensic psychiatrists, psychologists, neuroscientists, physicians, profilers, criminologists and sociologists studying the question of why and how the powerful sexual reproductive instinct is merged (paraesthesia) with the aggressive killing or feeding instinct, we still have not entirely figured it out. We suspect early childhood traumas in male children as young as five years old trigger paraesthesia which results in a variety of so-called "paraphilias" (literally, "unusual loves" or more commonly referred to as "sexual deviations" or "perversions".)[32] Almost exclusively an aspect of male psychopathology, a paraphilia is an obsession for a very particular and often unusual (minority practiced) type of sex, without which the paraphiliac could not be aroused otherwise. Paraphilias include specific fantasy scenarios, 'abnormal' preferences, an obsession with a particular part of the human non-genital anatomy ("partialism") or a preference for a sexualized inanimate object ("fetishes.")

We are not talking about someone occasionally on payday buying their girlfriend sexy lingerie or dressing in leather or latex on the weekend, but of a constant obsessive addiction to a particular paraphilia for a period of six months or more to the exclusion of being aroused sexually in any other way.[33] A subject may have several different paraphilias at the same time, and paraphilias can change and mutate, but one paraphilia usually predominates until a different one takes hold.

Some paraphilias on their own or with a willing partner, can be relatively harmless like: *absiophilia* (a preference for a disabled partner); *acrotomophilia* (preference for amputees); *agalmatophilia* ("pygmalianism" a desire for sex with dolls, mannequins or statues); *agnophilia* (a preference for a partner *pretending* to struggle); *altocalciphilia* (a fetish for high-heeled shoes); *coprophelia* (arousal from feces or from being defecated upon or defecating on a willing partner); *formicophilia* (arousal from being crawled upon by ants or other insects); *gerontophilia* (a preference for a partner from an older generation); *hyphephilia* (arousal at the touch of certain things, from skin or hair, to leather, fur or a particular fabric); *klismaphelia* (sexual arousal from receiving or giving enemas); *maschalagnia* (a partialism for armpits); *masochism* (arousal from being dominated, restrained or hurt); *mixoscopia* (desire to watch others having sex with their consent); *nasophilia* (a partialism for noses); *oculophilia* (partialism for eyes); *plushophilia* (a fetish for stuffed toy figures); *raptophilia* (*simulated* rape with a *willing* partner); *trichophilia* (fetish for hair). Most of the above paraphilias are not illegal as long as they involve a willing partner.

Other paraphilias are more blatantly transgressive and usually illegal: *amokoscisia* (desire to slash or mutilate females); *anthropophagy* (cannibalism); *anthropophagolagnia* (rape accompanied by cannibalism); *biastophilia* ("paraphilic rape"); *colobosis* (mutilation of male genitalia); *exhibitionism* (exposing oneself to strangers); *flagellationism* (sexual satisfaction from whipping or beating a person); *frotteurism* (rubbing against unwilling subjects); *hybristophilia* (a desire to partner with a serial killer, one of the few rare female paraphilias); *necrophilia* (sex with corpses); *necrophagia* (eating corpse flesh in advance stages of decomposition); *necrosadism* (mutilation of corpses); *mazoperosis* (mutilation of female breasts); *pedophilia* (sex with prepubescent children); *pederasty* (anal sex with male children); *perogynia* (mutilation of female genitalia); *piquerism* (sexual gratification through the use of a knife or other sharp object to penetrate, stab or slash a victim); *sadism* (sexual arousal from dominating, humiliating, and causing pain to an unwilling subject); *scopophilia* (voyeurism, watching others undress or have sex without their consent).

One sees in the psychopathology of serial killers various paraphilias like strands in a rope wound together into one super-paraphilia: *"erotophonophilia"* (lust murder), defined as "murdering sadistically and brutally, including the mutilation of body parts, especially the genitalia"[34] and "cruelty, torture, or other acts sexual in nature that ultimately culminate in the death of the victim and includes those acts of homicide commonly referred to as sexual sadism... This more broadly inclusive definition of sexualized torture includes conscious, unconscious, live, or dead victims."[35]

Current forensic literature when referring to the type of sexual homicides committed by "traditional" serial killers like Ted Bundy and Jeffrey Dahmer, are now using a resurrected archaic term "serial lust murder" or in academic-speak, serial "erotophonophilia" to distinguish these offenders from other types of serial killers who might kill for profit, political or ideological motives, thrills, revenge, attention seeking, visions as a result of mental illness or other apparently non-sexual motives. Because of its matrix of male paraphilias, this definition of serial erotophonophilia almost entirely excludes female serial offenders from the classification, except in those rare cases where women act willingly as accomplices of sadistic male erotophonophiliacs. (The Karla Homolka Charlene Gallego Syndrome – hybristophilia.)

\*\*\*

# Making serial killers

We believe serial killers are 'made' at a very early stage in childhood, as young as the age of five, when the child is experiencing a mess of reptilian sexual impulses, which he does not understand as "sexual", simultaneously with some kind of traumatic event. And trauma does not necessarily need to be what we as adults might perceive as "traumatic"--although often it is-- but *what the child perceives* at the time as traumatic; the range can be from being frightened by a kitten, parental divorce, to being yelled at or spanked, to more severe trauma like being beaten, assaulted or raped or witnessing such acts.

One of the more dramatic examples of typical childhood paraesthesia in a serial killer can be found in the case of Jerry Brudos who in 1968-1969 murdered four women, dressed their corpses in attire he had a fetish for, photographed them and had post-mortem sex with them. He cut off and kept the foot of one of his victims in a freezer to model it in his collection of women's high heel shoes he had accumulated through burglaries or from knocking women down in the street and fleeing with their shoes. Brudos had developed one of his paraphilias, this one for high heel shoes (*altocalciphilia*) at the age of five after he found a pair discarded pumps in a garbage dump. He recalled being fascinated by the strange and beautiful shoes, one of them still having a rhinestone clasp. The shoes in some way excited him and if it was sexual then at the age of five Brudos would not have understood the powerful sensation sweeping over him for what it was. In playful innocence and curiosity he brought the shoes home and put them on proudly to show his mother. His stern and repressed mother freaked-out at the sight of her five-year-old boy tottering about in oversized female high heels while in a state of innocent sexual ecstasy. Shrieking and admonished him for being 'wicked' she made a big show of burning the shoes and shaming Jerry. From that moment on for Brudos, female high heel shoes were forever sexualized and fused in his limbic system as he became saddled with a 'forbidden' secret fetish for the rest of his life.[36]

Alone the high heel shoes episode in Brudos' childhood did not make him a serial killer. Brudos had many other issues typical of serial killer childhoods, including a dysfunctional family and rejection and abuse by his mother who had not wanted him. Abandonment also featured in Brudos' childhood. As a child he became attached to a neighboring woman who treated him kindly and Brudos fantasized that she was his real mother and found comfort in her presence. The woman died of diabetes. At the same time Brudos also developed a close friendship with a girl of his own age, which he described later in very tender terms, who died of tuberculosis leaving him without friends or comfort from his emotionally barren home life. The two deaths and sense of abandonment deeply marked Brudos. He was sickly and not very bright and in Grade One he was caught stealing his teacher's high heel shoes and humiliated before his classmates. Small things that in a single dose might have been manageable, accumulated together to snuff out Jerry's childhood beyond salvation. His mother's disdain and other female's abandonment of him now fueled an irrepressible rage towards women in general. He escalated to violating their privacy and personal space by committing acts of 'fetish burglary' stealing female attire he was obsessed with. At the age of seventeen he was arrested when he went too far by incorporating a human victim into his fetish. He forced a neighborhood girl to pose and perform sexual acts while he photographed her and beat another girl with his fists when she refused to do the same. After receiving juvenile counseling, Brudos graduated school and found gainful employment as a broadcast electronics technician at a radio station; he also got married and fathered two children and seemed to settle down.

His wife testified that he was a gentle and considerate lover but that Brudos insisted she dress in lacy underwear and don high heel shoes before he could become aroused. She was happy to oblige and play along, but after the birth of their first child, his once compliant wife now found herself too busy and suffering from back aches to wear high heels; she began refusing to "dress up" to satisfy his paraphilias. Brudos retreated back into his fantasy world of infantile hurt, feeling abandoned by yet another significant woman in his life. He constructed off-limits "man caves" in the basement and garage of his home, fitting it out with an intercom to the house so that he would not be disturbed.  There he began accumulating a growing collection of female underwear and high heel shoes, in which sometime he would dress himself, posing in front of a mirror or taking photos of himself as he compulsively groped himself and masturbated to fantasies of possessing scantily clad females in high heels.  One last thing happened before he began killing:  Brudos was injured and lost consciousness in an electrocution accident at the radio station that nearly killed him.  Those who knew him commented on how "Jerry was never quite the same" afterwards.  Whether it was the final cause or trigger for his killing we will never know for sure, but shortly after the accident and the birth of a second child, which Brudos had planned to attend in the delivery room but was turned away by his wife to his shame and disappointment, Brudos at a serial killer's near-typical age of twenty-nine, began luring and kidnapping females to his garage and basement, murdering them, storing their corpses in the household freezer to take out and thaw to use as dress-up sex dolls before mutilating them and dumping their bodies into rivers, while his family lived and played upstairs on the other end of the intercom. (He insisted that his wife let him know over the intercom if she wanted anything from the freezer for lunch or supper and he would bring it up to her.)

Sexual paraphilias, some harmless, others very dangerous, combine together in the serial killer's fantasy and behavior.  A harmless fetish for high heels became deadly when a socially inept or psychopathic offender like Jerry Brudos feels compelled to kill to harvest a foot for his collection of shoes. The ostensibly harmless paraphilia of *agalmatophilia* ("pygmalianism" a desire for sex with dolls) has overtones of necrophilia. It is not that some serial killers want to necessary have sex with a corpse, but with an anatomically correct human doll.  They need to kill the victim to obtain the doll.  The killing is actually 'a chore' for some serial killers and not part to their fantasy except as a stepping stone to achieving it.  As the "Co-ed Killer" Ed Kemper explained his predilection for sex with both severed heads and the headless female bodies, "What I needed to have was a particular experience with a person, and to possess them in the way I wanted to:  I had to evict them from their human bodies."[37] Kemper described his murders as "making dolls" out of humans. Asked why he had to cut the head off to have sex with the corpse, Kemper responded, "The head is where everything is at, the brain, eyes, mouth. That's the person. I remember being told as a kid, you cut off the head and the body dies. The body is nothing after the head is cut off... Well, that's not quite true. With a girl, there is a lot left in the girl's body without the head. Of course, the personality is gone."[38]

Jeffrey Dahmer killed 17 male victims because he was lonely for their company to the point that he ate some of them to keep them "close" to him. He slept and cuddled with the corpses and attempted to find a non-homicidal method of finding companionship. For a while living in the basement of his grandmother's house he kept a store mannequin for sex and company until his grandmother forced him to get rid of it. Even after he began his serial killing, he tried to find ways of not killing his victims by attempting to reduce one of them into a lobotomized sex slave zombie by jamming a turkey baster full of battery acid into the victim's brain. Dahmer's mad experiment failed; the victim died.[39] In a remarkably similar case in England 1978-1983, David Nilsen killed 15 male victims "for company." He tenderly washed and dressed their corpses, cuddled and had sex with them, and once they began to decay he dismembered them flushing them piece by piece down the toilet. Eventually the buildup of fatty hunks of human flesh blocked the drains of the building and plumbers called out to service the problem discovered the remains and called in the police.[40]

*** 

## From fantasy to action: the serial addiction

While paraphilias give a conceptual structure to a serial killer's fantasies, a "signature" that profilers can detect and identify, by themselves these fantasies do not make a serial killer. Lots of people have paraphilic-like fantasies without necessarily acting them out or becoming obsessed by them. Surveys of non-criminal "healthy" college-aged males revealed that 62% fantasized about having sex with a female child and 33% fantasized of raping a woman but never conceived actually acting upon their fantasy.[41] Many males are turned on by the look of high heel shoes on a woman but they are not going to kill her and cut her foot off. Loving couples sometimes engage in some degree of 'rough sex' with groping, nibbling, scratching and biting; "spank me suck me fuck me I'm your bitch you're my slut" type of theatrical playful mating-ritual sex that stimulates the reptilian urges at their root in both the male and female; but to actually injure one's partner is inconceivable to them. What makes a serial killer is his compulsion to take these aggressive rape and cannibal urges off the fantasy track and out on reality road, to literally act them out, even if it injures or kills the unwilling subjects of their fantasy.

Again, research evidence suggests that serial killers can be formatively made as young as five years-old as a result of some sort of ill-timed trauma. The 'trauma control model' of serial homicide theory argues that the child not only develops paraphilias, but to survive psychologically withdraws emotionally from the trauma in an attempt to control it, forms an 'emotional scar' by developing what we call 'psychopathy'--a defensive emotional 'flatness' that protects the victim from the pain of trauma but results as well in flat range of limbic system emotions, especially empathy for others or a sense of conscience or responsibility. Noting serial killers who are adopted in infancy, there is an argument that 'psychopathy' can result as early as the infantile stage when a baby is not physically bonded with their mother--the "lack of cuddling" theory. David Berkowitz, the "Son of Sam" for example, was adopted as an infant and apparently raised by loving nurturing parents, yet grew up with an inexplicable rage that drove him to kill when he became an adult. Given up by his natural mother almost immediately after birth in a pre-arranged adoption, the hours-old child was torn from his womb mother, perhaps forcing the skittish little *Alien* infant to scuttle off into the emotional safety of psychopathy never finding its way out again. Fuse blown, wire melted, an irreparable micro break in the neuropaths. By the time the middle-aged childless Mr. Nathan and Mrs. Pearl Berkowitz brought their adopted little baby David home from the hospital, it could already have been a budding psychopath serial killer. He began as a child by killing his mother's canary and destroying her Matzo crackers for no apparent reason. Twenty years later he was fantasizing that a dog was ordering him to kill people and acting upon it with a .44 Bulldog magnum.

The problem is that while many serial killers score high on psychopathy tests, only a tiny minority of psychopaths become serial killers. Approximately 1 in every 83 Americans[42] and 1 in 166 Britons[43] are suspected to be a potential psychopath and it's very likely you have dated one, had one as a teacher or as a boss or voted for one. Many psychopaths end up as successful and productive CEO's, attorneys, performing artists, celebrities, Hollywood agents, television evangelists or congressmen, where a lack of empathy and concern for the feelings of others is a career enhancer, rather than a detriment. Some less functional psychopaths crash and burn destroying their lives and the lives of those around them with their lies and illusions, irresponsible behavior, their double-life secrets and crimes and misdemeanors, but without necessarily murdering anybody. A very rare few stack corpses in their basement or tend to remote forested body dumps where they return to feast on and have sex with the decaying remains of their victims. In over two centuries of serial killing in the United States we have identified (by mostly the three or more victims definition) a total of only 352 male serial killers and 64 female serial killers (18.1%).)[44] Serial killers are extremely rare even if you double that number.

A complex mandala of psychological disorders accompanied by trauma and familial instability are the common characteristics of most serial killer childhood histories. In adolescence a range of sexual paraphilias fuse with trauma-induced psychopathy (or one of its ancillary variants like sociopathy, asocial behaviour disorder, and other behavioral syndromes). [The simplest explanation I heard for the difference between psychopathy and a sociopathy, is that when tested, a sociopath is defined by what *they do*, while a psychopath by what *they are*.][45] The now famous FBI study in the early 1980s surveying twenty-nine male sexual serial killers and seven single sexual murderers, upon which the FBI developed its *organized/disorganized/mixed categories* profiling system, proposed that psychopathy is only the first of many factors in the making of a serial killer.[46] The FBI's 'fantasy motivational' model argues that rather than sexual abuse, exposure to a dysfunctional and abusive family environment translating into feelings of abandonment, is the most common 'trauma' experienced by serial killers as children. It causes them to withdraw into a fantasy world in which they seek control and revenge. Often their post-traumatic psychopathy or distancing leads them to behave in a way that results in them being further rejected by their childhood peers or subjected to bullying and abuse, fueling an increasingly deepening sense of abandonment, loneliness, isolation accompanied by a retreat into violent and vengeful fantasies in which the child finds comfort and control. For the serial killer it is all about control. All this is occurring at the same time as the child is developing a sexual reproductive impulse. While most children develop a 'normal' friendly boundary-defining instinctual sexuality through the experience of romp and play with each other, the lonely 'serial killer' child is withdrawn by itself into its own gloomy fantasy world. In that dark and dank hurt universe of reptilian sexual impulses the child and adolescent begins self-medicating at puberty with compulsive masturbation to their comforting aggressive control fantasies, a powerful conditioning process often involves the sensual interaction with increasingly fetishized dolls or inanimate paraphilic fetish substances or textiles as sexual totems of those who wear them; these items are often mutilated or destroyed in a child's rage that continues to pulse in the adolescent and adult offender.

Gradually they will begin "test driving" their fantasies out into the real world. Before he began killing, Ted Bundy recalled he used to disable women's cars with no concrete motive other than to see what the victim does and the satisfaction of controlling the victim's behavior.[47] Ed Kemper who mutilated dolls graduated to committing acts of voyeurism while clutching a knife. Sometimes offenders act out these fantasies as juveniles by committing "lesser crimes" like voyeurism, fetish burglaries, setting fires or acts of animal cruelty.

So-called "facilitators": alcohol, drugs and pornography, are believed to enhance fantasy scripting, masturbatory conditioning, and lower inhibitions on acting the fantasy out. The number one drug of choice for serial killers is alcohol, a depressant. One recent study of sexual killers found that majority 64% were consuming alcohol at the time of their offense.[48] Other drugs of choice reported by serial killers are amphetamines, cocaine and chemical hallucinogenics and marijuana. The daunting problem is that none of these things on their own can be definitively linked to serial killing. The Bible has been reported as a facilitator of serial murders of prostitutes, for example.

All that remains for this fucked up cocktail of escalating homicidal childhood fantasies of reptilian sexual revenge and control stewing for decades to unload into the real world of acting out his cruel and murderous fantasies is for it to be "triggered." Some last-straw event; a firing from work, a marriage collapse, a breakup, the birth of a child, an accident, the death of parent, even a scenario gone wrong resulting in an unintended murder. Often a preliminary investigation of a serial killer suspect begins with a survey of stressful event triggers in the suspect's life history plotted on a timeline of the suspected homicides.

Every serial killer has his first murder, when he is only a single killer, not yet transformed into a serial one. Some bungle it on the first try and are apprehended before they can kill again, leaving behind only a serial killer's signature, but not the requisite number of victims; some of them after serving a decade sentence for their first one or even two bungled murders are then paroled and begin killing again from exactly where they left off. Arthur Shawcross murdered two children in 1972, served a fourteen year sentence, and within two years of his release began a series of twelve necrophiliac murders of women in 1988-89. Profilers had estimated his age to be younger, not taking into account that he was "on ice" while serving a prison sentence. After Shawcross, profilers knew better. Some serial killers after evading arrest in their first murder, are so troubled by their act (for moral or personal risk factors) that they resist committing another murder for years before the fantasy or another trigger finally breaks them down, and having already done so once, they now become unbridled in an addictive serial killing cycle, (Jeffrey Dahmer for example) while others from their very first kill take to it like babies to mother's milk and begin a relentless reign of rape and murder that may go on for years. As symptoms of psychopathy seem to fade and flat line along with testosterone levels in males in middle-age, un-apprehended 'successful' serial killers begin to kill less frequently and even stop altogether. (Unlike female serial killers that seem to excel their killing in post-menstrual stages of their life.) Like in the case of Gary Ridgway the Green River Killer, these types of offenders can accumulate huge numbers of victims over the duration of their killings before going into retirement or semi-retirement, only to be identified in recent years by emerging DNA technology applied to evidence from cold case files decades old.

The second murder is the transformational one that makes all their killing serial from then onwards. Moors serial killer Ian Brady described his as "the psychic abolition of redemption" explaining that "the second killing will hold all the same disadvantages, distracting elements of the first, but to a lesser degree. This allows a more objective assimilation of the experience. It also fosters an expanding sense of omnipotence, a wide-angle view of the metaphysical chessboard. In many cases, the element of elevated aestheticism in the second murder will exert a more formative impression than the first and probably of any in the future. It not only represents the rite of confirmation, a revelational leap of lack of faith in humanity, but also the onset of addiction to hedonistic nihilism."[49]

The average male serial killer begins killing around the age of twenty-eight which means that sometimes it takes more than twenty years for these evolving, deeply harbored and escalating childhood fantasies to develop into literal acts.[50] With murder now as the ultimate act in the fantasy with nowhere to go afterwards, once acted out in reality, the offender is frequently overwhelmed and deeply depressed by how the reality is nowhere near as satisfying and comforting as the long held fantasy. Trapped between the disappointment of reality but unable now to return to the familiar comfort of fantasy having actually acted it out, the failure to realize as imagined a twenty-year fantasy now throws the perpetrator into a deep existential crisis and an addiction to "improve" and perfect the reality to the standard of the lost fantasy he had been compulsively masturbating to all these years, by repeating the killings over and over again.

Over time a serial killer will attempt to develop skills and techniques to gain more control over the victim to ensure that they "perform" exactly as the victims in his fantasy script. Making them into dead "dolls" is often the easiest way. The offender might also escalate the transgressive brutality of his fantasy goals and their limits trying to break through the 'time barrier' of his lost fantasies by imagining new and more transgressive ones in the new dimension of reality he is becoming familiar with. Serial killing is a constantly evolving learning process and a talented criminal profiler can discern the offender's learning curve and follow the perpetrator down it.

Despite this, the serial killer can *never* get the reality as perfect as his fantasy. (That's why they call it "fantasy", stupid.) The killing becomes a form of addiction in which the perpetrator is now serially chasing the dragon's tail of his sexual fantasy, never able to catch it. Some serial killers with no fantasy world left to retreat into or the imaginative talent to create new ones, disintegrate becoming sloppy and berserk, like Ted Bundy in his final murders, and are apprehended by the police. Some serial killers just stop killing and retreat into a new parallel non-escalated matrix of fantasies that might not involve murder (Albert Desalvo The Boston Strangler) while others vanish into the prison system for other dysfunctional offenses, commit suicide or just surrender and confess to the police. Some become dormant and had investigative technology not caught up to them, might have never been identified like Denis Rader, the BTK killer or Gary Ridgway. Some, like Jack the Ripper in 1888, the Cleveland Torso Killer of the 1930s, or the Zodiac Killer in California in the late 1960s, were never apprehended or even identified and remain mysteries to this day.

But why was there such a dramatic rise in serial murder since the 1950s and why is it still increasing. What is going on?

***

**The rise of serial killing today: a brief fifty year history.**
It should come as no surprise that the homicide rate in the United States, including serial killing, begins to rise dramatically in the 1950s after the most homicidal episode in human history, the Second World War (1939-1945.) In a relatively short span of six years the war killed 55 million people in Europe and Asia, an unprecedented number of dead for any war in human history. Unlike previous wars, this war was distinguished by an extraordinary number of non-combatant civilian deaths. Thirty million of the dead were civilians, many of them murdered; that is hung, shot, gassed, battered, mutilated, bayonetted, raped, beheaded, poisoned, tattooed, used for medical experiments or worked to death as slaves (as opposed to unintentionally or negligently targeted or killed in battlefield crossfire, aerial bombed or starved in military sieges or through deprivation ("collateral damage")).[51]

Nazi Germany dispatched battalion-sized mobile killing units of zombie-like elite *SS* paramilitary. They were actually state-induced serial killers called *Einsatzkommandos* ("task squads"). They and their local auxiliaries travelled in Eastern Europe from village to village in encrypted radio-equipped motorized columns, fueled by rations of alcohol and methamphetamine, hunting down and shooting unarmed men, women, elderly, children and infants into tank ditches, ravines or hastily dug mass graves.[52] Deployed to kill millions of people in an attempt to alter the racial composition and demography of Eastern Europe, these Nazi 'killer *kommandos*' did not murder in traditional military firing squads, but one-on-one, each killer paired to their own victim.

The officers sometimes were accompanied on these murder campaigns by their girlfriends, wives and children. At the end of

41

the day, after shooting a dozen or so victims, a killer would return home for supper, his wife would wash the blood and brain splatter from his tunic while he read the paper and played with his kids.[53] Cooled off, the next day he would rise and just like a serial killer he would hit the road to kill some more, week after week, month into month. Over a killing period of twenty-two months, the *Einsatzkommandos* killed 1.6 million men, women and children mostly by single shots to the backs of their heads. They even had a technical term in German for these state serial killers: *genickschussspezialisten*—"nape-of-the-neck shot specialists." The killing was eventually industrialized and depersonalized with the construction of mega-sized gas chamber-crematorium complexes that could kill and burn thousands of people a day transported to death camps built along railways lines for easy delivery of victims.[54] Some of the death camps were equipped with petting zoos for the families and children of the *SS* killers who ran them, while the mega-death camp Auschwitz had a swimming pool with high diving board for the killers' families.[55] The Nazi share in the direct state serial murder of civilians during the Second World War was 11 million victims, including 6 million Jews along with Poles, Russians, Ukrainians, Byelorussians, Serbs, Czechs, Roma-Gypsies and other eastern European Slavic peoples.

When this war ended in 1945 and Allied troops broke through the gates of these death camps, thousands of horrific photographs and film images of emaciated naked corpses and alleged lampshades made from tattooed human skin and shrunken head paperweights, flooded mainstream media back home, confounding a generation of children and adolescents in a state of sexual anxiety and curiosity: slavery, death, dismemberment, corpses, sex and nakedness colored some of their fantasies and imaginations. As these horrific images poured out into mainstream media in 1945 after the war, future serial killer Hillside Strangler Angelo Buono was eleven years old; Henry Lee Lucas and Andrei Chikatilo were nine; Jerry Brudos, Dean Corll, Patrick Kearney and Robert Hanson were six; Lawrence Bittaker and Richard Biegenwald were five and John Wayne Gacy and Rodney Alcala were three and two years old; Arthur Shawcross, Denis Nilson,

Dennis Rader, Chris Wilder, Randy Kraft were being born, and the next year in 1946, Ted Bundy, Richard Cottingham, Gerald Gallego, Peter Sutcliffe and Gerard Schaefer were born. As future serial killers they were going to be raised like mushrooms in the dark cultural shit of the coming world of the 1950s and 1960s.

Whether you like it or not or approve, when it comes to male sexual arousal, the primary sensory stimulus is the one that reaches fastest and furthest, at the speed of light, the visual one: the eye. From the graphic bright mating signals in the animal world of feathers, claw and fur to the human world of lipstick, silk and couture, the visual is what most frequently triggers first the sexual impulse, followed by scent, touch and taste in that order as one gets closer in proximity to the figure or object of one's sexual desire. It was only in the 1920s that technology became cheap enough for the mass printing and distribution of clear and high definition photographic images or artistic pictures in black and white and color. Photojournalist magazines like *Life Magazine* and visual narrative comic books arose in the 1930s to compete with the emerging visual power of motion pictures that began to dislodge in our civilization the predominance of mass text-based media since Sumerian cuneiforms of five thousand years ago. Text which requires analysis and interpretation through the neocortex became secondary to the image which is limbically captured by the eye and sent directly to the reptilian brain without the need of neocortex effort that text requires. That is why it's "easier" to watch TV instead of reading text. In many ways the power of the image over text appeals to this day to our infantile primitive cave painting origins before language. The image is still the most powerful tool in advertising, which essentially tries to bypass our neocortex to get at all our reptilian wants and desires directly and subliminally.

A wide spectrum of publications had always transformed popular erotic, true crime and horror textual narratives into visual media. The so-called Victorian era "penny dreadfuls", popular cheap pamphlets with salacious true crime or fictional narrative, by the 20th century were transformed into increasingly illustrated "pulp literature" with gaudy color covers, comic books, true

43

detective and men's adventure magazines and other cheap 'exploitation' media relying more and more for its sales appeal on the visual reptilian aggressive sexual signal rather than through a textual appeal to the neocortex.

When the Second World War broke out, a massive media industry turned to producing propaganda for the war effort in the form of movies, magazines, posters, and images including morale-boosting 'girlie' pinup magazines for GIs and war stories denigrating the enemy. When the war ended, this industry did not go away. Throughout the 1950s and 1960s Nazi atrocities became the entertainment staple of men's illustrated adventure pulp magazines, with stories and images of female sex slaves, cruel torture, naked women strapped spread-eagle on surgical tables for mad Nazi scientists to probe and mutilate, female Nazi '*Ilsa, She Wolf of the SS*' guards forcing males to sexually service them or collecting their tattooed skin for lampshades, or perpetrating lesbian blood lust torture rapes of female inmates. Even today nearly seventy years after the war, from *The Night Porter, Seven Beauties* to *Inglorious Basterds* and *The Reader,* the Nazis and their psycho-sexual cruelty remain a major theme in our popular culture and imagination.

By the end of the 1960s forensic psychiatrists were reporting among the characteristics of sexual murderers and serial killers their obsession with Nazi concentration camp atrocities.[56] In England, Ian Brady who raped and murdered with his female partner Myra Hindley five victims between the ages of 10 and 17 in 1963-1965, was fixated on reports and images of Nazi crimes. The pioneer of postwar serial killing, grave robbing necrophiliac Ed "Psycho" Gein, who murdered at least two female victims in 1954-1957, made furniture of human bones and greasy skin and rolled about in the grass under a full moon, his naked body clad in in a female 'skin suit' with breasts, later confessed that he had been inspired by images of Nazi and Japanese atrocities and tales of Pacific cannibalism as portrayed in a postwar generation of pulp war and adventure magazines like *Man's Adventure, True Adventure, Man's Story, Action For Men, Saga, See For Men* and even a magazine called *War Criminals,* along with true detective

44

magazines, another reported favorite in the reading and viewing habits of serial killers.[57]

All these magazines had virtually one thing in common: their covers usually featured a garish illustration of a restrained or prostrate female, thrown to the floor, or the bed, the table, the rack, a remote forest ground, scantily clad or her clothing in disarray, skirt hiked up exposing her thighs or stockings, being subjected to torture and on the brink of being raped or just raped, her face contorted in fear and submission, often gazing out from the magazine cover toward her unseen assailant, toward the male reader, as if *she* was the reader's personal slave who could be possessed merely with the purchase price of the magazine.[58] Serial killers, one after another, frequently confessed their obsessions with these magazines as children, adolescents and adults.[59] [For examples of cover art see my Facebook gallery at: http://bit.ly/FB-SK-Porn-Magazines

Although detective pulps with these kinds of cover images had been around in the 1920s and 1930s, there was a dramatic rise after the Second World War in pulp magazines which now included war atrocities. There was an escalation in their explicit sexual violence and homicidal scope, the sexuality of its female subject victims, cover color quality and the magazines' pervasive reach in terms of affordability and distribution to newsstands, grocery stores, drugstores, candy stores and other retail outlets. These stylized and gratuitous portrayals of violence, sex, rape, cannibalism and murder, were paralleled by the portrayal of real death and cruelty as increasingly revealed in the pages of mainstream photojournalist magazines like *Life, Look, Newsweek* and *Time.* It was all coursing through the veins of American mass culture.

The horrors of World War Two were followed by the fear and loathing of the Cold War, Korean War, brutal wars of liberation and decolonization, new terrorism and anxiety of the apocalyptic threat of thermo-nuclear war. A subgenre of grotesque crime tabloids from the *National Inquirer* (before it turned to "pure" gossip) to titles like *Midnight, Exploiter, Globe, Flash, Examiner,* along with the true detective magazines, featured headlines like: I WATCHED MY BABY BURN ALIVE; RETARDED SON MADE OWN MOM PREGNANT—THEN HELPED HER KILL 'SIN BABIES'; 39 STAB WOUNDS WAS ALL THE NAKED STRIPPER WORE; HE KILLED HER MOTHER AND THEN FORCED HER TO COMMIT UNNATURAL SEX ACTS; SEX MONSTERS! THE SLUT HITCHHIKER'S LAST RIDE TO DOOM; RAPE ME BUT DON'T KILL ME; BOUND AND GAGGED; STRIPPED AND ROPED; DUCT TAPED DAMSEL.[60]

A lot of this material was first directed at adult males who might have fought in the war, not necessarily teens. (The average age of a U.S. soldier in World War II was 26, unlike the 19 in Vietnam.) The enemy our fathers and grandfathers fought in Europe and the Pacific in that era was homicidally brutal and it is still taboo even today to discuss openly how our enemy's brutality rubbed off on our own soldiers. They sometimes shot prisoners-of-war in Europe, infrequently, but they did. In the Pacific U.S. soldiers mutilated Japanese corpses, cutting off ears, pulling teeth and even shrinking heads, collecting skulls and other body parts. The May 22, 1944 edition of *Life Magazine* featured a photo of a young American woman sitting at a table with a skull on it. The caption reads: "Arizona war worker writes her Navy boyfriend a thank-you note for the Jap skull he sent her."[61] President Roosevelt was presented with a letter opener with a handle made from a Japanese soldier's arm bone (which to his credit Roosevelt ordered to be decently buried.)[62] As American GIs were liberating Europe in 1942-1945, it is estimated that along the way the "good guys" raped 14,000 women in Britain, Italy, France and Germany.[63] Some of our fathers and grandfathers returned home with some dark secrets from the war about which they would never speak.

Many of the fathers and grandfathers of these serial killer-to-come children were significantly traumatized by their experiences in the Second World War as combatants or as civilians in an era before we defined Post Traumatic Stress Disorder (PTSD) and started talking about it and treating it. (That only came in the

1980s after Vietnam.) Our grandfathers and fathers had to suck it up after the war in silence.

The post-war world of the 1950s to 1970s was a world of broken old men. You would see them everywhere on the 'skid rows' of every city in a way you don't see them today: where did all the old "bums", "hobos" and "winos" go? Some of the older ones were already busted out by the Great Depression in the 1930s in which they lost everything, their jobs, their families, their pride and dignity and their will to live. In the late-1940s they were joined by a marginally younger war generation who had lost their minds and souls in that apocalyptic war and could never go back home again. On my way to school in the early 1960s I would catch glimpses of them through the greasy windows of a nearby flop-house hotel, old men sitting in the lobby smoking and reading newspapers with nothing to do. They would be out front crowded on the sidewalks each in various degree of dereliction, from men in stained dirty clothing with alcohol swollen faces marked by oozing open cuts from fighting the night before to dignified lonely men with tired eyes dressed in neatly pressed outdated fifth-hand suits, desperately trying to keep it together. When I hit New York City in my early twenties in 1977 to film punk bands at CBGB on the Bowery, the world's largest skid row save old downtown Los Angeles, many were still there, hundreds of single lonely old men living in chicken-wire flop houses, surviving day to day, meal to meal, bottle to bottle. Some of them had been there since the 1930s. Some of the older winos in front of CBGB eyed my *Arriflex* movie camera and told me their tales of when they were "in show business" or "the pictures" and asked me for a quarter when it used to actually buy something. I came to understand men's adventure true crime pulp for the sad and hopeless truss-set market it was directed at, that Charles Bukowski-Paul Schrader world of alcohol, pills and war-damaged single male sex: lonely sex, saggy stripper sex, cheap toothless suck sex, repressed sex, angry drunken blood sex, dead woman in a box sex, sick cannibal open wound war sex, but all of it sex nonetheless.[64]

If pulp magazine art and literature was culture, then skid row is where it sickened, infected, grew old and died. In fact right about the time that punk rockers were descending with electric guitars onto the Bowery in the late 1970s, pushing alcohol aside with speed, heroin and eventually crack, killing everything and everybody including themselves as storm troopers for condo gentrification, postmodern art galleries, high-end boutique hotels, shoe stores and rich New York housewife cocktail bars that rule the Bowery today, is exactly when pulp magazines began to vanish along with the oldskool skid row bums. Pulp magazines' last yelp before going under in the late 1970s was the *Punksploitation* porn genre: titles like *Sunk Punk, Puke Punk, Pink Punk, Punk Pussy* and *Punk Dominatrix.*[65] After that, it was over. The elderly winos and bums were literally driven underground into subway tunnels, exchanging the predictable confinement of their chicken-wire flops for the cold concrete jungle mad mobility of the shopping cart. There in the dark, the sick old men of the old world were beaten to death and eaten by the hungry broken crackhead generations of the new world, by younger raging sick insane male and female homeless--the new infected tribes of the walking dead displaced off skid rows to make room for Starbucks and the affluent condo zombies like maggots on a corpse picking clean the rotted bones of the dead American industrial age. The pulps were replaced by cable TV, MTV and the Shopping Channel, VHS cassettes, CDs and DVDS, game consoles, internet, social media and smart phones. But until that happened in the 1990s, this decaying brand of sick, sadistic, repressed sex was a major channel of titillating entertainment and obsession for the lonely, festering its way off skid row like a science fiction blob into the June Cleaver world of inner city working-class and middle-class suburban adolescents, where its dark and cannibalistic appeal found a fertile ground among lonely boys who were either fathered by the war damaged or had their own private demons twisting at their minds. In fact, skid row was not a place but a sickness raging in our culture beyond the derelict confines of chicken-wire, facial wounds and empty bottles.

I have not even mentioned so far the walking wounded who managed to get home from the wars without crash-and-burning on skid row along the way. With the horrors of the war locked into their psyches they somehow found brides and shambled into some semblance of marriage and family. Work was guaranteed and the gates to a middle-class open if one surrendered to a factory job like a Moslem to Islam (and not even that, as Islam calls on its followers to briefly pray only five times a day; industrial capital demanded forty hours and more of feudal kneeling a week or one did not eat or have a place to sleep.) How their war experiences later impacted their marital relations and their conduct towards their own children is an 'x-factor' that we cannot decipher until the taboo on our own atrocities during the "last good war" is lifted, even if the scale and scope does not hold a candle to the rape and murder perpetrated by Nazi Germany and Imperial Japan. (Interestingly, I cannot think of any examples of a World War II *combat* veteran who subsequently became a serial killer once home. Perhaps the reality of war death pre-empted any 'fantasy' they may have been engaged in.)

As the 1950s dawned, the sick sons and younger men who never went to war but stayed home and fantasized about it, began to stir in their adolescent puberty and grasp their knives and ropes. In 1957 thirty-year-old lonely mama's boy Harvey Glatman (who looked like a nerd geek exactly as his name sounds) in Los Angeles was obsessed with true detective magazine cover photos featuring bound women.[66] Having already served time for kidnapping and raping a woman when he was eighteen, Glatman learned he could no longer leave surviving witnesses. He began contacting models through their agencies pretending to be a detective magazine cover photographer. Glatman later described to police what happened when he successfully lured nineteen year-old Judith Ann Dull to his TV repair shop "photo studio" for a what he claimed was a modelling assignment: "I told her that I wanted to take pictures that would be suitable for illustrations for mystery stories or detective magazine stories of that type, and that this would require me to tie her hands and feet and put a gag in her mouth and she was agreeable to this, and I did tie her hands and feet and put a gag in her mouth and I took a number of pictures."

Once bound and pinned in a pose as per his magazine cover fantasy, he stepped into it and raped and murdered her,

49

photographing the process along the way, creating his own set of custom-made true detective magazine images to satisfy his obsession.[67] Glatman murdered three women this way before a fourth victim escaped and alerted police. Glatman is also suspected in a fourth homicide committed previously in Colorado, the victim in which was only identified in 2009 through DNA testing.[68] Glatman is among the earliest of many serial killers in the future who would record on film, sound or video their murders to later relive them again and again while masturbating.

*\*\*\**

*True Detective magazine covers from December 1941 to August 1976. Described by FBI behaviorists as "pornography for serial killers" popular pulp magazines were readily available everywhere mainstream magazines and comics were sold, and typically featured covers depicting a bound or prostrate female victim in a state of disarray and fear.*

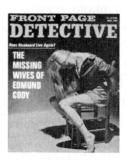

*Photos by serial killer of a victim forced to pose prior to being murdered, attributed to serial killer Harvey Glatman in 1957 (www.murderpedia.org).*

\*\*\*

In Maryland and Virginia 1957-1959, Melvin Rees, a talented meth-addicted jazz musician murdered five known victims. He would overtake his victims while they were driving in the country, forcing them off the road by flashing the lights of his green-colored police car-like vehicle. In Maryland he approached the female driver of the car and shot her in the face killing her. Her boyfriend escaped across the fields. When he returned to the scene with police, they discovered that the female was raped post-mortem. In Virginia, he overtook a family travelling with their five year-old daughter and eighteen-month infant girl. He tossed the infant into a ditch, and then shot the father dead, throwing his body on top of the infant which suffocated to death beneath the weight of the father's corpse. The mother and the five year-old girl he led away into the woods where he tortured, raped and murdered them both. Nearby the police found an abandoned cinder-block building in which there was an enormous stash of violent pulp and porn images taped to the walls along with morgue photographs of dead females. A button belonging to one of the victims was found in the room suggesting that he took his victims back there to rape and torture them surrounded by the images he had been fantasizing to for who knows how long. Reese was identified and arrested after bragging to a friend that murder was not wrong and just another human experience he wanted to partake in.[69]

Another serial killer, John Joubert, who murdered three young boys in 1982-1983, stated that when he was eleven or twelve he had seen detective magazines in the local grocery store and became aroused by the depiction of bound women on the covers. He began acquiring these magazines and masturbating to the images, eventually superimposing the fantasy of bound young boys over the images of the women. While a facilitator, detective magazines or porn on their own do not necessarily make people into serial killers. Joubert also stated that when he was six or seven, at least six years *before* he saw his first detective magazine, he fantasized about strangling and eating his babysitter. Joubert said that he could not recall whether these images brought on the masturbation or whether masturbation brought on the fantasies.

Violence and sex become merged into a murderous obsession, which often is kept secret. As one unnamed subject in the FBI sexual homicide study said, "Nobody bothered to find out what my problem was, and nobody knew about the fantasy world."[70]

There was a period (after the textual age of Brothers Grimm) that an adolescent flavor of comic books contributed to the ecology of necrophiliac fantasy. Garishly illustrated comics like *Tales from the Crypt* and *Weird Tales* portrayed explicit acts of murder, horror, death, dismemberment, zombies, ghouls and decay, until the comic industry was forced by the public concern over rising juvenile delinquency to self-censor crime and horror comics by its adoption of the Comic Code Authority in 1955. The demise of the horror comics turned adolescents to the adult pulp horror and crime literature. In Toronto in the 1960s in an era when magazines sold for a few coins, some street kiosk newsstands which carried these publications, along with soft erotica like *Playboy,* were sponsored by a charity for the blind, employing sightless or semi-blind clerks. Every month there would be lines of school boys formed up at these kiosks practicing their 'adult' deep voice, "I'll take a *Close-Up Detective, Murder Tales, Weird Fantasy, Bitchcraft, Sexorcists,* and gimme a *Playboy* and a *Big'uns* while you're at it." It was all available, one way or another, if not at a blind man's newsstand then from the secret stash underneath the mattress of an older brother or dad or the kid across the street. It was everywhere. All this pulp true adventure and true detective genre would fade only in the late 1970s, a victim of the economic realities of magazine publishing and fragmenting media but not before feeding the fantasies of several generations of serial killers.

***

### The Sixties and the rise of serial murder

As we sank into the 1960s we were battered by a wave of particularly savage and weird singular, multiple, mass and serial killers and assassins who killed for no reason that we could understand, and collectively appeared like an inexplicably rising wave of monsters. Anyone who has been recently watching the

TV series *Mad Men* has seen over the chronological arc of its seasons, episodes in which everyday life in the 1960s was interrupted by television and radio news reports that stopped everybody in their tracks gasping in horror: the October Missile Crises in 1962; the Kennedy assassination and the murder of Lee Harvey Oswald on live television in 1963 (perhaps the first murder in history carried on live TV); the reports of the Boston Strangler in 1964; the rape-murder of eight student nurses in Chicago on a single alcohol fueled night of butchery by a skid row drifter Richard Speck and a few weeks later the murder of 16 victims by crazed sniper ex-Marine Charles Whitman firing his rifle from a clock tower in Austin, Texas in the summer of 1966. Then came 1968, beginning with a widely televised color film news sequence showing a Vietcong prisoner summarily being executed with a shot to his head from a .38 snub-nosed revolver wielded by a Saigon police chief during the Tet Offensive in Vietnam. It was 'snuff TV' in primetime. In the spring of '68 reports of Martin Luther King's assassination and the race riots that followed, and two months later the assassination of presidential nomination candidate Robert Kennedy, completely threw us off balance as we began to feel a loss of control to some sort of dark conspiratorial invisible murdering forces, of being overrun by unexpected and inexplicable homicidal violence. The summer brought us live broadcasts of Chicago cops beating and brutalizing not only antiwar protesters, but ordinary citizens who happened to wander into the street on that day, the postman and the guy who stepped out to buy a quart of milk for his kids.

The overwhelming stopping power of these reports is not exaggerated in *Mad Men*. Unlike today with cable, satellite and internet, back in the 1960s there was no place to look away to: no MTV or Pet, Golf, or Food Channels to turn to, no kitty videos on a YouTube or Facebook. There were only three television channels run by the only three networks: ABC, NBC and CBS. With nothing but dead air on Channel 1, the television dial started with Channel 2 and ended at Channel 13. CNN was still twenty years away in the future. We were strapped in to whatever came at us in those three television feeds, like Malcolm McDowell in *A*

*Clockwork Orange* with his eyelids forciped open to the images of violence streaming at him. These three narrow video feeds fed into a vast reserve of illustrated print material ranging from mainstream to soft-core and hard-core imagery of rape and murder. Excited, horrified, compelled, titillated, obsessed by the violence streaming from the television screen, both real and simulated, there were no VCRs or videotape to capture and keep it, but the pulp print pictures one could fold up and take away behind a closed door to some private corner to masturbate and fantasize with at will, over and over, further fusing and conditioning in a disturbed mind the connecting process between the reproductive sexual impulse and death, rape and cannibalism.

It is hard to imagine George Romero making *Night of the Living Dead* in any year other than 1968. Unlike traditional zombies on isolated tropical island locations or the Hammer film zombies in basements and courtyards of medieval castles ruled by monsters, Romero's waves of new cannibal zombies swarmed among us, over a stark black & white Pennsylvania landscape, eating the living or infecting them with their bite, serving no master other than their hunger. The horror climaxes in the *Night of the Living Dead* not with the zombies, but with us, the parties of drunken zombie-killers, who like the Nazi *Einsatzkommandos* are hunting them down and piling their zombie corpses onto huge flaming pyres. The film ends with one of the protagonists who survived a siege of zombies in a farmhouse, being cavalierly killed by zombie-hunters who mistake him for an undead and casually shoot him through the head and toss his corpse into a bonfire of zombies. The monsters are us; the horror, the horror.

After 1968, there was one more year left to the 1960s and it was capped in the summer of 1969 when Charlie Manson and his crazed homicidal pseudo-hippies high on speed and acid came howling down the Hollywood Hills massacring Los Angeles's elite beautiful people in their homes and finger-painting graffiti in their blood on their designer walls. What Manson didn't finish in the summer of 1969, the US Army did when reports came out that back in March of 1968, in a little Vietnamese hamlet called My Lai, US troops in the defence of democracy and the American way massacred 347 elderly men, women and children, gang raping and mutilating some of the women before and after death. They say that after My Lai America lost her innocence forever; there was no coming back from something like that; even though truthfully, we knew it was lost long before then. By now a generation of young up-and-coming serial killers were matured and stirring out of this morass of blood and rape and hypocrisy: the hedonistic 1970s were coming, the American Decade of the Dead.

The serial killers of the 1970s to 1990s were being brewed as disturbed children with fantasies emerging in the 1940s to 1960s. Serial killing is not exclusively a reflection of the era in which it occurs, but of the era in which the serial killer was first nurturing his fantasies, as long as twenty years earlier.[71] If we look at this relatively random list of birthdates of some prominent serial killers and the years in which they were born and raised as children, and when they committed their killings, the chronological significance of the Second World War (1939-1945) and its aftermath is dramatically self-evident. To get a sense of why these serial killers are offending between the 1960s and 1990s, one needs to look at the world they were being hatched in as children in the 1940s and 1950s.

***

**Modern male serial killers chronologically by year of birth and period of principal killing activity. [Additional date indicated if the serial killer was incarcerated for murder committed prior to his principal serial killing period, or confessed to an earlier murder.]**

| Serial Killer | DOB | Killing Cycle |
|---|---|---|
| Ed Gein | 1906 | 1954-1957 |
| Harvey Glatman | 1927 | 1957-1958 |
| William Heirens | 1928 | 1946 |

| Serial Killer | DOB | Killing Cycle |
|---|---|---|
| David Carpenter | 1930 | 1979-1980 |
| Albert Desalvo | 1931 | 1962-1964 |
| Melvin Rees | 1933 | 1957-1959 |
| Juan Corona | 1934 | 1970-1971 |
| Angelo Buono | 1934 | 1977-1979 |
| Andrei Chikatilo | 1936 | 1978-1990 |
| Henry Lee Lucas | 1936 | 1976-1983 and 1960 |
| Ian Brady | 1938 | 1963-1965 |
| Jerry Brudos | 1939 | 1968-1969 |
| Dean Corll | 1939 | 1970-1973 |
| Patrick Kearney | 1939 | 1965-1977 |
| Robert Hansen | 1939 | 1980-1983 |
| Lawrence Bittaker | 1940 | 1979 |
| Richard Biegenwald | 1940 | 1958-1983 |
| Fred West | 1941 | 1967-1987 |
| John Wayne Gacy | 1942 | 1972-1978 |
| Rodney Alcala | 1943 | 1971-1979 |
| Arthur Shawcross | 1945 | 1988-1989 and 1972 |
| Denis Nilson | 1945 | 1978-1983 |
| Dennis Rader | 1945 | 1974-1991 |
| Chris Wilder | 1945 | 1984 |

| Serial Killer | DOB | Killing Cycle |
|---|---|---|
| Randy Kraft | 1945 | 1972-1983 |
| Paul Knowles | 1946 | 1974 |
| Ted Bundy | 1946 | 1974-1978 |
| Richard Cottingham | 1946 | 1977-1980 and 1967 |
| Gerald Gallego | 1946 | 1978-1980 |
| Peter Sutcliffe | 1946 | 1975-1980 |
| Gerard Schaefer | 1946 | 1971-1972 |
| William Bonin | 1947 | 1979-1980 |
| Ottis Toole | 1947 | 1974-1983 |
| John N. Collins | 1947 | 1967-1969 |
| Herbert Baumeister | 1947 | 1983-1998 |
| Herbert Mullin | 1947 | 1972-1973 |
| Edmund Kemper | 1948 | 1972-1973 and 1964 |
| Charles Norris | 1948 | 1979 |
| Douglas Clark | 1948 | 1980 |
| Gary Ridgway | 1949 | 1982-1993 |
| Richard Chase | 1950 | 1977 |
| William Suff | 1950 | 1986-1992 and 1974 |
| Randy Woodfield | 1950 | 1980-1981 |
| Gerald Stano | 1951 | 1970-1980 |
| Kenneth Bianci | 1951 | 1977-1979 |

| Serial Killer | DOB | Killing Cycle |
|---|---|---|
| Robert Yates | 1952 | 1975-1998 |
| William Hance | 1952 | 1978 |
| Carlton Gary | 1952 | 1977-1978 |
| David Berkowitz | 1953 | 1976-1977 |
| Coral Watts | 1953 | 1974-1982 |
| Robin Gecht | 1953 | 1981-1982 |
| David A. Gore | 1953 | 1981-1983 |
| Danny Rolling | 1954 | 1980 |
| Keith Jesperson | 1955 | 1990-1995 |
| Michael Hughes | 1956 | 1986-1993 |
| Wayne Williams | 1958 | 1979-1981 |
| Joel Rifkin | 1959 | 1989-1993 |
| Anthony Sowell | 1959 | 2007-2009 |
| Jeffrey Dahmer | 1960 | 1987-1991 and 1978 |
| Richard Ramirez | 1960 | 1984-1985 |
| James Rode | 1960 | 1991-1993 |

\*\*\*

### The Dawn of the Less Dead

Finally, there is another way at looking at this increasing phenomenon of serial murder. Maybe it's not that there are more serial killers but that there are more available victims. From the time of the first modern 'celebrity' serial killer, the still unidentified Jack the Ripper in London in 1888, there has been the debate as to whether serial killers are a product of modern crowded industrialized urbanized society. The theory is that when society was agrarian and people lived in small rural villages and hamlets where everybody knew each other and travelling strangers were feared, suspected and closely watched, it was difficult for a serial killer to murder several victims without calling attention to himself unless these gruesome crimes were blamed on werewolves, vampires and demons. It is argued that the crowded anonymity of huge cities rising with industrialization cloaked the identity of the serial killer while at the same time provided him with a large victim pool of strangers to prey upon among the displaced urban industrial masses living in a state of degradation about whom nobody really cared. It was one thing to kill a peasants' daughter in a village where the entire community, kin and clan raise an alarm, and another to snatch a victim from the teeming slums of London, New York or Chicago where nobody knew anybody and nobody cared. Jack the Ripper was killing the exact same kind of victim that many serial killers prefer to this day: street prostitutes.

Criminologist Steven Egger argues that there is an increased climate today of social encouragement to kill a type of person who, when murdered, is "less-dead" than other categories of homicide victims. Prostitutes, cruising homosexuals, homeless transients, drug addicts, runaway youths, senior citizens, minorities and unemployed inner-city poor, according to Egger, are perceived by our society as "less-dead" than a white college girl from a middle-class suburb or a fair-haired innocent child. Egger explains: "The victims of serial killers, viewed when alive as a devalued strata of humanity, become "less-dead" (since for many they were less-alive before their death and now they become the "never-were") and their demise becomes the elimination of sores or blemishes cleansed by those who dare to wash away these undesirable elements."[72]

News media is probably the single worst contributor to the 'less dead' syndrome. In the mid-1990s, the trial of William Lester Suff who murdered thirteen women in the Lake Elsinore region of California from 1986 to 1992 went virtually unreported. Suff killed drug-addicted street prostitutes and left their bodies behind strip mall garbage dumpsters, posed so as to call attention to their drug habits. But Suff went on trial in the middle of the O. J. Simpson case. What are thirteen dead crack whores compared to two shiny, tennis white Starbucks victims in Brentwood at the hands of an enraged celebrity? And how about Joel Rifkin, who murdered seventeen street hookers in the New York–Long Island area? The media abandoned his story in the rush to cover the massacre of six "respectably employed" train commuters by Colin Ferguson. The trial of Joel Rifkin was wrapped up in relative obscurity despite the seventeen murder victims. We might not even know his name if an episode of *Seinfeld* had not made it a butt of jokes. For the press covering serial murder these days it is not the sheer number of snuffed-out lives that count, but their celebrity status or visible credit rating; the trade-off comes around at one SUV in the garage for every five dead hookers in a Dumpster.[73]

Essayist and environmentalist Ginger Strand recently challenged the theory that the increase in serial killing in the USA after the 1950s can be attributed to the rise of the postwar modern American interstate freeway system that gave serial killers rapid mobility to strike far from their home territory in the anonymity of the road.[74] The FBI's recent Highway Serial Killings Initiative launched in 2009 to investigate over 500 unsolved homicides linked to interstate freeways further bolsters this image of the highway system 'circulating' serial killers like bad blood throughout the body of the America. But the image of the highly mobile interstate 'drifter' serial killer is a myth. In reality a 74% majority of serial killers stay close to home, preferring to kill in their own state.[75]

Ginger Strand argues that the rampant building of the American interstate freeway system, especially in the way it was built in the 1950s and 1960s through urban centers, has indeed contributed to rising serial murder not by mobilizing killers, but by increasing the victim pool through its destruction of inner-city communities and the scattering of people into soulless, depressed public housing ghettos. Strand reports, "In its first decade [1956-

1966], the interstate highway program destroyed some 330,000 urban housing units across the nation, the majority of them occupied by minorities and the poor. After that the pace picked up. No one knows the exact number, but estimates are that the highway program displaced around a million Americans."[76]

Strand describes how Atlanta's vital and prosperous Auburn Avenue neighborhood known as "Sweet Auburn" once described by Forbes Magazine in the 1950s as "the richest negro street in the world" was ripped through by an elevated interstate freeway in 1966 destroying viable African American owned neighborhood businesses, community cultural institutions, churches and family homes and forcing them into bleak anonymous institutionalized high-density cinder-block public housing complexes.[77] Strand argues that the construction of American freeways through cities in the 1950s and 1960s often targeted poor and minority neighborhoods, destroying their communities, expropriating homes and businesses and forcing families into ghettos which produce not only 'less dead' victims, but in the chaos and degradation of families, serial killers as well. In the expropriation and destruction of Atlanta's Sweet Auburn to connect the I-20 interstate freeway, Strand says that a decade later Wayne Williams would find his vast victim pool. She writes, "1-20 would play a key role in Atlantans' understanding of why, in the late seventies, their children began to disappear."[78]

The destruction wrought by the building of freeways in the 1950s to 1960s through the hearts of once vibrant functioning African American and other minority communities in New York, Miami, New Orleans, Detroit, Nashville, Boston, Atlanta, Los Angeles, and other cities, twenty years later is taking its toll. While in the past serial killers were perceived as being mostly white males, today (2004-2011) 56% of all serial killers are African Americans and the proportion is increasing.[79]

When one considers the recent devastation of the American working and middle classes by the loss of industrial and clerical jobs to globalization, and by the loss of homes in the financial collapse of 2008 along with the horror and death we experienced on 9/11 and the brutality of the 'war on terror' that our young sons and daughters now are called upon to wage, we should not be anticipating a reduction in serial killing anytime in the near future.

We are living in a 'killing for culture' world. Since the public coining of the word "serial killer" in 1981 and the release of the movie *Silence of the Lambs* in 1991, serial killers have become a staple of popular entertainment. Those 2,514 instances I cited earlier that the term "serial killer" appeared in the *New York Times* during the 1990s were increasingly in the context of movie and book reviews. Making matters worse, since the introduction in *Silence of the Lambs* of the fictional sophisticated Chianti-sipping serial killer Dr. Hannibal "The Cannibal" Lecter, there is a genre that celebrates serial killers as symbols of rebellion, bold courage, individuality and unique cleverness. Many transform the serial killer into a figure which allows them to fantasize rebellion or the lashing out at society's ills. The serial killer becomes a symbol of swift and effective justice, cleansing society of its crime-ridden vermin. The serial killer's skills in eluding police for long periods of time transcend the very reason that he is being hunted. The killer's elusiveness overshadows his trail of grief and horror.

The movie *Silence of the Lambs* separated monsters into "good" and "bad" serial killers. The sophisticated and charming fictional Hannibal Lecter as portrayed by Anthony Hopkins was a "good" serial killer, while the sexually confused, dirty, poverty-ridden, rural shack-dwelling, pseudo-transsexual Buffalo Bill, who kept his victims in a stinking pit and skinned them, was the "bad" serial killer. Buffalo Bill was himself "less-alive." As one critic pointed out, many would enjoy the company of the cannibal Dr. Lecter at a dinner party (as long as they weren't on the menu), but who would want to be even seen in public with Buffalo Bill? There is no better example of a "good" serial killer today than *Dexter,* a TV serial killer who kills other serial killers. This celebration of serial killing in popular culture is as American as the Western. In fact as one critic argued back in the 1990s, American Westerns were "really about serial killing all along."[80]

Television portrays serial killers as devilishly clever and creative rogues, as worthy opponents of the television investigators who weekly catch one. Movie stars like Anthony Hopkins, Kevin

Spacey, Brad Pitt, Christian Bale are brought in to create charismatic serial killer screen characters whose bizarrely Hollywood scripted murders are always 'works of art' or *Se7en*-like symbolic philosophical ruminations on the meaning of life and death. The pain, degradation or the foul smell of death are never elements in these fanciful works of fiction or television shows.

Death stinks. Even true crime literature and interviews with serial killers rarely touch on the fact that when a victim is murdered they often soil themselves as their bowels release upon death. In one rare exception, veteran true crime author Michael Newton in his book based on his interviews with serial killer Eddie Cole, describes how after killing his female victims Cole would wipe them clean of their post-mortem excrement, sometimes gagging or vomiting on the floor from the stink, until the victim was sufficiently clean for him to perform sex with the corpse.[81] For other serial killers it was all about the stink. As James Rode, who while incarcerated in Florida for sex crimes, befriended Ted Bundy and with his 'advice' after his release went on to kill five female victims in 1991-1993, told a psychiatrist afterwards, "I want to watch them shit and piss for the last time."[82]

Through the 2000s most mainstream comic publishers abandoned the Comic Code Authority. DC and Archie Comics were the last holdouts until 2011 when they also left the code.[83] Immersive video games enable players to simulate serial killing. Snuff films, once a myth, are now a reality with the posting on the internet of horrific homemade videos like "3 Guys 1 Hammer" recorded in 2007 by three young Ukrainian serial killers as they battered and stabbed elderly derelict victims to death with a hammer and a screwdriver.[84] They eventually murdered 21 people. In Canada a celebrity wannabe Luc Magnotta is awaiting trial charged with murdering, performing sexual acts upon, dismembering and cannibalizing a male victim. It is alleged that he recorded himself on video stabbing with an ice pick the corpse of his victim tied to a bed, performing acts of necrophilia and dissecting it with a knife and fork and feeding parts to a dog. He then posted segments of the video to the internet entitling it "1 Lunatic 1 Ice Pick" as homage to the "3 Guys 1 Hammer" video.

After mailing the body parts to Canada's political parties and two elementary schools, Magnotta fled to Germany where he was arrested and extradited back to Canada. At this writing he is awaiting trial.

***

*Nineteen year-old team serial killers Viktor Sayenko and Igor Suprunyuck convicted for 21 homicides in the Ukraine in 2007, pose for a third accomplice with a camera with animal and human victims in videos they made of themselves. Posted after their arrest to the internet under the title "3 Guys 1 Hammer" their gruesome murder videos inspired other recent celebrity wannabe serial killers.*

\*\*\*

Again in Canada, inspired by and obsessed with *Dexter,* wannabe serial killer and filmmaker Mark Twitchell ("Dexter Killer") lured a male victim to his garage movie studio where he killed and dismembered him. Twitchell was arrested after he lured a second victim to his garage and attempted to subdue him with a stun baton but the victim managed to escape. Convicted in 2011, it was recently reported that Twitchell had purchased a television for his prison cell in order to see every episode of *Dexter* that he missed since he was arrested.[85]

As I write this in the summer of 2013, news is breaking that a man in Florida after murdering his wife posted the image of her corpse on his Facebook Page before surrendering to police. We are hurtling through a post-9/11 brave new world of technologically enhanced serial killing that is likely to get a lot worse as our current generation of children raised on *Dexter, Grand Theft Auto,* split zombie heads and internet snuff video, grow into adulthood. To paraphrase John Fogerty, looks like we're in for nasty weather, there's a bad moon on the rise...[86]

***

# Chapter 1: Timothy Wayne "T.K." Krajcir
## Inmate C96201:
## By Dane Ladwig

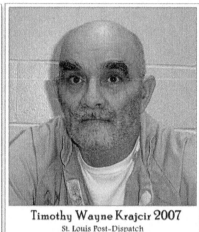

Timothy Wayne Krajcir 1979
St. Louis Post-Dispatch

Timothy Wayne Krajcir 2007
St. Louis Post-Dispatch

*Stltoday.com Police Handout*

The information herein is intended for the purpose of promoting public awareness and to further endorse and encourage public safety. The author of this article does not advocate on behalf of the criminal. The victims who are immortally etched in history as true sacrifices of a violent criminal's final acts are the divine messengers to humanity.

How does covetous greed and lust turn an innocent east coast boy into a barbaric hell-bent fiend determined to impose his will upon the innocence and purity of women he desires? What demented thoughts drive serial killers to the brink of murder? Does the conscience play a role in a serial killers conduct when he targets physically weaker victims only to fulfill profound sexual fantasies, then desecrates and ravages those he covets?

For this killer, if victims did not conform to his ideal of "perfection," whatever that twisted concept of "perfection" consisted of – in his convoluted adult mind – he felt his victims were better off "extinguished" and he would see to it that the deed was carried out. These unfortunates met their ends amidst cruel and undeserved circumstances.

He was determined that no other person would ever partake of his victim's glorious virtues, lest he permit them life beyond the present... and he had no intention of such a benevolent expression. This twisted individual, and all like him, who elevate themselves in their deranged minds, taking what they want from humanity simply because they can, stands as a true testament of a diabolic, malignant spirit spat directly from the deepest bowels of Hades.

As a predator, he evaded arrest. He did not fit the common profile, the conventional form or design of a serial killer. Who was this notorious lunatic, who kept authorities at bay for years chasing an elusive shadow as obscure as the baffling and deceptive phantom they called "Jack the Ripper;" and what made this criminal tick?

I began corresponding with convicted serial killer, Timothy Wayne "T.K." Krajcir [pronounced CRY-cheer] in the winter of 2012. By the spring of 2013, I had visited the inmate at Pontiac Correctional Center located about 100 miles southwest of Chicago's magnificent Lake Michigan shoreline and serene, picturesque skyline.

T.K. is serving two consecutive forty-year terms and fifteen consecutive life sentences for the murders of nine women spanning four states: Illinois (2); Missouri (5); Pennsylvania (1); and Kentucky (1). The murders date back to as early as the 1970's. All of his victims were women. Shooting, stabbing, and strangling/asphyxiation were his chosen methods of murder. His weapons of choice ranged from guns, knives, curtain cords, phone cords, and his bare hands.

When I first began correspondence with "T.K.," as his cellmates refer to him, I wondered how much of the "real" man would actually respond to me and how much might be mere fabrication of the man T.K. perceived himself to be, or perhaps even a distorted version of the man he wished he was. Because of this probable illusion, I sought the more credible avenue of face-to-face contact.

Having never sat down with a convicted serial killer before, prior to our first meeting, I began to imagine scenarios... Kind of like a heads up of what to expect. And I learned from experience, it is probably best not to run things through your mind, or review your notes, right before bedtime as it makes for sleepless nights.

Interviewing a serial killer bares no glory and is not what I would consider an honorable assignment. The person sitting across from the interviewer has performed acts most of us have only read about or watched in fictionalized dramatic horror films. With their victim's spilt blood forever leaving its mark on history, the criminals have etched out a place on the notable red-letter timeline; unfortunately, the victims are soon forgotten, but the criminal acts live on. The more victims they kill, the more gruesome the murders become, and the more notoriety they gain over a period of time. This is why it is so important to know how to interview a serial killer, and not allow them a platform to parade themselves and their heinous crimes before the families of the victims or the public.

In memory, I have listed the names of each known victim of Timothy Wayne "T.K." Krajcir at the end of this chapter. I urge you to please take a few moments at the conclusion of your reading to consider each victim and remember. These women did not invite him into their lives, nor were they women of questionable character; they were simply women who were chosen out of a veritable smorgasbord of innocent sacrifice from society's bounty. They had families and loved ones who were forced to endure a lifetime of horrific, haunting memories as a result of one man's selfish desires and grotesque fantasies. One man who forever destroyed the lives of hundreds, including family, friends and the beloved of the nine women he murdered.

From my research of T.K., I learned he was not only an educated man, but also quite adept when it came to exposing faults and weakness in others. He was a master of deception and manipulation from his many years of honing his skills in those areas. At the beginning of our correspondence, I held nothing back. I got straight to the point with my first question. "How would you categorize your murderous rampage as it equates to society and your contribution as a citizen currently in this place and time in history?"

I certainly did not expect the truth in his letter, but I was shocked at the audacity of his answer. "The same way you are an artist with your words, because of what you do [author books], I was sort of an artist like Van Gogh. At the time I committed the crimes, people [women] in my path were the canvas and I was the artist, an artist of intimidation and terror. The best ever!" He gloated as though he deserved the Pulitzer Prize of destruction.

*This perception of murder as an art form really made me wonder about all the other serial killers in history and whether they too viewed themselves as a "Van Gogh" of murder. It does seem fitting when you consider the way serial killers have evolved throughout history, and become more clever, crafty and cunning.*

When TK compared himself to an artist and author, I was appalled. Then I thought to myself, *that's exactly what he wants... to provoke me... he wants to control the interview and he probably knows the best way to do that is to get the best of me; hit me where I am most vulnerable – my passion for writing... my career.* To put his crimes and my writing on an equal plane, is to say, I too am a criminal, a lawless self-centered immoral fiend who is capable of every deplorable act an individual can commit against humanity... only I do it with my words.

In his demented criminal mind, he was merely attempting to justify his wrongs and he was trying to gain the upper hand of the interview. I would not allow such insanity. He is the convicted criminal. I am the innocent free man. He surrendered certain rights when he crossed over the lines of morality into the abyss of ruthless tyranny.

T.K. was born Timothy Wayne McBride in 1944. Now, a mere shell of an aging man, in his heyday, he was quite handsome, robust and virile. He had rich jet-black hair and a full thick mustache. Thick bushy eyebrows complemented his piercing eyes. His strong dimpled chin and distended cheekbones offered him an appearance more akin to a Greek demi-god. Later in life, he preferred to shave his head. He felt it made him look more "unique". T.K. was not a small man; he appeared healthy, strong, and his stare seemed to pierce my soul as if to be assessing my moral fiber through the deep recesses of my eyes. A dark presence was noticed and it was not attached to me or the guard present in the room. Although the guard was very intimidating, it was TK's foreboding glare that sent shivers up my spine and made the hairs on the nape of my neck stand at attention. I began recollecting his childhood...

A year after T.K. was born his paternal father, Charles McBride, abandoned T.K. and his mother, Fern Yost. When he was five years old, his mother met and married Bernie Krajcir and they relocated to Harrisburg, Pennsylvania.

By all accounts, T.K. did not display your typically damaged or psychologically destructive childhood nature that most other serial killers are prone to displaying. His academic grades were higher than most, he was a good-looking boy, he was not aggressive, nor did he "experiment" with animals or pets. However, he did act out from time to time.

T.K. was charged with his first crime: petty theft – stealing a bicycle – when he was an adolescent prior to his teen years. In 1953, Bernie Krajcir legally adopted T.K. and in turn, the family unit (Bernie and T.K.'s mother) changed his last name from McBride to Krajcir. It is at this time in T.K.'s life (at the age of ten) when he admits to beginning an unhealthy sexual obsession involving his mother.

*Sigmund Freud termed the psychoanalytic theory "Oedipus complex." Many serial killers are diagnosed with having experienced a degree of the Oedipus complex when sexual deviation is a motive or part of the killer's modus operandi. The Oedipus complex broken down is repressed subconscious desires and thoughts of sexually possessing a parent of the opposite sex. In the case of females, it is referred to as the "Electra" complex, introduced by psychotherapist and psychiatrist Carl Gustav Jung.* (encyclopedia 2013)

By the time T.K. reached puberty, he had begun exposing himself publicly. He said, "At first, I wanted to see how people would react, but then I realized it aroused me so I would do it more and more."

In 1962 (at the age of seventeen), T.K. enlisted in the U.S. Navy Reserve and was shipped to Great Lakes Naval Training Base in Great Lakes/Waukegan, Illinois. A few months later, he met Barbara Jean Kos. The two fell in love, or so Barbara thought, and in February of '63 they were married.

Three months after T.K. and Barbara wed, he was brought up on charges of rape. In addition to raping the Waukegan, IL woman, he brutally stabbed her several times. Miraculously and to his surprise, she survived. While awaiting the conclusion of the trial he committed another rape in the North Chicago area.

As a result of his sexual crimes, and his incarceration for the crimes while enlisted in the Navy, in 1963 the Navy Reserves dishonorably discharged him after only 14 months of service. T.K. stated, "They taught me a lot about discipline, but that was about all they were good for. I didn't mind when they cut me loose."

In May of 1963, while he was incarcerated pending the outcome of the trial for raping and stabbing his first victim, T.K.'s wife Barbara gave birth to their daughter, Charlotte. Until this day, T.K. never met his only child.

In June of 1963 the guilty verdict made headlines. T.K. was sentenced to 25-50 years and incarcerated at Joliet Prison in Joliet,

Illinois. Two years later, Barbara filed for divorce and it was granted.

In the ensuing years, T.K. continued an uncontrollable sexually motivated path of destruction spanning four states. The average IQ is 90-109, his IQ is 125, and he is highly intelligent. As such, he was difficult to catch. His formal criminal history diagnosis is "Sexual Deviancy Serial Killer." His acts include assault, attempted murder, home invasion, murder, rape, theft, and robbery. The victim's ranged from ages 21 – 65.

According to a state mandated psychological evaluation dated July 27, 1983, by Paul K. Gross M.D. Timothy Wayne Krajcir (38 years old at the time), psychiatric treatment "[]... has not helped to control his [Krajcir's] sexual deviancy. (Campbell 2011) (Campbell 2011)"

During the evaluation, while Krajcir was incarcerated at the Lehigh County Prison for "... breaking into a house with the purpose of raping its occupants, although it was thwarted by a phone call to the police. He [Krajcir] wound up threatening the occupants and masturbating in their presence. (Campbell 2011)"

Dr. Gross made it clear that Timothy Wayne Krajcir is a deviant sexual predator. Krajcir is detached from his feelings and feels no remorse for his actions. His deviant acts have included public masturbation, cross-dressing, homosexual contact, rape of a minor, forcible rape (at gun and knifepoint), fantasies of sexual contact with his mother, and other peculiar and bizarre fantasies.

In short, Krajcir's crimes were driven by his bestial sexual appetite, directed by demented fantasies, and a narcissistic outlook on life. At no time did he display an ounce of compassion for his victims or the desire to repent or accept responsibility for his crimes against humanity. A cold-blooded killer to the core.

## Krajcir's Crimes Abridged

In 1944 in West Mahoney Township in Pennsylvania, a small town by the name of Ironton, welcomed a little baby named Timothy Wayne to Charles McBride and Fern Yost. McBride abandoned his son and Fern Yost. Five years later, his mother met and married Bernie Krajcir. Soon after Bernie Krajcir adopted Timothy Wayne. Timothy was a troubled adolescent who had a history of sexual perversion and criminal intent. His sexual crimes escalated to forced rape at a very young age. In and out of penile institutions, his crimes continued and intensified to include murder. To Krajcir, the killings turned to a cat-and-mouse game with the authorities. Now serving several back-to-back sentences for his crimes, Krajcir will never see the light of day outside a prison for as long as he lives. He shows no outward expressions of contempt or remorse for his actions.

## The Bust and the Deal

It has been conjectured throughout the past several decades that Krajcir attacked women he could overpower with very little effort. Combined with his dedication to committing crimes strictly at night, and his devotion to complete silence and never speaking of his crimes to anyone; these are convincingly the very reasons Krajcir evaded the authorities for over nine years. After Krajcir was released from prison on his first rape conviction he was under a court mandated order to gain full-time employment or option for academic education at an accredited college. In December of 1981 Krajcir graduated from Southern Illinois University in Carbondale, where he earned a degree with a minor in psychology, and a major in Administrative Justice, typically reserved for individuals pursuing a career with the police department, although not restricted to law enforcement personnel. With the advantage of his degree and education in law enforcement and criminal justice, Krajcir was able to stay one step ahead of the police at all times. Police believed throughout the investigation that perhaps a police officer was behind the crimes – that is how well he masterfully confused the crime scene investigators.

What Krajcir did not know at the time, was that twenty-five-years later technologic advancements would link him to the scene of the crime through DNA – it simply didn't exist at the time he unleashed his vengeance on the victims in his path. However, as time passed, Krajcir knew his day would come. He was fully aware that eventually advances in forensic technology and investigation would lead back to him. He knew he had to make a very important decision.

When Krajcir was serving time for rape charges of a Southern Illinois University student, Deborah Sheppard, in 1982, he received a life sentence. Krajcir plea-bargained for a deal that would spare his life. If he surrendered the names, dates and details of his criminal acts, his sentence would be reduced from the death penalty to consecutive life sentences. For Krajcir, the idea of execution was the most horrific and disrespectful demise a human could endure – even one who subjected innocent victims to appalling humiliation, and final moments that ended in terror and merciless annihilation.

Krajcir was earmarked as a "sexually dangerous person" (Estrada 2007). However, shortly after he enrolled at Southern Illinois University, it was later learned that Krajcir drove just one hour from the campus to stalk, rape and murder five of his nine victims. Utilizing the education he was gaining, he perfected his skills with each murder. He changed locations, drove several miles to stalk the next victim, and the important details left to forensics, such as fingerprints, shoeprints, and hair fibers all varied with each killing. Krajcir was convinced that if he mixed things up enough and confused the cops he could go on killing indefinitely. However, when the anvil landed and the news of DNA matching hit the airwaves, Krajcir feared that the electric chair or lethal injection would soon mark the end of his reign of terror.

*Although Krajcir remains and his victims are gone, his arrogance and deeds finally caught up with him. Krajcir is far from a model of reformation or rehabilitation. In the following interview, you will meet a man whom you may feel deserves to die. By God's grace, and justifiably so, he is dying daily and will forever pay the price for his crimes. If you are compelled to believe justice was not served, I urge you to consider the nature of a beast as uncaring as this hardened criminal. As unfortunate as it is, it seems that for the world to understand the harmony of peace and paradise, we must also experience the injustice of hatred and discord.*

At his trial after the plea bargain was accepted and Krajcir was off the hook and free from facing his worst fear; the death sentence, he remarked, "I don't know if I could have been so generous if I were in the same situation. Thank you for sparing my life."

# The Interview

*The Welcoming Center of Pontiac Correctional Center in Illinois*

*Razor Wire Garnishes the Iron Fences*
*SurroundingPontiacCorrectional Center*

After checking in at the guard's quarters, I was escorted through a brightly lit corridor covered in that ubiquitous drab gray paint, that adorns the walls of most underground parking garages and hospital basements. Proceeding further, I noticed a firearm securely strapped to the waist of the guard walking directly in front of me; a can of pepper spray, an ASP Tactical baton (the type of baton, which has a handle and a steel rod, similar to an old timer's Billy club), a ring of keys, and nylon tie straps (zip tie restraints), strategic gear enabling a measure of security from the psychopathic killer behind the steel gates.

We finally made it to a room with several steel tables encircled by steel benches permanently connected to the concrete floor. I looked up toward the high ceiling and noticed small steel-gated windows enveloping the room allowing just enough sunlight to form a halo-like glow in the room. Just then the guard sought direction from his handheld receiver. I missed the first part of the conversation as his security radio quavered, but I was able to make out, "Then give me a few minutes and I'll get him over there."

It turned out, we were not allowed to conduct the interview in such a "high risk" area, but we were allowed in a controlled environment with supervision, far from the reach of the general prison population. If those terms were not acceptable, I was informed I would be forced to "forfeit the interview based on a lack of following prison protocol." I refused to come this far without interviewing Krajcir so I complied, and we were soon in an "Interrogation" room, although someone had taped a handmade sign over the nameplate which now read "Interview".

Furnishings consisted of a cold steel table with a comfortable looking padded chair at one end and a seemingly uncomfortable steel chair at the other end. The guard escorted me to the padded chair, and then gave me specific verbal instructions.

"You are not to pass anything across the table. You are not to touch the inmate. I will remain inside with you standing behind the inmate at the door... the other guard will be stationed outside the door. You are not to get up from your seat under any circumstances unless I inform you to do so. Do you understand?" I nodded my head.

"I said... DO YOU UNDERSTAND?" He repeated barking like a Marine Drill Sergeant.

"Yes sir!" I responded in an orderly fashion.

He then radioed to the guards out the door to escort "Inmate C96201" into the room.

I stood, but as soon as T.K. made his way to the table, the guard pointed his index finger signaling me to sit. I sat per his instructions.

As T.K. sat, he gleaned over his spectacles just below an unmanicured unibrow studying me. Then I began with small talk, first introducing myself and then thanking T.K. for the opportunity to conduct the interview.

It is a bit unnerving sitting across from a convicted serial killer. But then again, *This is about the man and his psyche. I reminded myself, and I am not a criminal investigator, nor a judge. His acts sicken me, indeed but he has been judged, convicted and is serving his time.*

Still, haunting images of victims invade my thoughts. I could only imagine the raw heart-wrenching emotion felt by a beloved family member as they sit in a court of law enduring the process of a painful trial with their loved ones killer just a few feet away.

After we finished with the formalities of introductions and legal clarification involving the purpose of the interview, I proceeded with the questioning.

Q. "Would you say, your childhood was a good experience or a bad experience?"

A. "It was a childhood. I dealt with the hand that was given to me."

Q. "What about your time in the Service?"

A. "That was a joke. They thought they could teach me something. I guess in a way they did. They showed me how ridiculous this system is... our government is, and our laws are. They helped to open my eyes to a lot of things wrong with our system."

Q. "You were able to take advantage of that system and your victims paid the ultimate price for your acts; are you saying you blame the system for what you did?"

A. "No, I take full responsibility for my acts. I'm saying the system allowed me to see the flaws and learn ways to get away with what I was doing for as long as I could without being caught, that was their fault. If there were better laws or surveillance or dedication to catching me, they could have long before I committed all those crimes."

N. *(Deflection of blame is a common reaction when the conscience is burdened with guilt. Diverting responsibility for ones actions is also a telltale sign of not accepting accountability for the actions he or she has committed.)*

Q. How does it make you feel knowing those people would still be alive if, as you say, the laws or system would have caught you prior to you taking their lives?"

A. "It pisses me off. I'm not what you would call a very religious man, but why did God allow it to happen? That pisses me off too. He [God] allowed me to be the way I am [*interesting that he did not say, "the way I was"*], and He allowed those people to be where they were at that time and place. You could say He orchestrated the whole damn thing."

Q. You say the system and the laws could have helped to avoid the crimes and that God was the architect behind the design of the crimes. I am curious as to where that leaves Timothy Krajcir and his responsibility in the crimes?

N. *T.K. gave a long stare. I felt as though he were contemplating ending the interview as if perhaps I had triggered an ethical dilemma. If in fact he publicly proclaimed his role and accepted responsibility (as he did in his most recent parole board hearing), why the flip-flop as to who is responsible for his actions?*

T.K. answered in a very rigid tone, which confirmed my suspicion of his agitation over my questioning.

A. "In the first place, I do regret what I did. It's just unfortunate that things like this happen and are allowed to happen. I mean… why me, why not the guy at the hardware store or a bank. Why are they the way they are and I was made the way I am?"

Q. You mean, why are you a convicted serial killer as opposed to a store clerk or a bank teller?

A. "Yeah. I didn't ask to be this way, it wasn't a choice, it just happened."

Q. Are you saying, serial killers do not make choices, moral or otherwise, which dictate their behavior?

A. "I believe, when I did the women [raped and murdered them], I was acting out of an uncontrollable desire and an overpowering need to fulfill some kind of emotional, physical, and psychological obligation or ambition, to perfect the illusion I had of being more superior than the victims, the cops, and I guess of God."

*N. I had made a note that T.K. had now started expanding his vocabulary and his depth of thought as it pertained to his actions in the crimes he had committed, and therefore it seemed like a good time to advance the level of questioning.*

Q. "T.K., while thinking back, do you recall any early indicators or predetermining factors that you now consider may have bound you to the criminal element?"

A. "Well, sure. Way back when I was a kid… I didn't have what you would call the ideal childhood. Then as a teenager, I was more into taking what I wanted. If I saw something, I didn't have and I wanted it, I created the perfect plan and just grabbed it. I don't ever remember *not* having to do what people call immoral or illegal things to get what I wanted or needed."

Q. "Do you recall the first time you ever killed someone?"

"Sure," he responded. "For me to do what I did, many things had to come together, and all of them had to be allowed from above [God]. Right?"

Q. "Your analogy, that is, if God is the ultimate designer in the end, where does free-will come into play? Are we not given the power to choose or decide, good versus evil?"

T.K. responded with a question, "How can you choose, when you are saturated in evil from the very first breath you take?"

N. *Many criminals feel they are disowned and shunned in the sight of God, and as a result they feel they are not worthy of His bounty and His forgiveness, which perpetuates an already declining situation.*

I asked the inmate, "I'm curious, how does a serial killer choose his victims?"

He replied with a smirk and snidely said, "Me? I liked them."

I interjected, "That would imply you knew your victims. Did you?"

He had no reservation in discussing the subject and explained matter-of-factly, "I would sit in the Walmart parking lot, or the Kroger [Supermarket] lot, and I would watch them. I wanted to know their every move before I approached them."

This response begged the question, "So, you stalked them?"

Instantly he responded, "I suppose you could say that."

N. *At that very moment, I envisioned my daughter at the local department store with a monster like T.K. in his car, parked in the rear of the lot photographing her, and then following her home. After the conversation with T.K., I called my daughter during the ride home and read her the "riot act" about safety. She snickered incessantly, and wanting to know what I was so "freaked out" about. I was stuck in a restless state of turmoil the remainder of the evening.*

T.K. would either stalk the women, abduct them, and take them to his residence, or break into their homes and await their arrival. As soon as his chosen victim arrived and was cozy in the comfort and safety of her home, he pounced like a predator on his prey. He would then bind the victim, rob them of their worldly possessions, and rape them. In one diabolical instance he forced a woman's son to witness the crimes as the son was an unexpected intruder whom T.K. had every intention of killing afterward. So T.K. violated his victim sexually, and then executed her in front of her son, all the while pointing a gun in the young man's face, and rendering him helpless.

T.K. never made any attempts to hide from the authorities; in fact, many times he revisited the scene within minutes of committing the crime. And in 2007 when he confessed to these ruthless killings in an attempt to avoid the death penalty, he was convinced that his fifteen consecutive life sentence terms would be decreased. Although he had been before the parole board claiming full responsibility for his actions, and professing to be "a changed man," the fact remains he will never see the light of day outside the walls of a state penal institution.

Q. Are you saying if things in your life were different from the very beginning, you would have been a different person, not a serial killer or rapist?

T.K. responded, "I guess it doesn't matter, 'cause we'll never know!"

I proposed, "Does that mean you wouldn't change the things, the events, which have led up to this time and point in your life?"

He said, "I'm just saying, sittin' around thinking about how things might have been, don't change a damn thing. I did what I did and here I am, and those are the facts."

*N. I wondered about my next question and I wanted the answer to one very specific basic question, but I knew it was not going to be easy to extract the truth, but I just went for it.*

Did you ever think about the victims after you killed them but before you were apprehended?

*N. In a strange way, I felt as though I was now the defendant and T.K. was the jury, as though he held the verdict a sentence was about to be imposed. After a long deliberation, T.K. delivered the ruling.*

"No. Not really!"

*N. It was as short of an answer as a guilty or not guilty verdict.*

Q. When was the first time you started thinking about them? *I wanted to see if T. K. would change his story. If he would fess-up to having a conscience and thinking about the women he killed.*

A. "I would try to do things a little different each time [murder] so I would recall what I did, and not do the exact things twice. I guess in a way that was thinking about them. How else do you learn unless you go over it in your head and I had to mix things up, 'cause I didn't want to give the cops too much to go on."

I then asked, "What would you have done differently if given the opportunity?"

He pondered the question for a moment, "Well, I probably wouldn't have got caught!"

I followed with a piercing question, if you could face your victims right now, what would you say to them?

*He turned his head slightly towards the guard elevated his voice and replied...*

"I'm sorry!"

Then he smiled at me, raised his bushy eyebrows, and under his breath he whispered, "Tough loss!"

I propositioned one final question, "What would you say to anyone who would consider taking the same path as you in life... becoming a serial killer?"

He thought for a few minutes. Just when I thought he was going to blow off the question, he blurted out, "Think about what you're going to do. You're taking the life of someone else and you're forfeiting your life. In a way you are kinda saying their life is more important than yours, because they're dead and you have to pay for it... for their death... so it makes their life kinda more important than you or what you want. When you think about it that way, it's really not worth it. If you think you can pull it off and never get caught, you're wrong. You're dead wrong. If you really want to end it all, cause that's what you're doing really, then just off yourself, 'cause it ain't worth the hell of serving a life sentence."

The Psychological Evaluation

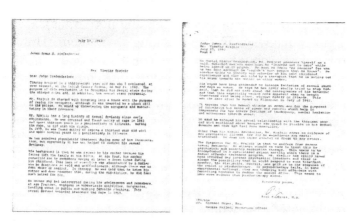

The above letter is directed to Judge James N. Diefenderfer, dated July 27, 1983. It consist of a court ordered psychological evaluation of Timothy Krajcir. Although the evaluation was conducted over thirty years ago, not much has changed regarding Krajcir or his emotional or mental state. Below is a word-for-word transcription of the evaluation.

*Warning: Graphic in nature.*

July 27, 1983

Re: Timothy Krajcir

Dear Judge Diefenderfer,

Timothy Krajcir is a thirty-eight year old man who I evaluated at your request, at the Lehigh County Prison, on May 23, 1983. The purpose of the evaluation is to determine his mental state during the alleged crime and, in addition, his mental state currently.

Mr. Krajcir is charged with breaking into a house with the purpose of raping its occupants, although it was thwarted by a phone call to the police. He wound up threatening the occupants and masturbating in their presence.

Mr. Krajcir has a long history of sexual deviancy since early adolescence. He was arrested and found guilty of rape in 1963 and spent thirteen years in a penitentiary in Illinois. During the rape, he did stab his victim. In 1979, he was found guilty of raping a thirteen year old girl and spent several years in a penitentiary in Illinois.

He has received psychiatric treatment during some of his incarceration, but apparently it has not helped to control his sexual deviancy.

His background is that he was raised by his mother because his father left the family at his birth. At age four, his mother remarried and he remembers moving at least a dozen times during his childhood. This lack of stability was accentuated by who he describes as cold and unaffectionate, although there was no real abuse or neglect. In therapy, he was told that he hates his mother and does remember that, during the mid-sixties, he did feel much hatred for her.

He became shy and introverted during his adolescence and remembers, at age fourteen, engaging in voyeuristic activities, burglaries, fondling women in public and wearing feminine clothing. This sexual deviant behavior preceded the rape in 1963.

July 27, 1983

On Mental Status Examination. Mr. Krajcir presents himself as a cold, detached man who says that he "learned not to care" while being locked up in prison. He says he feels "no remorse" for what he has done although he "couldn't hurt people that he knows". He somehow tries to justify his behavior on his past childhood experiences and once was told by a therapist that he is acting out his anger towards his mother on other women.

His rapes have been proceeded by intense fantasies of sexual abuse and rape on women. He says he has never really tried to stop himself, that he did not care about the consequences of his behavior and that this especially became more apparent when he became frustrated with being alone, without family or friends. This was the case after he moved to Allentown in July of 1982.

It appears that his sexual attacks on women are for the purposes of increasing his sense of power and control which help to compensate for his severe feelings of inadequacy, social isolation and bitterness toward women.

He says he enjoyed his sexual relationship with the thirteen year old girl mentioned above because she would be pliable to his sexual demands and made him feel more masculine.

Other than his sexual deviancies, Mr. Krajcir shows no evidence of any psychiatric illness, nor did he experience any mental breakdowns. He does not abuse alcohol or drugs to any extent.

The diagnosis for Mr. Krajcir is that he suffers from severe sexual deviancy. An attempt should be made to treat this by psychiatric and possibly medication therapy. This needs to be accomplished in a specialized prison setting where there is a sexual offender treatment program. Mr. Krajcir has never been afforded any intense psychiatric treatment and there is always the possibility that he would respond to such treatment. However, the statistics, overall, are grim as to the response of the rapist to psychotherapy. If psychotherapy fails, in some experimental settings, they are treating such offenders with feminine hormones to reduce the sexual drive. This seems to have more success than psychotherapy alone.

Sincerely yours,

Paul M. Gross, M.D.

## Victims of Timothy Wayne "T.K." Krajcir

L-R Top Row – Mary Parish, Cape Girardeau, FL. (58-years-old) died August 12, 1977, Brenda Parish, Cape Girardeau, FL. (27-years-old) died August 12, 1977, Southeast Missouri State University student Sheila Cole. Sheila's body was found November 17, 1977 at a roadside highway rest area near McClure, Ill. Her car was later located in a Walmart parking lot in Cape Girardeau, FL. Second Row – Margie Call (57-years-old), Mildred Wallace (65-years-old), Deborah Sheppard a Southern Illinois University (SIU) student (raped and murdered in Carbondale, Ill. in 1982). Bottom Row – Virginia Lee Witte (strangled and stabbed to death in 1978), Myrtle Rupp (51-years-old), and Joyce Tharp (29-years-old) Krajcir traveled from Paducah, KY. where he first murdered Joyce, to Sothern Illinois (SIU) then traveled back to Paducah, KY. with Joyce.

# The Nature of a Serial Killer

Some years ago, our cable television system was on the fritz. We had gone back and forth with the cable company trying to resolve the problem. In the end, we cancelled the cable service, not because of the repeated issues, but because the most recent technician that came to my home was disturbingly strange.

My wife was at work, and I was in college at the time, but this particular day I was home catching up on a backlog of homework. When the technician entered our home, he "scanned" the outlay of the Duplex, similar to how a bank robber might "case the joint." Upon noticing a picture of my daughter, he began getting a little too personal. To make a long story short, I asked the technician to leave before I called the authorities, or took the huge risk of taking matters into my own hands while introducing him to the "tool-shop" in my garage.

I am not a small man, and can be quite intimidating to someone who doesn't know me. I am built well, and sport several tattoos. I also ride a motorcycle and don't mind getting my hands dirty. To put it politely, the technician made a wise choice in leaving of his own accord.

About two weeks later while watching the evening news a special report grabbed my attention… "A [Cable Company] employee has been arrested on charges of multiple murder. [Technician] has been charged with five counts of murder. [Technician] would gain access to customer's homes and when there was only a woman present; he would strangle the victim, commit rape, and then place her body in the bathtub. Investigators found the bodies of five women, all customers of [Cable Company], who allowed [Technician] in their home."

The photo flashed on the television screen of the alleged criminal confirmed my deepest fears. His fixation on my wife's whereabouts and my daughter's photo became clear.

The fact is I observed very unsettling characteristics about this same serial killer when he was in my home. It was horrifying to think that a serial killer was in my home and mere circumstances made the difference between my loved ones being protected and kept safe from this sexual predator and serial killer. I was glad that I was the one home that day to meet the cable Technician.

While researching the behavior of serial killers, I learned that the so-called "indicators" experts point out when discussing behavioral traits and characteristics of serial killers are based on case study analysis of convicted criminals. To speculate or assert that an individual can be identified as a serial killer or murderer prior to committing the crime is impossible. Based on the top ten indicators known to cause emotional breakdowns or "psychasthenia" psychologists suggest they can determine who will have a breakdown before they actually experience the breakdown. The problem with this is psychologists do not have a crystal ball although they do know the top indicators, some people react differently than others. Not all serial killers are fashioned alike. I would think most serial killers tell the State appointed evaluators what they think the evaluator wishes to hear or what the parole board wishes to hear. What comes into play is; exactly how trustworthy is the research of the "indicators" based on these seasoned cons and masters of deception?

The question remains, how is a serial killer made and what drives his or her behavior, or lack of conscience?

Serial killers can be adept at blending into society. They may attend church and contribute to worthy causes such as volunteering at homeless shelters. As demonstrated by Timothy Krajcir, they might sit in their cars in grocery or department store parking lots, stalking their prey. To a serial killer the shadows we fear are the places they find most comfortable. Serial killers are driven by one compulsion – to drive fear into their victims and slaughter them in the most lethal manner possible. They crave Death!

In the mind of a serial killer nothing is off limits. The intrigue of baiting the police, watching investigators on the chase, and outsmart the sharpest legal minds is a driving force and exactly what T.K. attempted and ultimately failed to do. But a person does have to wonder if there is a point where the game is over and the serial killer wants to get caught because, as seen in the many years T.K. frustrated the authorities, many serial killers can successfully elude the authorities. Yet eventually they let their guard down and are caught and convicted with the simplest of slip-ups or mistake.

Some serial killers murder for money; others enjoy the sheer thrill of killing... and then there are those like T.K. who kill for sex. I have always been baffled by those who kill for sex when it seems sex is so readily available today without having to sacrifice the innocent life of another person. When I asked T. K. why he didn't just pay for sex or pick up a 2:00a.m. barfly, he simply responded, "Why should I... I took what I wanted."

My assessment of the interview with the serial killer and rapist Timothy Wayne "T.K." Krajcir" is that he was not completely honest. Some of his answers seemed forced; others fabricated. Nevertheless, Krajcir is an intelligent individual who knows the system inside and out and offered what he felt I wanted to hear. In no way am I convinced that the penal system has reformed him, nor do I believe he is a willing subject in any reformation project. I am thoroughly convinced, however, that if T.K. were a free man and had the opportunity he would no doubt continue inflicting his reign of terror and destruction on society.

After my visits with the serial killer, I began to question our legal system, our culture, and society. This is one of hundreds of serial killers that have prowled the streets. Thousands of victims have perished because demented butchers like Timothy Krajcir "take." Perhaps I should have felt compassion for the incarcerated prisoner as the final interview concluded. As a God fearing Christian I should have. When his shackles clanked and handcuffs rattled, my faith and security were realized in the steel bar and concrete reinforced enclosure holding this abomination until he breathes his last breath. I take refuge in knowing that T. K. and the cable Technician who was in my home will perish behind prison walls.

The lives of Timothy Krajcir's victims were obliterated for one reason only – to satisfy the sexual whims of a self-centered lunatic. He is not the first narcissistic serial killer in history, nor will he be the last. When I think of his victims, I wonder if justice was really served. At a cost to the public in excess of $80,000.00 a year, Timothy Krajcir is allowed to continue aging, while the casualties of his acts no longer subsist. I am not the judge. I am not the jury. If I find solace in anything, it is this: for his atrocities Timothy Krajcir will have to face the ultimate Judge who created him and when that day inevitably comes, T.K. will be held eternally accountable for his crimes.

To the victim's families and friends...

For the duration of this research, the interviews and beyond, your loved one was held dear to my heart. Though I did not know her personally, I did make a connection. She left indelible footprints not only in my memory, but more importantly in my heart!

Special thanks to Pontiac Correctional Center Pontiac, Illinois and Warden Randy Pfister.

# Chapter 2: Frank Spisak

## By Michael Newton

"My Aim Was Pretty Good"

On the first Monday of February 1982, Frank Spisak went hunting. It was not a conventional safari, but rather a "search and destroy mission." Spisak was hunting humans on the campus of Cleveland State University, sprawling over eighty-five acres in the heart of Ohio's largest city.

Spisak's morning began with a restless feeling. He called in sick to his job at the Edward W. Daniel Company, an industrial hardware manufacturer on Harvard Avenue, and made his way to CSU. His first stop was the Michael Schwartz Library in Rhodes Tower, rising twenty-one stories above Euclid Avenue. He dawdled in the stacks, selecting a volume of 1930s Nazi propaganda in the original German, and spent some time browsing the text before moving off in search of a restroom. There, on entering, he spied a pair of shoes beneath the half-door of the nearest stall and slipped into the one next-door. Someone had bored a glory hole through the partition separating one stall from another. Stooping down and peering through thick glasses, Spisak eyed the restroom's other occupant.

Reverend Horace T. Rickerson, a 57-year-old African American, was pastor of the Open Door Missionary Baptist Church on Woodland Avenue, known beyond his congregation to Clevelanders who heard his sermons broadcast over Radio WJMO on a Sunday show called "Heart to Heart." His latest offering, aired the previous morning, had been titled "How to Know You Are Saved." He would find no salvation that day, however, during a break in researching his next week's message.

Reports of what happened next differ radically. Spisak would later claim that Rickerson "was bothering me. He was making obscene lewd gestures at me. He wasn't leaving me alone." Prosecutors countered with a claim that Spisak asked the minister for sex and was rebuffed. The end result is indisputable. Spisak drew a .22-caliber automatic pistol, poked its muzzle through the glory hole, and emptied its seven-round magazine from a distance of eighteen inches. Even with his poor eyesight and the excitement of the kill, he couldn't miss.

Despite Spisak's claim that he then "ran out quickly because he was scared," he must have spent a moment scrambling after his weapon's spent brass. Police would later find four empty cartridges, with three left unaccounted for. Despite initial fear, Spisak felt "pretty good" about the shooting, as if he had "accomplished something," and he celebrated his achievement with a cup of coffee from the library's snack bar. When that was done, he drifted back toward the men's room, where a student had found Rickerson's corpse in the meantime and raised the alarm.

Amidst the crowd of onlookers, Spisak noticed one he thought was eyeing him suspiciously. Timothy Sheehan, CSU's fifty-year-old assistant superintendent for buildings and grounds, didn't know Frank Spisak from Adam, but his glance unnerved the fledgling killer. Had he seen something? Did he suspect? Rather than wait and take a chance, Spisak turned tail and made for home.

\*\*\*

Frank George Spisak Jr. was born in Cleveland on June 6, 1951. Frank Senior was a factory worker who played trumpet in a polka band, while his wife, described in court documents as "an extremely strict mother," handled discipline on the home front. Both parents were bitter racists: Frank's father moved the family from Buckeye Road to Middleburg Heights to escape black neighbors, while his mother—again, in the court's words—"taught him to hate people of color and others whom she deemed to be 'undesirable' or 'repulsive.'"

Frank Junior, as it turned out, fell into that class himself. A childhood victim of bipolar disorder, further plagued by gender confusion, Spisak suffered maternal beatings and verbal humiliation at any display of sexual behavior. By the time he entered Midway High School, Frank was an awkward nerd, singing in the choir, joining the chess club, working part-time as a library aide. The flip side of his character was an obsession with Adolf Hitler's Third Reich, aired in racist harangues and swastika sketches. He planned to study history in college, and enrolled at CSU in 1969, but dropped out in his sophomore year when cash for tuition ran short. By 1972 he was following in his father's footsteps, taking a factory job "because I wanted to buy myself a car and do other things."

Frank got the car—a Mustang, candy-apple red—and started sporting stylish clothes. Co-worker Laverne Lampert caught his eye and Spisak pursued her, offering flowers and Elvis Presley albums. They married in 1973, and Laverne was soon pregnant with daughter Sally Ann. It wasn't quite a normal marriage, though. Spisak pursued his Nazi mania, and Elvis soon gave way to recordings of Hitler and Rudolf Hess ranting in German. Frank joined the National Socialist White People's Party—formerly the American Nazi Party, renamed by founder George Lincoln Rockwell shortly before a disgruntled ex-member killed him outside a Virginia laundromat—and he began collecting guns. After a street mugging, he kept a pistol on his person at all times. He poured over Nazi texts so incessantly that his eyesight failed, requiring thick spectacles.

Laverne might have endured Frank's mania for fascism, but that was not his strangest quirk, by any means. In 1976, she would recall, a car crash "messed his mind up" worse than ever. He began to dress in women's clothes on weekends and interrupted his lectures on Hitler with talk of a sex change. Sometimes, at night, he would slip out in drag to turn tricks on the street. Laverne told Frank he was "sick in the head"—an opinion shared by his sister, Nadine, who told him to his face that "he was crazy" and "there was something wrong with him." On December 18, 1977, Spisak was arrested on a prostitution charge, but the case was not pursued to trial. Its disposition remained "unknown" to authorities when he was nabbed for murder five years later.

Still, Laverne stood by her man until the night in 1978 when he brought another transvestite home to have sex in their bed. As Laverne described the incident, "I told Frank it's either me or that thing." He chose the "thing," and Laverne left him flat, taking Sally Ann, their furniture, even their home's stove and refrigerator. They would reconcile briefly, in 1980, but Laverne gave up for good after she caught Frank taking estrogen to prepare himself for transgender surgery.

Free at last, Spisak found his last real-world job, as a machinist with the Edward Daniel Company, banking $220 per week as a member of Teamsters Local 507. On the job, he regaled weary coworkers with talk of Nazism and gay pornography. Off duty, Spisak dressed as a woman full-time and had the Bureau of Motor Vehicles change the name on his driver's license to "Frankie Ann Spisak." He took male hustlers home for sex, and on occasion violated his Aryan code with black prostitute Beverly Murphy. If funds were sparse, Spisak paid Murphy with guns from his ever-growing collection.

Perhaps unfortunately, for his future victims, Spisak made a lousy woman. With his frizzy hair, thick glasses, pockmarked face and amateurish makeup, he became a laughing stock around his neighborhood. The whistles he received from young men on the block were pure and simple mockery. In time, he even came to loathe himself in drag. It was at that point, Spisak later testified, that God reached down to rescue him. He said good-bye to Frankie

Ann, threw out his dresses, sprouted a Hitlerian toothbrush mustache, and began to strut his Nazi stuff in earnest.

It was time, Spisak had decided, to "clean up the city."

\*\*\*

Spisak's first homicide gave him a rush, and also amped his paranoia off the charts. Four months after Reverend Rickerson's murder—on Friday, June 4—he went hunting again, this time with fellow Nazi Ronald Reddish, prowling Cleveland's West Side in Reddish's Buick LeSabre. They wanted a black man and found one.

John Hardaway, a onetime Georgia sharecropper born in 1927, had migrated to Cleveland at age twenty-six, struggled with alcohol over the next dozen years, then turned his life around. By June 1982, he had been working at the Production Finishing Company's factory for seventeen years, and he followed an unwavering routine. Each Friday after work, he stopped by the Black Horse Tavern at Madison and West 117th, cashed his paycheck and drank two small cans of orange juice, then walked to the nearby rapid-transit station on West 117th and took the train home.

This Friday, Spisak saw Hardaway enter the station, jumped out of Reddish's Buick, and followed him inside. Hardaway saw the stranger approach him, then drop to a crouch as he aimed his . 22 pistol. As with Rickerson, Spisak emptied the weapon, seven bullets striking Hardaway in the arm and torso, leaving his victim for dead. Unknown to Spisak, however, his kill shot was deflected by a medallion Hardaway wore on a chain, dangling over his heart. An RTA driver found Hardaway at 11:30 P.M., sprawled on the station's platform, surrounded by blood and forty dollars he'd dropped as he fell. She called police in time to save his life, and he was back at work a month later. Detectives recovered seven spent cartridges from the crime scene.

The failure galled Spisak, but failed to put him off the hunt. On Monday, August 9, he went back to CSU, roaming the campus in search of black targets. Instead, however, he decided on Coletta Dartt, a white employee at the university's chemistry lab, when he heard her "making some derisive remarks about us"—that is, the "White People's Party"—to friends. At 5:00 P.M. he trailed Dartt from her office to a women's restroom, then followed her inside. His plan, Spisak later admitted, was to "slap the shit out of her and rob her." Dartt found him waiting for her as she emerged from the stall, barking at her to back up. She bolted instead, shoving Spisak aside. He pursued her into the corridor, fired a wild shot that missed Dartt completely, then fled.

Dartt offered a description of her would-be killer to police, while their technicians dug his bullet from a wall. Rewards were posted for the restroom shooter's capture, but they brought no takers. Meanwhile, stung by yet another failure, Spisak couldn't wait to try again.

On Friday, August 27, Timothy Sheehan looked forward to celebrating his son's fifteenth birthday. The day had been routine for Sheehan, rising at 5:00 A.M. and catching the bus to work at CSU, supervising the university's maintenance staff at their various tasks. At 2:00 P.M., Sheehan left his office to answer reports of a faulty door lock, then dropped out of sight. His pager went unanswered, and in time a search began. Two hours after he went missing, a security guard found Sheehan dead in one of CSU's restrooms, shot four times at close range.

Spisak's accounts of Sheehan's slaying were the most confused he offered to authorities in custody. One version claimed that he recognized Sheehan from February 1, as a possible witness to Reverend Rickerson's murder, and seized the opportunity to silence him. On second thought, Spisak floated the claim that he thought Sheehan—a Catholic, born in Ireland's County Cork— might be "a Jewish professor perverting youth." Finally, Spisak said he had approached Sheehan for sex and was rebuffed, spending a restless hour in the library afterward, then decided to rob and kill Sheehan. Spisak told police that he "thought in his mind that it was not fair that this man had money and he did not," further reasoning that "if he did take money from him and let him live, the victim might identify him in the future."

After killing Sheehan, Spisak rifled his pockets for cash, picked up his empty brass because "it's sloppy to leave it laying around," and then left "real quick because he did not want to get caught." With him, he took the beeper whose insistent buzzing in the next two hours would precipitate the search for Sheehan's corpse.

So far, Spisak's one-man war of ethnic cleansing was a monumental failure. By his own account, he hoped to "get as many niggers as I could before I got caught, one thousand, a million, the more the better," but his death toll stood at two—and one of them was white. Aryan honor spurred him on to try again.

On the night of August 29, Spisak went hunting again with Ron Reddish. They took Spisak's car, driving aimlessly around Cleveland's east side and downtown for most of the night, before Reddish got bored and Spisak dropped him at home. On the verge of giving up himself, Spisak circled back toward the CSU campus and found Brian Warford, a seventeen-year-old African American, dozing in a bus shelter on Euclid Avenue.

Warford was trying to make a new start as a student. Two years earlier, he had dropped out of Collinwood High School during his sophomore year, then was thrown out of his parents' home for stealing his father's van and credit cards. Warford's father tagged him as "a loner who lacked discipline," but Warford still hoped for the best. While living with his sister, he enrolled in CSU's alternative education program, working toward his GED. He might have made it if he hadn't nodded off that evening, while waiting for a bus to take him home.

Spisak approached Warford on foot, determined to kill him because he was "one of our enemies." He fired five shots at Warford from close range, missing with four, but one drilled Warford's skull and killed him instantly. Frank looked around for cartridges, but could not find them in the darkness, so he left without them. As he later told police, "I was just worried about getting back across to the other side of the campus to where I put the car because I figured in the early morning hours it was so quiet somebody was bound to hear all the shots. I didn't want to get caught that time because I wanted to be able to do it again and again and again and again."

His worry was wasted. There were no witnesses; nobody heard the shots. A passerby found Warford's cooling body in the early hours of August 30 and called police, who picked up Spisak's brass as evidence.

At last, it seemed, he might be on a roll.

\*\*\*

What happened next can only be attributed to drunken hubris. On September 4, the beginning of Labor Day weekend, Cleveland police received a report of gunshots fired from a second-story apartment window at 1367 East 53rd Street. Two patrolmen came knocking, and Spisak admitted firing one round through the window. He invited them inside, where a shotgun and a .22-caliber pistol lay in plain sight. Frank was drifting toward the sofa when the officers stopped him and lifted its cushions, revealing a .38-caliber pistol and a two-shot derringer.

The cops arrested Spisak and transported him to Cleveland's Justice Center, where they booked him on charges of possessing unregistered handguns and discharging firearms within the city limits. He posted bond and left for home, although his shooting irons remained in custody.

Frank might have skated, even then, if he had ever learned to curb his tongue. Paranoid as he was, Spisak had talked about the shootings with ex-wife Laverne, sister Nadine, and a girlfriend. Early on September 5, a still-unidentified woman phoned police, suggesting that they double-check Spisak's guns against bullets from the unsolved slayings. The confiscated .22 automatic matched Brian Warford's death slug, and ejector markings on the test-fired brass matched shell casings found at the various crime scenes. A warrant was issued. Police returned to East 53rd Street in force.

Spisak was not home when they arrived the second time, but officers proceeded with their search, uncovering newspaper clippings on the shootings, together with a cache of Nazi paraphernalia—and Timothy Sheehan's lost pager. Detectives knew they had identified the shooter, but where was he?

Spisak came home with the search still in progress, to find his street swarming with cruisers and uniforms. He drove on past, but a neighbor saw him leaving and tipped off the manhunters, thoughtfully including Spisak's license number. The car was registered to Ron Reddish, which in turn led raiders to his home on Marvin Avenue. There, they found Spisak hiding in a basement crawlspace and arrested both men, Frank for murder and attempted murder, and Reddish on preliminary charges of obstructing justice.

When confronted with the evidence against him, Spisak copped to everything. He described switching out the .22 automatic's barrel between crimes, to frustrate ballistics experts, and spun tales of defending himself against homosexual advances from Reverend Rickerson and Timothy Sheehan. Police suspected that the opposite was true, pegging Spisak as the sexual aggressor, and noted Frank's confession that he'd killed Brian Warford during a racist "hunting party." In custody, Spisak seemed proud of his "achievements," grabbing a pen to autograph one of his swastika t-shirts for the arresting officers.

On March 29, 1983, the Cuyahoga County Grand Jury indicted Spisak on four counts of aggravated murder (two separate counts for Tim Sheehan), one count of attempted murder (for John Hardaway), three counts of aggravated robbery, and one count of receiving stolen property. Pursuant to Ohio's capital punishment statute, the aggravated murder charges included nineteen specifications permitting imposition of the death penalty. Ron Reddish found his charge of obstructing justice upgraded to include one count of attempted murder, for the wounding of John Hardaway. At his arraignment on April 8, Spisak declared himself a follower of Adolf Hitler, then pled not guilty on all counts by reason of insanity.

*** 

Prior to trial, Judge James Sweeney ordered a psychiatric evaluation of Spisak by Dr. Phillip Resnick. Defense counsel Thomas Shaughnessy requested and was granted parallel evaluations by four other psychiatrists: Dr. Kurt Bertschinger, Dr. Oscar Markey, Dr. Sandra McPherson, and Dr. S. M. Samy. Four of the five agreed that, while Frank clearly was abnormal, his mental state did not meet Ohio's legal standard for insanity—that is, inability to tell right from wrong or to physically obey established laws. Dr. Markey disagreed, diagnosing Spisak as suffering from a schizotypal personality and latent atypical psychotic disorder that rendered him incapable of controlling violent impulses, even though he recognized their illegality. Judge Sweeney accepted Dr. Bertschinger's report and found Spisak competent to stand trial.

When those proceedings opened on Monday, June 7, 1983, Spisak seemed the very picture of zany confidence, walking into court with head held high, his Hitler mustache on display, toting a copy of *Mein Kampf* and greeting Judge Sweeney with a stiff-arm fascist salute, responding to questions from the bench with "*jawhol*" instead of "yes." Lawyer Shaughnessy scarcely helped in his opening statement, telling jurors, "Part of the job that you've undertaken is going to be sitting in judgment of a sick and demented mind that spews forth a philosophy that will offend each and every one of you. Make no mistake about, you will be offended."

Spisak, testifying in his own behalf, lived up to that prediction. The shootings, he said, were carried out under direct orders from his "immediate superior"—namely, God. His transvestite phase had not been his fault, either. Spisak blamed it on "the Jews," who had "seized control of my mind when I wasn't looking." That said, he seemed proud of his crimes. Sister Nadine recalled Frank boasting of one homicide, reporting that he "seemed to take delight in the killing." She had not reported it immediately, she explained, because "I thought he was crazy. He had that wild look in his eyes."

Attorney Shaughnessy called Dr. Markey to the stand on July 11, hoping Markey's dissenting view might persuade jurors that Spisak was insane. Alas, it did not go as planned. Judge Sweeney excused the jury to question Markey himself. Markey first repeated his diagnosis of Spisak's "schizotypal personality disorder" and "atypical psychotic disorder," then hedged, admitting that Frank's mental illness was "latent" and that "the potential is there," but that he "cannot be diagnosed as having an active psychotic illness." When Sweeney asked if Spisak knew the difference between right and wrong, Markey replied, "In our society...I know that he knows that we believe it is wrong, and that in this society in which he is trying to cure these ills, society thinks what he did was wrong. However, in his view he did the right thing and there is nothing to apologize for."

Prior to trial, Markey had claimed that Spisak was "unable to control his impulses to assault, though he was at the time, aware of its being socially wrong." On the stand, he acknowledged that "certainly, there are times when he would refrain, and I think he must have refrained in the past from acts like this because the consequences might be uncomfortable for him." That admission prompted prosecutor Don Nugent to bore in with the following exchange.

Q. Do you know what the legal test for insanity is?

A. Yes.

Q. What is that?

A. Did he know right from wrong, was he able to control any impulses which would have interfered with his knowledge of right from wrong.

Q. And would he be—or was he able to refrain from committing the acts that he committed?

A. It was obvious, I think he knew the difference, but remember he is changing the world by this act.

Q. Well, if you believe what he says, that he killed the Reverend because the Reverend made a homosexual pass, you would agree that has nothing to do with his Nazi theory?

A. That's right.

Q. You also agree that he refrained from killing any Jews because as far as we know, he is not charged with killing any Jews?

A. Because of what?

Q. He has not killed any Jews. Even if he espouses the philosophy of killing Jews, he has not done so. Therefore, we can conclude that he has refrained from killing the Jews. Fair enough?

A. Yes.

Q. I don't think we have any disagreement. You do say in all of the instances he knew the difference between right and wrong, and you do say in all of the instances he was able to refrain from committing those acts if he would have decided to refrain from doing it?

A. Yes.

Judge Sweeney permitted Markey to testify before the jury, then struck his testimony from the record at the trial's close, ordering jurors not to consider it. Sweeney also refused to admit any further expert testimony on Spisak's mental state, and declined to instruct the jury on ground for returning a verdict of not guilty by reason of insanity. After presentation of sixty witnesses and 250 exhibits, Tom Shaughnessy ruefully admitted, "In this segment of the trial, the defense has no defense."

The jurors agreed. On July 15 they convicted Spisak on every charge except one count of aggravated robbery and one death penalty specification in Tim Sheehan's case. Leaving court for his cell, Spisak seemed surprised that the panel had cleared him of any charges. "I thought it was going to be a straight shot all the way down the line," he remarked.

***

The penalty phase of Spisak's trial convened the next day, July 16. It was Shaughnessy's chance to present mitigating factors, hopefully swaying the panel away from execution and toward life imprisonment. In a bid to prove diminished capacity, Shaughnessy recalled Dr. Markey to the stand, reminding jurors that Spisak was "Mentally unwell. He lacks finer feelings. He is governed by fear, by anger, by circumstance, and not by remorse, by tenderness, or feelings of modesty." Dr. McPherson agreed, to a point, noting Spisak's bland, remorseless recitation of his crimes. "It was like discussing what I had for breakfast," she recalled. During his Rorschach inkblot test, Spisak saw only spattered blood and body parts. Still, in McPherson's opinion, it fell short of anything resembling legal insanity.

Shaughnessy took a strange tack in his closing argument, telling the jury, "Ladies and gentlemen, when you turn and look at Frank Spisak, don't look for good deeds, because he has done none. Don't look for good thoughts, because he has none. He is sick, he is twisted. He is demented, and he is never going to be any different. Every one of us who went through this trial, we know we can feel that cold day...or see that cold marble, and will forever...see Horace Rickerson dead on the cold floor. Aggravating circumstances, indeed it is...the reality of what happened there...you can smell almost the blood. You can smell, if you will, the urine. You are in a bathroom, and it is death, and you can smell the death...and you can feel the loneliness of that railroad platform...And we can all appreciate, and you can understand, and we can all know the terror that John Hardaway felt when he turned and looked into those thick glasses and looked into the muzzle of a gun that kept spitting out bullets...And we can see a relatively young man cut down with so many years to live, and we could remember his widow, and we certainly can remember looking at his children...you and I and everyone of us, we were sitting in that bus shelter, and you can see the kid, the kid that was asleep, the kid that never [*sic*] what hit him, and we can feel that bullet hitting, and that's an aggravating circumstance...There are too many family albums. There are too many family portraits dated 1982 that have too many empty spaces. And there is too much terror left in the hearts of those that we call lucky."

In effect, he made the prosecution's case. On July 19, jurors recommended death for Spisak. Judge Sweeney accepted that advice in sentencing Spisak on August 10. Aside from the death penalty, Spisak also received a superfluous sentence of seven to twenty-five years on each count of attempted murder and aggravated robbery. Rising to comment on the sentence, Spisak said, "Even though this court may pronounce me guilty a thousand times, the higher court of our great Aryan warrior God pronounces me innocent. Heil Hitler!"

Accomplice Ron Reddish, tried separately, was also convicted of attempted murder and obstructing justice. On the first count, he received a sentence of seven to twenty-five years and a $10,000 fine; on the second, eighteen months and a $2,500 fine. Reddish entered prison on November 22, 1983, but unlike Spisak, he would not die there. Paroled on July 11, 1990, Reddish discharged his sentence on August 13, 1991.

***

Frank Spisak fit no better in prison than he had in the free world. His work assignments varied—tutor, recreational worker, laundry attendant and barber—but he declined participation in any educational or therapeutic programs. Meanwhile, he logged a series of bad conduct reports inside the big house.

His first offense, cursing and spitting on a chaplain who denied his request for a religious medallion on July 12, 1984, earned Spisak ten days in "disciplinary control," otherwise known as solitary confinement. Next came four complaints of disobeying direct orders, recorded on April 10, 1985; on January 7, 1986; January 30, 1986; and on March 4, 1986. On April 12, 1985, he was reported for possessing and consuming an intoxicating substance. Two years later, on April 11, 1987, Spisak graduated to "possession or manufacture of a weapon or contraband" *and* "seductive or obscene acts, including indecent exposure or masturbation." His next ten-day jolt in solitary came on June 23, 1987, when he cursed a guard who asked him if he wished to make a phone call. Charges of encouraging or creating a disturbance followed on August 17 and 19, 1987; on November 11, 1992; and on December 23, 1993. The latter incident also included accusations of disrespect to an officer, staff member or visitor, and "excessive loud noises, such as from radio, TV, or shouting." His final recorded offense—performing fellatio on a fellow inmate in a recreation area—earned him another thirteen days in solitary.

When not busy getting himself into trouble, Spisak kept up a lively correspondence with free world admirers and journalists. A letter to *Cleveland Scene* magazine, penned from "Death Row, U.S.A." in 2006, bemoaned the general public "ignorance" surrounding his case. In that epistle, Spisak denied any allegiance to Nazism and offered his first expression of remorse for the CSU murders. "Mental illness caused the crimes," he wrote, "and I'm sorry that I got mentally ill enough to hurt and kill others [sad face]." Reverting to a bygone time and personality, he signed the letter: "Miss Frances Ann Spisak, a.k.a. STARGIRL, WHITE ROSE in a concrete jungle."

***

Between rambling letters and violations of prison rules, Spisak pursued appeals of his conviction and death sentence. He had no realistic hope of winning freedom, but hoped that legal maneuvers might buy him "a year, two years, or maybe ten" before he sat in Ohio's electric chair. In fact, he would stall execution by nearly three decades, during which time the state changed its mode of execution from electrocution to lethal injection.

Spisak's first appeal went to Ohio's Court of Appeals for the Eighth District, in 1984, complaining that Judge Sweeney had improperly excluded Dr. Markey's testimony and should have instructed jurors to consider an insanity verdict. The appeals court disagreed on both counts, but did find Frank's conviction on two counts of aggravated murder for a single victim improper. Accordingly, the court vacated one conviction and four death penalty specifications, while affirming Spisak's sentence on all other counts.

Next, on November 24, 1986, Spisak appealed to Ohio's Supreme Court, alleging sixty-four specific legal errors from his original trial. Again, Frank won a partial victory, with the court's April 13, 1988 ruling that "for purposes of sentencing...[e]ach aggravated murder count should...contain only one specification," rather than piling on a total of fifteen. Still, the court upheld his conviction and death sentence, finding that "the remaining aggravating circumstances outweigh the mitigating factors beyond a reasonable doubt."

From there, Spisak petitioned the U.S. Supreme Court for a writ of certiorari, seeking a review of all lower court decisions thus far, but that plea was routinely rejected in 1989. On December 15, 1995, Spisak petitioned the U.S. District Court for the Northern District of Ohio for a writ of habeas corpus (seeking release from "unlawful detention"). Judge Solomon Oliver Jr. denied that petition, prompting Frank to try the Sixth Circuit Court of Appeals on April 9, 1997.

That petition stalled Spisak's execution for six years, and he was not idle in the meantime. He filed motions seeking state support for transgender surgery, and failing there, in 1999 he launched a federal lawsuit demanding that Ohio authorities treat him as a woman. While those pleas went nowhere, Spisak enjoyed a measure of success at the Sixth Circuit. On April 18, 2003, that court granted a certificate of appealability on thirteen of his thirty-three procedural complaints. Still not satisfied, Spisak went back to the same court once more, winning an amended judgment certifying appealability of a fourteenth claim on July 29, 2003. Two days later, Frank filed his formal appeal with the Sixth Circuit Court.

Another thirty-two months passed before Sixth Circuit Judges Eric Clay, Boyce Martin Jr., and Karen Moore heard oral arguments for Spisak's appeal on March 14, 2006, then another seven before they announced their judgment on October 20, 2006. While rejecting most of Spisak's complaints, the panel agreed that late defense counsel Shaughnessy "abandoned the duty of loyalty owed to Defendant" with his denigrating comments in the trial's penalty phase, essentially promoting a death sentence. The panel also found errors in Judge Sweeney's jury instructions during penalty deliberations, granting Spisak a conditional writ of habeas corpus on those two issues and forbidding his execution. Judge Moore alone found Sweeney's handling of the insanity plea improper, but her vote on that count was overruled by a two-to-one majority.

Now it was the state's turn to appeal, seeking a writ of certiorari which the U.S. Supreme Court granted in 2007, reversing the Sixth Circuit's judgment and remanding it for further consideration. Unimpressed, the Sixth Circuit reinstated its original opinion in 2008, again sparing Spisak from execution. Ohio officials climbed back on the seesaw with another Supreme Court appeal, leading to oral arguments on October 13, 2009. State spokesmen claimed that the Sixth Circuit panel had contravened terms of the 1996 Anti-terrorism and Effective Death Penalty Act (ADEPA) and exceeded its authority under that federal statute by presuming that Spisak "suffered prejudice from several allegedly deficient statements made by his trial counsel during closing argument instead of deferring to the Ohio Supreme Court's reasonable rejection of the claim." Rather remarkably, *amicus curiae* briefs supporting Ohio's position were filed with the Supreme Court by state attorneys general from Alabama, Arizona, California, Colorado, Delaware, Idaho, Illinois, Kansas, Kentucky, Montana, Nevada, Oklahoma, Pennsylvania, South Carolina, South Dakota, Texas, Utah, Virginia and Wyoming—all fearful that pending executions might be jeopardized if Spisak won his case.

They need not have worried. On January 12, 2010, Justice Stephen Breyer delivered the high court's opinion, once again reversing the Sixth Circuit. According to that judgment, the ADEPA barred federal courts from overriding a state court's decision unless said decision "was contrary to, or involved an unreasonable application of, clearly established Federal law, as determined by the Supreme Court of the United States." Judge Sweeney's jury instructions were found to be valid, while Shaughnessy's final rant to the jury did not "fall below an objective standard of reasonableness," nor did it suggest a "reasonable probability" that any more sympathetic summation might have influenced jurors to vote for life imprisonment.

A year after that decision, on January 4, 2011, Spisak appeared before Ohio's Parole Board, again admitting his crimes but blaming the acts on mental illness. He told the board "the death penalty should be reserved for the few most deserving murderers. He does not feel that he fits that category, and views his offenses as no different from other murders committed by offenders who were not sentenced to death. Spisak also stated that a lot of people who committed murders are out of prison."

Dr. Chester Schmidt, a psychiatrist from Johns Hopkins Hospital in Baltimore, spoke to the board on Spisak's behalf, noting examples of Frank's delusional thinking. Despite his death sentence, Schmidt reported that Spisak hoped to earn a college degree, find a job at the U.S. Holocaust Memorial Museum in Washington, D.C., and uncover Hitler's secret genocidal orders to counter arguments from Holocaust deniers. "It's completely off the wall," Schmidt told the board. "It's an expression of delusional thinking." Prosecutors and survivors of Spisak's victims thought otherwise, dismissing Frank's latest fantasy as one more cynical attempt to dodge execution. On January 21, the Parole Board advised Governor John Kasich against granting clemency to Spisak. Kasich agreed with that decision, formally rejecting Spisak's plea on February 11. Four days later, the U.S. Supreme Court rejected his last-ditch appeal.

Spisak had come to the end of his road.

***

On Wednesday night, February 16, Spisak ate a last meal of spaghetti, salad, chocolate cake and coffee. The next morning, clean-shaven and minus his glasses, he entered the execution chamber before an audience including his attorneys, surviving victim John Hardaway, relatives of Brian Warford, and Timothy Sheehan's children. In lieu of personal last words, Spisak opted to read from the Book of Revelations, verses one through seven of Chapter 21. That text says:

And I saw a new heaven and a new earth: for the first heaven and the first earth were passed away; and there was no more sea.

And I John saw the holy city, new Jerusalem, coming down from God out of heaven, prepared as a bride adorned for her husband.

And I heard a great voice out of heaven saying, Behold, the tabernacle of God is with men, and he will dwell with them, and they shall be his people, and God himself shall be with them, and be their God.

And God shall wipe away all tears from their eyes; and there shall be no more death, neither sorrow, nor crying, neither shall there be any more pain: for the former things are passed away.

And he that sat upon the throne said, Behold, I make all things new. And he said unto me, Write: for these words are true and faithful.

And he said unto me, It is done. I am Alpha and Omega, the beginning and the end. I will give unto him that is athirst of the fountain of the water of life freely.

He that overcometh shall inherit all things; and I will be his God, and he shall be my son.

Spisak skipped the eighth verse, which reads: "But the fearful, and unbelieving, and the abominable, and murderers, and whoremongers, and sorcerers, and idolaters, and all liars, shall have their part in the lake which burneth with fire and brimstone: which is the second death." He also elected to read off the scripture in German, from handwritten notes, which posed a problem without his glasses. As Spisak was strapped to a gurney, Warden Donald Morgan held a microphone before him, while a guard held Spisak's translation of scripture.

"It's too far away," Frank complained at one point. "I can't read it. It's blurry." From the audience, Tim Sheehan's daughter opined, "He's making it up." A brother of Brian Warford called out, "Speak English, you fool!" After five fumbling minutes, Spisak concluded, "Heil herr"—loosely interpreted by one reporter as "praise God." (In fact, "praise God" in German is *Lob Gottes*.)

Warden Morgan signaled for the execution to begin at 10:29 A.M., with a flow of sodium thiopental into Spisak's veins. A physician pronounced Frank dead at 10:34, Ohio's forty-second inmate executed since 1999 and the last to die by sodium thiopental, whose manufacturer—Hospira, Inc.—had ceased production on January 21, 2011, in protest against its use in lethal injections. Henceforth, authorities declared, they would be killing prisoners with pentobarbitol, a sedative often used during cardiac surgery (and, in the Netherlands, for physician-assisted euthanasia).

*\*\*\**

It was, perhaps, inevitable that Frank Spisak's "search and destroy" raids in Cleveland would spawn a crop of conspiracy theories. First in line to claim his fifteen seconds of reflected glory was Keith Gilbert, a neo-Nazi convicted in 1965 for possessing 1,400 pounds of stolen dynamite, with which he planned to murder Dr. Martin Luther King Jr. during a speech in Los Angeles. In August 1983, Gilbert granted an interview to *People* magazine, claiming Spisak as a lieutenant in an Aryan Nations splinter group he called the Social Nationalist Aryan People's Party. According to Gilbert, Spisak's murder spree was carried out "under direct orders of the party." The order: "Kill niggers until the last one is dead." Authorities found nothing to substantiate Gilbert's claim, but they kept after him. In May 2007, at age sixty-six, Gilbert received an eight-year prison term for trafficking in illegal weapons.

A stranger, more perplexing story comes from author Peter Levenda's *Ratline: Soviet Spies, Nazi Priests, and the Disappearance of Adolf Hitler* (2012). Therein, we find the tale of an Indonesian physician, Dr. Sosro Husodo, who in 1960 reported a curious encounter on the island of Sumbawa, east of Bali. There, Dr. Husodo met a sixty-something German physician who introduced himself as Dr. Pöch, residing with a woman named Gerda and a boy, around seven years old in Husodo's estimation, who was introduced to him as "Frank G. Spisak."

Fact or fantasy?

It seems improbable at best, particularly since Lavenda's source was first published in 2010, but the final answer must remain a mystery. Like Spisak, Dr. Husodo has long since gone to his reward, whatever that may be.

The rest is silence.

# Chapter 3: Robert Pickton
## By RJ Parker

In a roughly twenty year period from 1983 to 2002, Robert William Pickton preyed on drug addicted prostitutes in Vancouver, Canada's east side. While in jail, he confessed to murdering forty-nine, but was only charged with and convicted of six. How he got away with his crimes for so long continues to be a hotly debated topic to this very day. He's known as Canada's worst and most prolific serial killer, and it cost over one hundred million dollars to investigate and prosecute him...making him one of the most expensive, as well. His story is one with many unanswered questions.

The Pickton family first show up in Port Coquitlam in 1905, owning a pig farm of thirteen acres near a mental hospital. This is where Robert, often called Willy, is born on October 24th, 1949. He was born with the umbilical cord wrapped around his neck, and it's unknown if he suffered any type of injury from this. It's worth noting that he was in special education classes in elementary school, and that he failed the second grade twice and the third grade once. Yet, he was quite smart, as you will find out later in this story. He was close to his mother, and his older sister, Linda, has stated, "Robert was kind of a mom's boy." Perhaps his mother, Louise, who is said to have been a stern and take-charge kind of woman, felt that this boy of hers was different and needed extra care and looking after.

His father, Leonard, who was born in England, shocked his family in the early 1940's when he married Louise who was born in Raymond's Creek, Saskatchewan, Canada, as he had never been known to have a relationship with any women. All of a sudden, he gets married to Louise, who was older than him. They met at a hamburger place, where he was picking up garbage to feed his pigs. Louise was living in a small place where they had the house in the front, chickens in the back behind the house, and Robert says she enjoyed it.did they live there together? Or was this where she lived before they met? Robert and his dad did not seem to have a close relationship, due to his father working so much and not really being big on conversation.

A spacing mechanic who worked for the Pickton family in the 1960's says he heard stories that Leonard violently abused Robert. Whatever was going on, young Robert took to hiding in dead pig carcasses when he was afraid. The work never ended on the pig farm. From sun up to sun down, Robert and his younger brother, Dave, did their chores, even on school days, which left little time for imagining or playing. Louise was in charge of making sure the hogs were taken care of, while Leonard ran the meat business in town.

When Robert was about three- or four-years-old, he says that he was sitting in the driver's seat of his father's truck while it was being loaded with hogs, and he somehow shifted it into neutral, the truck starts rolling, and pigs start jumping off. His father starts running behind the truck, hollering for him to stop. Robert doesn't know what to do so the truck smashes into a telephone pole. The truck is totaled and he says, "Boy, I sure got the hell beaten out of me, but that's what happens."

In 1960, Robert got a pet calf at the auction. It was three weeks old, and had a beautiful black-and-white face. Robert loved that calf, and even slept with it. He told the calf not to go down to the barn, known as the "piggery", where the butchering took place. But, one day, when he came home after school and after he fed the chickens and mixed the feed up for the other stock, he couldn't find his calf and learned that it had been butchered. The barn door was wide open. He asked his family, and they said it must have gotten out even though Robert knew he had locked the door and taken a stroll down to the piggery. He was afraid to go look, but carefully crept down to take a peek. His one-time friend and companion was strung up, skinned and cleaned out. There is no doubt that this was a very scarring experience for young Robert. When his father offered to get him a new calf, he refused, saying, "I wanted that one."

He says that he "couldn't talk to anybody for about three or four days". He was so mad he "locked everybody out of my own mind and everything else". He learned "that was the name of the game. You buy today you sell tomorrow". That was when he "started realizing that that's life; we are only here for so long and when your time is over, it's over and you let somebody else take over". He had planned on keeping that calf "for the rest of my life and now it's gone". Even his mother tried to get him to move on from the calf, accept some good money for it, and get another one. He admits that really upset him, but he said he had to face the fact that it happens. What else can you do?

In 1963, the family moved when the farm was in the way of a major highway construction project. They moved to the now infamous farm site on Dominion Avenue. Linda went away to Catholic boarding school, and never really lived on this farm. Robert and Dave were taunted with names like "Piggy" because they always smelled of pig manure, and people who knew the family say the house was messy with farm animals wandering in and out. Robert developed an aversion to bathing, and was terrified of showers. This fear would stick with him into his adult years.

Interestingly, then sixteen-year-old Dave has an experience on October 16th, 1967, that gives us an insight into the family

118

values that young Robert was learning. On that evening, Dave, who had just gotten his driver's license, gets into Leonard's 1960 truck and runs down a neighborhood kid named Tim Barrett, age 14. Dave sees that Tim, who is lying in the road, is hurt bad. He freaks out and hurries back home to tell his mother what happened. Louise hurries to where the boy is, looks him over, rolls him into a deep ditch along the side the road, and goes back home. Dave goes to the family mechanic, gets the dent in the truck pounded out, and a broken turn signal replaced, but the mechanic refuses to paint the truck to cover the damage.

Tim's poor parents look everywhere for their son. At about 1am, his dad goes to the police to report Tim as missing. The next morning, he and a neighbor go out to search more. They find one of his shoes on the side of the road, look down into the ditch, and see his body. The autopsy shows that Tim died from drowning, not the fractured skull, brain hemorrhage or fractured pelvis. He could have recovered from those. Dave ends up going to juvenile court, was convicted of leaving the scene of an accident, and is not allowed to drive until he's 21. Tim's death is ruled accidental, and Louise never faced any charges. Robert relays this story to one of his friends in later years, and that friend tells an investigative reporter. Author's note: Once again, it's the mother who plays a role in shaping a serial killer. She shows her child a total disregard for human life.

Robert, in an audio memoir he made in 1991 for a woman in the United States who is only known as Victoria, recounts many harrowing times on the farm. He talks about how they lived poor, getting water from a stream that ran beneath the floorboards of the farm. He talks often about hard work. He dropped out of school in 1964 because he was only going to school two days a week and working long hours five days a week.

Listening to interviews Robert has done, as well as his audio memoir to Victoria, you learn quickly that this man knows his dates and numbers. He has a good memory for details, can tell you the sizes of buildings he worked on, prices of grain, and

119

differences between the U.S.A and Canada. Author's note: This is important to make note of because many descriptions of Robert describe him as being a simpleton, and unable to understand or articulate himself very well.

In February 1974 at the age of 24, Robert goes on a trip to the United States to meet pen pals, and notices that all the men aren't around because of the Vietnam War. He wanted to go into the Army, but "Mother said no. I have to stay and keep the farm going". He stayed on his trip for 6 weeks, traveling by plane to Kansas City, Missouri, and then on the bus to St. Louis on George Washington's Birthday, where he kept getting free cherry pie. From there, he went to Chicago, where "you have to be careful and can't be out at nighttime; lots of black people there". From Chicago, he went to Detroit, Michigan, where he seems to have had a good time.

In Detroit and Utica, Michigan, Robert, "a plain old farm boy", tells Victoria that he had the chance to be a model making $40 an hour. He turned the opportunity down, and enjoyed just meeting people. Most likely hippies, as he says that a lot of them wanted to come back with him. But Robert is on his vacation and out to have a good time. He doesn't want the responsibility of bringing someone into another world, worry if they will be happy there, or figure out what their goal is. He was too young to even rent a car.

What he doesn't tell Victoria, but later tells police, is that he went to Pontiac, Michigan, to meet Connie Anderson, a girl he says he was engaged to. He described her as blond, 5" 10' or 11', heavy set 140 lbs., nice body. He felt she was the girl for him right away, and they spent five weeks just spending time together and going around meeting people. Neither were into the bar scene. They just enjoyed sightseeing and traveling around. They never had sex. This seems like it was the happiest time in Robert's life. But, sadly, he had to go back to the farm and Connie, he says, couldn't leave her job to come up to Canada to be with him. She wanted him to stay there, but he never got away from the farm to go back down to the states again.

He never talked to his father about being engaged, but his mother was fine with it, as long as it didn't interfere with the work on the farm. Linda couldn't help on the farm because she didn't know anything about hogs and farm stuff, and was off living her own life. He said that Dave also knew nothing. And when asked if they knew it was the love of his life that he was leaving behind, he says, "Well, shit happens."

Victoria, the other woman from the states, wasn't being told about Connie. Robert had lots more stories of farm life to share with her. do you really need this paragraph? You already said that he didn't tell Victoria about Connie

He tells her about getting in between two boars who get into a fight. He doesn't latch one into a pen as securely as he thought he did, while trying to breed a sow. He gets "chewed up" pretty badly in his leg. The wounds end up putting him in the hospital. The doctor orders him to stay in bed, with his leg propped up, for three weeks to let the wound drain. Robert can't let the work pile up at the farm so he ignores the doctor's orders and half-crawls, half-drags himself out to a tractor to get to work. His wound is so bad that pus runs down his leg. He ends up taking off his clothes and is just in his shorts. However, this causes him to get a bad sunburn, along with blisters, on his back.

Most of his stories of "the good old days" match up fairly closely in both his audio to Victoria in 1991 and his police interview in 2002, lending some credence to them being fact.

Life back on the farm was about to change for Robert, leaving him even less time to pursue his fledgling social life. Leonard dies in 1977 at the age of 77.

He spends time with Bob Kourac, a Croatian who helped butcher on the farm. He taught him how to kill 34 pigs in one day. The most lambs he butchered in one day was about twelve.

In 1979, his mother, who has cancer that had spread all through her body, suffers two months at home and another two months of suffering in the hospital. She then passes away. Robert can't even spend much time with her. He was too busy on the farm. "You never own a piece of land, the land owns you." His mother's will stipulates that Robert's inheritance from the farm would remain in trust until he is 40-years-old, another ten years.

He keeps on working the farm, staying up until 2 or 3 in the morning, and doing it all over again when the sun comes up the next day. "Gee, I'm telling you. I mean, morning comes early and here you got, holy geez, your eyes are getting watery, and you want to keep...you gotta keep on going, but you're...you don't know exactly how to, and the problem is that you're just getting more tired, you just put longer hours in and...just slow down a little bit when you really feel tired. Then I just stop and rest for about 15, 20 minutes, then there I go again. I mean that little...that little rest sure means a lot."

He tells Victoria that he wants to build a new house for himself, when he figures out what he wants to do, because he's considering selling the farm in 1991. He tells Victoria that he's tired, and he wants to let somebody else take over so he can settle down if he finds somebody...or "whatever".

He wants to build up to six rooms in his house and have a planetarium, a spiral staircase, a tennis court out back, and a built-in swimming pool. Not that he does any swimming, but he wants to keep up with the times.

Dave, his brother, is going through a break-up with his live-in girlfriend of eight years, and Robert tells Victoria that he is just trying to stay out of it. Not that Dave would take his advice anyway. "My brother brings his trucks over here for me to work on. I tell him how to do this, and tell him how to do that. He doesn't do it that way and then it becomes a problem about the only way you can do it. But the biggest thing is that there's so many other people out there always trying to challenge you because when you're on top, it's hard to stay there. It's very had to stay there. They're always trying to knock you down one inch, or knock you down another way and...um, it's different. It's different, but I kind of like it. I kind of like it because the problem is, I mean...they always try to do it their own way, and then they always come back to me and they want my...my ideas and everything else. Believe it or not, they do it my way, no matter whatever. Whatever which way I say it or whatever, I'm always right. It's hard to believe. It's hard to believe."

He goes on to explain to her about all the vehicles he is working on, and then tells her he is waiting on some photographs that he will mail along with this tape. He plans on putting some songs on the tape that he picked out for her.

Media reports all describe Robert as a pushover, a loner with no intelligence and no social skills; Dave's lackey. It's true that he was a dirty looking guy and smelled badly, but he had some charm and he knew how to talk to people. It was this charm, and the persona of the little pig farmer who helped other people, that allowed him to fool so many and lure his prey to the farm.

At one point during the early 1980's, Robert and Dave were involved in an investigation concerning some stolen cars that were buried at the farm. Robert had helped the police recover the vehicles...a yellow Mustang and a couple of Ford pick-ups. The two men stated that someone else had been dismantling the vehicles, and were putting them underneath a hog feed pile. Robert had been able to walk right over to the spots and show the police right where everything was buried.

On December 21st, 1981, the first day of winter, Robert had to euthanize his 1,400 pound stallion, Goldie, at 5:30 or 5:45 pm. He was trying to board some girls' mares, and one of them kicked his horse in the back leg. The horse had been born on March 20th, 1977, his mother's birthday, at 4:28 am. He had trained him to do everything, even took it to shows. He looked after it, he says. He had to have the veterinarian come out to put the horse down because he couldn't do it. He decapitated the horse and took the head to a taxidermist. He had to wait 11 months for it to come

123

back mounted. He had this hanging proudly in his trailer. He tried 30 or 40 other horses to try to get one to match his beloved Goldie, but never did get one that was the same.

Vancouver's east side is notorious for the dark and desperate lives of the downtrodden and drug-addicted. In June 1983, Rebecca Louisa Guno disappeared and was never seen again. She was a 23-years-old with a bright cheery smile, dark brown eyes, and black hair. Her addiction to drugs led her to sell her body as a prostitute sometimes. She is believed to be the first victim of Robert Pickton.

Sherry Lynn Rail was 27 in January 1984 when she went missing. She had long, light brown hair, green eyes, and a butterfly tattoo on her left shoulder blade. No one reported her missing until 1987.

Elaine Auerbach told her friends she was moving to Seattle in April 1986, but she never showed up.

Teressa Ann Williams, a 26-year-old Aboriginal woman, went missing in July 1988.

Ingrid Soet, a 40-year-old mental patient, went missing in August 1989.

Sometime in the early 1990's, Robert meets Gina Houston. Gina is a crack addict that, for unknown reasons, Robert adored. He placed her on a pedestal and wanted to get married to her, she said. He wanted to settle down and start a family, but Gina wasn't interested. She already had children and Robert bought them toys and stuffed animals, and taught them to ride horses.

In 1992, another woman from the east side went missing. Kathleen Wattley disappeared in June, but would not be reported missing until 1996. It should be noted that Dave was convicted of a sexual assault in 1992. He was fined $1,000 and given 30 days probation. The victim told police how Dave had attacked her in a trailer at a pig farm, but she managed to escape when a third party came in and distracted him.

In February 1993, Inga Hall disappeared, and was reported missing the following month.

In 1994 and 1995, the Pickton's, including Linda, sold part of the farmland for $5.16 million. Then they owned P&B Salvage and, later, a dirt hauling business. Dave moved about a mile away and built his own place, eventually building "Piggy's Palace".

In March 1995, Catherine Gonzales went missing; in April, Catherine Knight disappeared. Dorothy Spence vanished in August, and Diana Melnick went missing in December.

The Pickton brothers opened Piggy's Palace in 1996. They registered it with the Canadian government as a non-profit, charity organization known as the Piggy Palace Good Times Society. They were supposed to be organizing special events, dances, and shows on behalf of service organizations, sports organizations, and other worthy groups. The mayor was seen in attendance at one such function. Robert was something of a local celebrity chef for his barbecuing hogs.

New paragraph Tanya Holyk went missing in October and Olivia Williams in December 1996.

In 1997, the killer was in a frenzy. Sadly, the police were under-funded so finding missing prostitutes and drug addicts was not a priority. Piggy's Palace was starting to be known for its drug-fueled, wild parties featuring prostitutes and Hell's Angels bikers. In March of that year, Stephanie Lane went missing, and Robert Pickton was charged with the attempted murder, assault with a weapon, and forcible confinement of a prostitute named Wendy Lynn Eistetter.

On March 23$^{rd}$ , Robert Pickton picked up Eistetter and took her to his farm with the promise of $100 and a ride back into town for an hour-an-a-half of sex. On the ride out to the farm, she found a woman's bra and asked him who it belonged to. "Oh, just a date I had last weekend," he said.

Eistetter started to feel weird about the whole thing, but never saw an opportunity to bail out. When they got to the farm, Robert got out of the pick-up truck and unlocked the gate. She says she didn't know it was a farm. It looked more like a junkyard with beat up, wrecked cars.

Robert drove up near the trailer, and they got out and went inside. Walking towards the back room, she remembers how dirty and grubby the kitchen was. She noticed a large butcher knife sitting on the table. They walked further along and went into a room that had no furniture, no bed. There was just a big roll of plastic and a sleeping bag in the middle of the floor.

After they had sex, she asked him if she could use his phone because she wanted to call her boyfriend to tell him where she was, and that she was on her way back into town. As she leaned over the phone book on the table looking for the number to the hotel where her boyfriend was, she felt something behind her and turned around. Robert grabbed her left hand and started caressing it, before quickly slapping a handcuff on.

Fighting to keep him from getting the cuff on her other hand, Eistetter starts throwing stuff at him. Wondering if Robert is planning on raping her or killing her, she grabs the knife off the kitchen table and stabs him. She knows she must kill him or be killed. In the fighting, Robert stabs her four times...twice in her abdomen, a deep cut on her left arm, and in her ribcage, puncturing a lung. She feels something hot running down her chest, and knows it's blood. She manages to get away, seriously injuring Robert almost as bad as he has injured her.

Maria Mills and her husband are driving down the road when she notices a woman coming down from the driveway. As they get closer, they can hear the woman's pleas. "Help me! Please, help me!" They stop the car, and Maria sees the large kitchen knife in her hand and the handcuff on her wrist. Eistetter continues to plead with them for help, and Maria realizes this is not a woman who has "had an accident. This is something serious and evil". Maria calls for an ambulance for Eistetter, who is taken to the hospital, her heart stopping twice on the way.

Coincidentally, Robert manages to drive himself to the same hospital, and an orderly finds a key in Robert's pocket. The key fits the handcuff on Eistetter.

The Royal Canadian Mounted Police investigate and bring charges, but the prosecutor believes a conviction would be unlikely due to Eistetter's life as a drug addict. The charges are dropped, and Robert remains a free man to continue preying on the prostitutes on the east side.

As more people come to the farm to take advantage of Robert and his money, more women go missing. More than a dozen disappeared in 1997, but there was still no real investigation going on. Robert must have healed from his injuries sometime around June when Janet Henry disappeared.

August 1997 saw Helen Hallmark, Jacqueline Murdock, and Marnie Frey disappear. In September, Cindy Beck vanishes. Also in 1997, Andrea Borhaven went missing, but it was not reported until 1999.

Lisa Yelds and her ex-husband, Dave, were friends and employees of Robert Pickton. Lisa, a loud and brash woman who "hates cops" because "they twist what you say", says that Robert cut the penis and skin off of a hog he was butchering, and made a belt from it. He tied it around his waist, and as   Dave Yelds was bent over working on something, Robert walked up behind him and goosed him with it. Dave Yelds says Robert had a weird sense of humor.  When he had been butchering, he would take the pieces of entrails, and chase him around with them.

January 1998, Kerry Koski and Jacqueline McDonnell go missing. In April, Sarah Jane deVries disappears and is reported missing the same day. Also in April, Port Coquitlam authorities seek an order to destroy, under the Livestock Protection Act, one of Dave Pickton's dogs. The proceedings were later dismissed without explanation.

In July 1998, Shelia Egan is never seen again. In October, Julie Young disappears, followed by Angela Jardine, who was said to have the mental capacity of a 10-year-old. In November, Michelle Gurney vanishes, and Marcella Creison, who had just gotten out of jail on the 27th and did not show up to a belated holiday dinner with her family, disappears in December. Also last seen in 1998 was Ruby Hardy, but she is not reported until March 2002.

August 1998 brought investigators. Bill Hiscox, who worked on the farm, had suspicions of something going on, and all the women disappearing that he read about in the paper. He told police that Lisa Yelds told him that she had found female purses and identifications that Robert was keeping as a sort of trophy. He also suggested that an associate of the Hell's Angels biker gang had been murdered, ground up, and fed to the hogs on the farm. Lisa Yelds denies any knowledge of that.

On December 31st, 1998, the Pickton's had a New Year's Eve party that resulted in an injunction banning future parties and public gatherings on the farm. This was an attack from Port Coquitlam against Piggy's Palace, which violated city ordinances. The parties drew as many as 1,800 people, and the injunction gave police authority to arrest and remove anyone attending these parties. The so-called "Society" lost its non-profit status in January 2000 for failure to supply mandatory financial statements.

In 1999, Andy Bellwood, who met Pickton through a mutual friend, moves to the farm, fresh out of a month stay in treatment. He and Pickton get along well and quickly become close friends. Robert comes into the trailer where Andy is watching television, and tries to talk him into going with him to go get a hooker. Andy refuses several times and says he isn't into hookers. Robert then shows him what he does to hookers. He takes out a belt, some wire, and a pair of handcuffs from a hidden spot in the room. He pretends he has a hooker on all fours on the bed, and mimics that he is stroking her hair, brings her arm up behind her back, and slaps a handcuff onto it. After he mimics handcuffing the pretend woman, he shows how he wraps the belt around her neck, strangling her while telling her "Gonna be all right. Gonna be over now". He tells Andy he wouldn't believe how many actually believe that. Then Robert tells him that he then takes them to the barn, hangs, and guts them. Some of Robert's associates threaten Andy a few days later and tell him to forget that conversation. They then proceed to beat him up.

Lynn Ellingson, another crack addict friend of Gina Houston, meets Robert and moves onto the farm to help with phone calls and paperwork. One night in March 1999, she accompanies Robert to Vancouver where they pick up Georgina Papin, buy some drugs, and head back to the farm. Lynn says she got $150 and so did Georgina. While she went into her room to smoke crack, Georgina went into another room to have sex with Robert. Lynn then said she heard a noise and when she went to check, no one was in the other room. She noticed a light coming from the slaughterhouse. She walked out to see what was going on and when she opened the door, a strong smell hit her nose. She saw a body hanging from a chain the way he hung his pigs. The legs were at her eye level, and she saw red nail polish on the toes. Robert was cutting something on a big shiny table. Lynn couldn't say what it was, but said that it was covered in blood and had long black hair like a horses tail. He told her that if she said anything, she would be right up there hanging next to her. She promised him she wouldn't say anything, but she just needed money for drugs. She left the farm soon after that. She admitted to blackmailing Robert whenever she needed drug money afterward.

The media's coverage of the missing women, including a visit by John Walsh from America's Most Wanted, spurred a public outcry so the police began seriously investigating the disappearances. A rally was held that was attended by Sereena Abbotsway, who was just out of the hospital recovering from a beating by a bad john. She would go missing in July 2001 despite stating, on camera at the rally, that she would rely on her sixth sense to keep her from going on a "bad date".

In the fall of 1999, police started surveillance on Robert Pickton. He soon found out about it when he was pulled over by police one night, and had a female passenger in his pick-up. The passenger was Gina Houston's 13-year-old daughter. That year, he also learned that he had contracted Hepatitis C from a prostitute.

On January 19th, 2000, Robert is finally interviewed by the RCMP about suspicions they had of his involvement in the missing women cases. In a very informal interview, attended by Gina Houston, he denied any wrongdoing. When the subject of the 1997 stabbing of Eistatter came up, he stated that he wanted to see her picture on the board of the missing women. Some have said that in this police interview, he was shaking in fear while reminiscing on the stabbing incident. However, when one watches the recording, it seems more of a controlled rage and anger. He also appears to be very articulate, and able to understand everything during this interview. Later, Gina said that Robert had been very cooperative with the investigators, and had told them that they were welcome to come out and look; that he "just wanted this to be all over, this all to stop".

In the fall of 2000, Dinah Taylor starts staying at the farm, and says she was there to do housekeeping, while trying to break her drug addiction.

Early in 2001, Andrea Joesbury is reported missing. Later, it is discovered that she was brought to the farm by Dinah Taylor.

In July of 2001, Dinah Taylor brings Seerena Abotsway to the farm, and Gina Houston sees them doing drugs. Gina goes and tells Robert, who doesn't believe her. By the time they make their way back to the trailer, Dinah and Sereena have everything cleaned up. Sereena is never seen again.

That fall, Diane Rock and Mona Wilson go missing. Gina says that she is on the phone with Robert when she hears some sort of argument in the background, and hears the name Mona. A few days later, she goes to the farm to pick up a pig Robert has butchered for her. In the piggery, she notices the freezer near the door has something covered up on top, and all his tools are laid out very precisely. When she steps closer to look, Robert comes up behind her and, with a tear in his eye, shakes his head.

Everything came to a head in 2002 when Scott Chubbs, another drifter who had been staying at the farm, tipped police off that Robert had illegal guns on the property. He had been hoping to get a reward; instead, it gave police the evidence they needed to obtain a search warrant and check out the farm. They converged on the property on February 5th.

The search yielded them the guns, as well as some female clothing, an id, some syringes, and an asthma inhaler with Sereena Abotsway's name on it. Realizing they were onto something big, they returned the next day with another search warrant to look for evidence related to the missing women.

Robert was charged on February 22$^{nd}$, 2002, with the first two of an eventual 27 counts of murder. The discovery of two pails containing decomposing body parts, which had begun to liquify, sparked the largest investigation in Canadian history. In the first pail was a head that had been split in two, and looked as if the skull had been manually separated, and it contained hair, an ear, skin, and a tooth belonging to Andrea Joesbury. In the second pail were remains that were not as decomposed as the others. It consisted of a skull, with the second vertebrae still attached, that had been cut from the rear of the head and cut again through the center of the face to the middle of the forehead. It showed evidence that this person had been shot by a .22 caliber bullet near one of the ears. Hands and feet later determined these remains as belonging to Sereena Abotsway.

Jawbone fragments belonging to Marnie Frey and Brenda Wolfe were found. Large amounts of Mona Wilson's blood, as well as blood splatter which indicated a struggle, was found in a Dodge motor home. Her DNA was also found on a dildo, that was attached to the end of a gun, which was found in Robert's bedroom. Her necklace was found in Robert's office. Hand bones belonging to Georgina Papin were also found. Bones, teeth, blood and other DNA were found on the property, as well as personal belongings from those and 23 other women. 235,000 pieces of evidence were collected form the farm and analyzed. 60 items were ultimately linked to specific individuals and to Robert himself.

On March 10th 2004, it was revealed that some of the victim's flesh may have been ground up and mixed with pork from the farm.

Dinah Taylor, Pat Cassanova, and Lynn Ellingson were also arrested but, in exchange for their testimony, no charges were ever brought against them. Lynn became the star witness for the prosecution. Pat Cassanova, who helped Robert with butchering, admitted to having sex with some of the prostitutes, including Andrea Joesbury. He called her an "Angel".

On January 22nd, 2007, Robert Pickton's trial began. The judge in the trial decided that since Pickton was being tried for over two dozen murders, it would be best to split the trial into two parts, so as not to overload the jury. He also rejected one charge in the case of Jane Doe, due to a lack of evidence, leaving him charged with a total of 26 murders. There were many facts and witness statements not heard by the jury.

In December 2007, Robert Pickton was found guilty of second degree murder of six of the women because the jury was not convinced that he had planned the murders beforehand. The judge sentenced him to the maximum sentence allowed under Canadian law...25 years with no early parole.

An inquiry was made into the investigation of the missing women, and it was decided that Pickton's second trial for the remaining 20 women would be stayed. Inquiry commissioner Wally Oppal blamed years of inadequate and failed police investigations for allowing Pickton to prey, undetected, on prostitutes in Vancouver's troubled east side. He went on to say that "The police investigations into the missing and murdered women were blatant failures, and the causes included discrimination, a lack of leadership, outdated policing approaches, and a fragmented police structure". In his December 12, 2012, summary, he said, "The women didn't go missing. They aren't just absent, they didn't just go away. They were taken...taken from their families, taken from their friends, taken from their communities. We know they were murdered." The inquiry was called to look into the police investigation of this serial killer, and their mishandling of cases involving missing women from Vancouver's east side.

# Chapter 4: Mary Bell

## By Sylvia Perrini

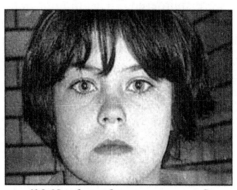

*(1968 when she was arrested)*

**The child who kills is the child who never had a chance**

Crimes by juveniles (arson, robbery, assault with weapons, manslaughter, murder, and rape) have all increased significantly in the western world over the past few decades. However, one story which sent shock waves through a nation happened as early as 1968 in the northeastern city of Newcastle upon Tyne in England.

Newcastle upon Tyne sits on the north bank of the River Tyne 8.5 miles (13.7 km) from the North Sea. In the 19th century, shipbuilding, coal mining, and heavy engineering made the city prosper, and it became a powerhouse of the British Industrial Revolution.

However, in the 1960s, Newcastle was a decaying city. The decline of the shipbuilding and mining industries had virtually brought the city to economic ruin. The city, during this period, held the highest crime record, highest unemployment figures, and the highest rate of alcoholism in the whole of the United Kingdom.

### Scotswood

And nowhere was this poverty so clearly seen than in Scotswood, an impoverished slum area of approximately half a square mile on a hillside, three miles west of the city centre; it was an area that had barely changed since the end of WWII and was an area notorious in the 1960s for its social problems and difficult families that accompany years of deprivation and neglect. With the high unemployment figures, it was common for the men in the area, husbands and fathers, to be drunk. Many of the residents in the area were well known to the police for drunkenness and petty crime. Calls to the police for domestic abuse and fights in the streets were frequent. Here rundown, back-to-back government housing stretched down the hillside to the industrial wasteland on the banks of the River Tyne. The local children played out in the derelict streets and the wasteland, which the children called the "Tin Lizzie," often for hours without parental supervision and without fear of molestation. The "Tin Lizzie" sat next to railway lines and was littered with construction materials, old cars, and dangerous wreckage. Of course, there was the occasional accident and certain areas parents warned their children to stay away from like some of the old derelict houses, in what was known as "rat's alley" which they considered unsafe. Here the children, as a pastime, would throw stones at the windows. However, generally, the parents never considered their children might be at risk.

The majority of the homes in the area didn't have much, just the bare minimum of furniture and a TV. Despite the poverty and problems, it was a close-knit community where almost everybody in the neighborhood knew one another and looked out for one another and each other's children; there was a small local shop, "Dixon's" and the "Woodland's Crescent Nursery" with a sandpit that was another favorite play area with the local children.

On May 11, 1968, John Best, a three-year-old boy, was found at the bottom of an embankment behind some empty sheds near the Delaval Arms public house, bleeding from the head and dazed. He was taken to the public house and claimed that he had been pushed off a ledge but would not say by whom. Even for young children in the area telling the authorities anything was considered bad form. The police and ambulance were called, but the incident was considered accidental and no action was taken.

The following day, seven-year-old Pauline Watson and two friends were playing in the Woodland's Crescent Nursery sandpit when two local girls, ten-year-old Mary Bell, a cousin of the little boy John Best, and her best friend thirteen-year old-Norma Bell (no relation despite the same surname) joined them. Mary told Pauline to get out of the sandpit and when she refused, Mary put her hands around her neck and squeezed hard, while simultaneously attempted to shove sand down her throat. The other two girls managed to pull Mary off, and Pauline ran home in tears to her mother and reported what had happened. Mary and Norma then scuttled off. Mrs. Watson, despite Pauline's protests as she was terrified what Norma and Mary might do to her, called the police. The police questioned Mary and Norma about the incident, and each girl blamed the other. Norma declared afterwards that Mary was no longer her friend; a declaration that lasted no more than one night. According to the May 15th official police report, both Mary and Norma were warned as to their future conduct.

Mary and Norma lived next door to each other on Whitehouse Road, one of the roughest streets in the area, and had become best friends since Norma Bell had moved in to the house next to Mary in 1967. Norma, the third of eleven children, lived with her ten brothers and sisters ranging in age from a handicapped brother of sixteen to a small baby of a few months old.

Mary lived with her mother Betty Bell, her stepfather (whom Mary thought at the time was her father) Billy Bell, a drunkard and petty criminal, and her younger half brother and two younger half sisters who she didn't realize were half-siblings. It was a chaotic household.

Her mother was a depressive, erratic, alcoholic who was frequently away working as a prostitute in Glasgow. Betty Bell's specialty was sadomasochism, which the police later believed, although it was never brought up in court, that Mary must have witnessed on a daily basis when her mother was working from home. Betty was later to tell a social worker,

"I always hid the whips from the kids."

## Martin Brown

On Saturday the 25th of May in 1968 blond, shiny, blue-eyed, four-year-old Martin Brown, while his parent's were enjoying a morning lie in, carried up some milk and a Rusk biscuit to his one-year-old sister Linda, whom he shared a bedroom with. It was his normal weekend routine.

Martin lived in a two storey house at 140 St Margaret's Road with his father Georgie and his mother June. His aunt Rita and her five children lived a few doors away on the same street at number 112.

After having given Linda her milk and biscuit, Martin carried the baby into his mother before scuttling down the stairs to eat his own breakfast of "Sugar Pops," his favorite breakfast cereal. Martin then slipped on his anorak before calling upstairs to his mother "I'm away, Mam" and then shot out the door to play with his friends.

That was the last time June Brown heard or saw her young, mischievously faced son alive.

Other people saw him that morning. Two city electricians, Gordan Collinson and John Hall, gave him a biscuit as he watched them work. His Aunt Rita saw him when he called into her house and was fed an egg on toast. She also saw him again in the afternoon when he dropped by and asked for a piece of bread. His father saw him briefly when he returned home at 3 p.m. to ask for some change to buy a lollypop from Dixon's.

At 3.30 p.m., three teenage boys who were foraging for wood in a derelict house, number 85 St Margaret's Road, found Martin in an upstairs bedroom, flat on his back, his little arms outstretched, and blood and saliva dribbling from his mouth. They called out to the city electricians, still working in the street, for help. Gordan Collinson phoned for an ambulance, and John Hall gave him CPR. Neighbors hearing the commotion ran out of their houses, this included June Brown and her sister Rita, who arrived at the scene to see John Hall attempting to revive Martin. Martin was transported to Newcastle Hospital and was pronounced dead upon arrival.

The police found no signs of violence, Martin's clothes were undamaged, and there were no broken bones. He had no visible strangulation marks or any other marks. A bottle of aspirin was found in the rubble of the room, which made the police think briefly of possible accidental poisoning, until the toxicity report came back negative. The authorities concluded that Martin's death was accidental, although they had no idea of what caused it. The official report declared the "cause of death open." The residents of the area blamed Martin's death on the dangerous conditions of the derelict houses. The residents organized protests, calling on the authorities to have the derelict buildings demolished rapidly.

On Sunday the 26th of May, Mary Bell, known to friends and neighbors as May, celebrated her eleventh birthday with her friend Norma Bell. During the celebrations, Norma's father saw Mary attempt to throttle his ten-year-old-daughter, Susan, and smacked Mary's hands loose. At the time, Mr. Bell dismissed the incident as over excitement.

A couple of day's following the death of Martin, on hearing a knock at her front door, June Brown, Martin's mother, opened it to find Mary and Norma standing there smiling. Mary asked to see Martin.

June replied, "No, pet. Martin is dead."

"Oh, I know he's dead. I wanted to see him in his coffin," Mary replied grinning.

June, deep in grief, slammed the door on them and their strange request.

Mary and Norma also plagued Martin's Aunt Rita. They would knock on Rita's door and ask her, as they grinned,

"Do you miss Martin?" and "Do you cry for him?"

In the end, Rita, unable to stand it anymore, told them to stop bothering her and to never again call at her house.

The following morning on May the 27th, teachers at the "Woodland's Crescent Nursery," which young Martin Brown had attended, discovered a break in. School supplies had been recklessly strewn about, cleaning materials splattered over the floors, and four disturbing handwritten notes were discovered.

Notes:

"Look out THERE are Murders about"

"I murder so THAT I may come back"

"fuch of we murder watch out Fanny and Faggot"

"we did murder Martain brown F*** of you Bastard"

The police were called and took the notes, which they noted had each letter written alternately in two different handwritings, and filed them away as a sick prank. The nursery school, following the incident, had an alarm system installed.

That same day at the Delaval Road Junior School that Mary and Norma attended, Mary wrote in her school notebook:

*'On Saturday, I was in the house, and my mam sent Me to ask Norma if she Would come up the top with me? we went up and we came down at Magrets Road and there were crowds of people beside an old house. I asked what was the matter. there had been a boy who Just lay down and Died.'*

Next to the story, Mary had drawn a picture of a child in the same position as that in which Martin Brown had been found; close by the body she had drawn a bottle with the word "TABLET" labeled on it. Mary's school notebook story did not strike her teacher, Eric Foster, as strange as it was a momentous event in the small community, although Mary was the only student who wrote about it.

The schoolteachers at Delaval Road Junior School found Mary to be a highly intelligent child but worried occasionally about her seemingly lack of feeling for other people. Mary was a sweet-faced, very pretty child, with a heart-shaped face and pretty blue piecing eyes under a dark heavy fringe. One morning, Eric Foster noticed one of his young girl pupils with what looked like a burn mark on her face. He questioned her about it. The girl said that Mary had snubbed a cigarette out on her cheek. Eric Foster then questioned Mary about it and asked her if she had done it.

"Oh yes," she had replied.

Mr. Foster then asked her if she was sorry about it, and she had replied, "Yes," but without much conviction. Tragically, nothing was done about Mary's violent behavior. Most of the children at the school tried to avoid Norma and Mary on the playground.

Norma was also a pretty girl with dark brown hair and soft brown eyes in a round face. The teachers found her to be slow-witted, with a variety of learning difficulties. The joke among the teachers and others in the neighborhood was that if Mary had asked Norma to jump off the Tyne Bridge she would have done it.

In early June, a twelve-year-old boy, David McCready, witnessed Mary scratch her friend Norma, knock her to the ground, and kick her in the eye in the Nursery sandpit. He later said that Mary screamed,

"I am a murderer!" as she pointed at the house where Martin Brown was found. "That house over there, that's where I killed..."

The boy dismissed the comment as Mary had a reputation among the local kids as being a show-off and a liar.

Early in July, the recently installed alarm went off at the Woodland's Crescent Nursery. Mary Bell and Norma Bell were caught breaking in, but both denied having broken in before. They were both charged with breaking and entry and a date was set for them to appear at Juvenile Court before being released to the custody of their parents.

Towards the end of July, Mary visited the Howe family, close neighbors, and declared,

"I know something about Norma that will get her put away."

She told them that, "Norma put her hands on a boy's throat. It was Martin Brown -- she pressed and he just dropped."

To illustrate her statement, she clutched her own throat in a choking gesture and then left the house.

### Brian Howe

On the 31st of July in 1968, fourteen-year-old Pat Howe was at home at 64 Whitehouse Road making supper for her younger brothers: seven-year-old Norman and three-year-old Brian. Pat lived in the house with her father, Eric, her two younger brothers, and an older brother Albert. The mother had walked out on the family some eighteen months previously. Pat had taken on the role of surrogate mother, ran the house, and looked after the two younger children with the help of neighbors and friends.

When at 5 p.m. Brian hadn't arrived home for his supper, Pat began to worry and went outside to call him. Down the street outside number 66, Pat saw Mary Bell sitting on the doorstep. She called out,

"Mary, have you seen our Brian?"

"No, but I'll come and help you look for him," Mary offered helpfully.

The two girls set off to look for the three-year-old toddler, and Norma shortly joined them. They first made their way to the local shop "Dixon's", asking along the way if anyone had seen the small boy. They continued searching the streets and neighborhood with Pat becoming progressively more worried. They went up to the railway bridge from where they could get a good view of the industrial wasteland the "Tin Lizzie." From this vantage point, they could see no signs of any children.

"He might be playing behind the blocks or between them," Mary said as she pointed to some large slabs of concrete blocks.

141

"Oh no, he never goes there," Norma said, who knew Brian well as she sometimes babysat Brian and his best friend John Finlay. Pat agreed with her, as she knew her baby brother didn't like to stray too far from home. The girls had another walk around the streets and popular play areas of the local kids and checked to see if while they had been out he had returned home. At 7p.m., Pat phoned the police and reported Brian missing.

The police began a search. By this time, most of the neighborhood had heard that the toddler was missing and joined in the search party.

The police found Brian Howe shortly after 11 p.m. He was lying between the concrete slabs Mary Bell had pointed at hours earlier. His little body, still dressed, had been covered with grass and purple weeds that grew in abundance over the "Tin Lizzie." Brian had been strangled. There were scratch marks on his nose, blood-stained froth had oozed from his mouth, and his lips were blue. On his neck, there were pressure marks and scratches. Found lying in the grass close to his body were a pair of scissors with one blade bent back and one blade broken.

A murder inquiry was launched. Initially, the police suspected that there was a pervert loose. However, following the autopsy they changed their thinking.

Residents of the area began to wonder if Martin Brown's death was not an accident after all.

During the autopsy on Brian's body, six puncture marks were found on his thighs, and the toddler's genitals had been partially skinned. On his stomach, the letter "M" had been cut into his skin with a razor blade. On closer examination, it looked as if the initial had originally been an "N," but then changed. He put the time of death down to between 3:30 p.m. to 4:30 p.m. on the 31st of July in 1968.

The pathologist, Mr Bernard Tomlinson, thought that due to the lightness of the pressure marks on Brian's neck and the six puncture wounds indicated that the injuries had been caused by a child or children.

## Investigation

Police began conducting house-to-house inquiries and interviewing all of the children in the neighborhood. Within 24 hours, over a thousand homes in the area had been visited and 1,200 children between the ages of three to fifteen were interviewed and asked to fill out questionnaires.

The police then examined all the questionnaires and selected twelve children they wanted additional information from; two of the children were Norma Bell and Mary Bell.

Detective Kerr first visited Norma Bell's house. Part of the replies on her questionnaire were unreadable, in particular her answer to when she had last seen Brian Howe. Detective Kerr found Norma's behavior strange. He was investigating the murder of a toddler she had known well, and Norma had kept grinning at him as if it was a joke.

Norma made a new statement saying that she had last seen Brian Howe at about 12:45 p.m., on the 31st of July when he was playing with his brother and two little girls on the corner of Whitehouse Road.

Asked what she was doing on the afternoon of July 31st, she stated that between 1-5 p.m., she played in the street with Gillian and Linda Routledge. They then went into the Routledge house at 59 Whitehouse Road and made pom poms.

Detective Kerr then went next door to 70 Whitehouse Road, where Mary Bell lived. However, her stepfather Billy, a big rough gypsy type, at first refused him access to Mary and threatened to set the family Alsatian on him.

If her parents were somehow responsible for young Mary's behavior, she would not talk about it. She had been taught to keep quiet, especially around authority figures. Mary and her younger brothers and sisters were instructed to always call Billy "Uncle," in front of authority figures so that their mother could collect government assistance as a single mother.

When Detective Kerr was finally allowed access to Mary, he wanted clarification on two questions from her.

When had she last seen Brian?
Was she playing near the Delaval Arms public house near to the railway lines between 1 p.m. and 5 p.m. on Wednesday the 31st of July?

Mary stated that she had last seen Brian Howe on Whitehouse Road at about 12:30 p.m. playing with his brother. She denied being near the Delaval Arms or the waste ground near there on Wednesday the 31st of July.

Over the next few days, police interviewed Norma and Mary on a number of occasions.

On Friday August the 2nd during an interview, Mary told Detective Sergeant Docherty that she had remembered seeing a boy on his own on Delaval Road after Brian had been killed. He was covered in grass and little purple flowers. She claimed he had scissors in his hands and something was wrong with them "like one leg was either broken or bent. And I saw him trying to cut a cat's tail off with those scissors."

The police interviewed the boy mentioned by Mary, and he had a solid alibi for his whereabouts on the afternoon in question. He had been all afternoon at Newcastle airport, eight miles away, with his parents. He was immediately eliminated from their inquiries.

At this time, no details of the scissors found lying in the grass close to Brian's body had been photographed or described in any way in the newspapers. By mentioning the scissors, Mary became a prime suspect along with Norma Bell, who had already changed her statement twice. It was becoming clear to the detectives that either Mary, Norma, or both girls had seen Brian die and that one or the other of them was the killer.

Also, the police had several witness statements that Norma and Mary had been seen together that afternoon; yet, neither girl had mentioned this fact in their statements. The police returned to Norma's house, and this time took her to Westgate police station where she was cautioned about her rights and questioned.

Norma now claimed that Mary had told her that she had killed Brian and had taken her to see his body at the blocks. She said that when she saw Brian, she knew he was dead, "because his lips were purple." Norma stated that Mary had said,

"I squeezed his neck and pushed up his lungs; that's how you kill them."

The police detained Norma in a children's home overnight. They then had Mary picked up shortly after midnight and brought to Westgate Road police station accompanied by her Aunt Audrey, as her mother was away working in Glasgow, even though it was late at night and Mary was asleep in bed. Mary, despite three hours of questioning and having been told that Norma had made a statement implicating her in Brian's murder, stuck to her statement although she conceded that she had taken her Alsatian dog to the park for a walk and that Norma had briefly joined her.

The police were astounded by Mary's intelligence and the sophisticated way she second-guessed their questions. Mary would answer the first question before it was even finished and continue answering more questions before they had even been asked.

Detective Dobson, the lead detective in the case, said to Mary,

"I have reason to believe that when you were near the concrete blocks with Norma, a man shouted at some children who were nearby and you both ran away from where Brian was lying in the grass. This man will probably know you."

"He would have to have good eyesight," Mary replied.

"Why would he need good eyesight?" Detective Dobson asked, thinking he was about to catch the eleven-year-old out in a lie.

"Because he was... "Mary said, and after a pregnant pause added, "clever to see me when I wasn't there."

She refused to make another statement.

"I am making no statements. I have made many statements. It's always me you come for. Norma's a liar; she always tries to get me into trouble."

The police sent Mary home at 3 a.m. having no solid evidence to hold her any longer.

The following day, August 7th, was the day of little Brian Howe's funeral. It was a hot August day. Over two hundred people turned up for the funeral, many of them strangers to the Howe family. Masses of flowers were sent from all around Britain.

Detective Dobson stood outside the Howe's house as the tiny coffin was carried out so, too, was Mary Bell. Detective Dobson later said,

"I was, of course, watching her. And it was when I saw her there that I knew I did not dare risk another day. She stood there laughing. Laughing and rubbing her hands. I thought, *'My God, I've got to bring her in, she'll do another one.'*"

Norma, also in the morning, made a fourth statement claiming to have been with Mary earlier and had gone with Mary and Brian to the concrete blocks on the Tin Lizzie. Brian had with him a pair of scissors given to him by his brother. At first, they had all climbed inside an old tank but immediately all climbed out because it was smelly. Norma said it was shortly after that Mary told Brian to lift his neck. Norma continued: She got him down on the grass, and she seemed to go all funny. You could tell there was something the matter with her. She kept on struggling with him, and he was struggling and trying to get her hands away. She let go of him, and I could hear him gasping. She squeezed his neck again, and I said,

"Mary, leave the baby alone," but she wouldn't.

She said to me, "My hands are getting thick; take over."

Then I ran away. I went back the way we had come. Norma claimed she had then gone back to Whitehouse road and played with some other children. Then Mary arrived back twenty minutes later and asked Norma to revisit the scene of the murder. This Norma did and said this time Mary had a razor blade with her which is when she cut the initial 'M' on Brian's tummy. Norma said Mary had then hidden the razor blade.

Norma said they again revisited the murder scene at about 5.30 p.m. This time Norma said Mary cut off lumps of Brian's hair and stabbed his legs with the scissors. Norma, accompanied by police officers, revisited the crime scene and showed them where Mary had hidden the razor blade. This blade was then taken into evidence.

### Arrest

Later that afternoon, Mary was again picked up from home and taken to the police station. This time, Mary appeared nervous and not quite so sure of herself. She made a new and full statement. The following is Mary Bell's official statement:

*I, Mary Flora Bell, wish to make a statement. I want someone to write down what I have to say. I have been told that I need not say anything unless I wish to do so but that whatever I say may be given in evidence.*

*Signed, Mary F. Bell*

*Brian was in his front street and I and Norma were walking along towards him. We walked past him and Norma says,*

*"Are you coming to the shop Brian?"*

*and I says, "Norma, you've got no money, how can you go to the shop? Where are you getting it from?"*

*She says, "Nebby" (keep your nose clean).*

*Little Brian followed and Norma says,*

*"Walk up in front."*

*I wanted Brian to go home, but Norma kept coughing so Brian wouldn't hear us.*

*We went down Crosshill Road with Brian still in front of us. There was this colored boy, and Norma tried to start a fight with him. She said,*

*"Darkie, whitewash, it's time you got washed."*

*The big brother came out and hit her. She shouted,*

*"Howay, put your dukes up."*

*The lad walked away and looked at her as though she was daft.*

*We went beside Dixon's shop and climbed over the railings, I mean, through a hole and over the railway. Then I said,*

*"Norma, where are you going?"*

*and Norma said, "Do you know that little pool where the tadpoles are?"*

*When we got there, there was a big, long tank with a big, round hole with little holes around it. Norma says to Brian,*

*"Are you coming in here because there's a lady coming on the Number 82, and she's got boxes of sweets and that."*

*We all got inside; then, Brian started to cry, and Norma asked him if he had a sore throat. She started to squeeze his throat, and he started to cry. She said,*

*"This isn't where the lady comes; it's over there, by them big blocks."*

*We went over to the blocks and she says,*

*"Ar--you'll have to lie down"*

*and he lay down beside the blocks where he was found. Norma says,*

*"Put your neck up."*

*And he did. Then she got hold of his neck and said,*

*"Put it down."*

*She started to feel up and down his neck. She squeezed it hard. You could tell it was hard because her finger tips were going white. Brian was struggling, and I was pulling her shoulders, but she went mad. I was pulling her chin up but she screamed at me.*

*By this time, she had banged Brian's head on some wood or corner of wood, and Brian was lying senseless. His face was all white and bluey, and his eyes were open. His lips were purplish and had all like slaver on, it turned into something like fluff. Norma covered him up, and I said,*

*"Norma, I've got nothing to do with this. I should tell on you, but I'll not."*

*Little Lassie was there, and it was crying, and she said,*

*"Don't you start or I'll do the same to you."*

*It still cried, and she went to get hold of its throat, but it growled at her. She said,*

*"Now now. Don't be hasty."*

*We went home, and I took little Lassie (Brian's dog) home an all. Norma was acting kind of funny and making twitchy faces and spreading her fingers out. She said,*

*"This is the first, but it'll not be the last."*

*I was frightened then. I carried Lassie and put her down over the railway, and we went up Crosswood Road way. Norma went into the house, and she got a pair of scissors, and she put them down her pants. She says,*

*"Go and get a pen."*

*I said "No. What for?"*

*She says, "To write a note on his stomach."*

*And I wouldn't get the pen. She had a Gillette razor blade. It had Gillette on. We went back to the blocks, and Norma cut his hair. She tried to cut his leg and his ear with the blade. She tried to show me it was sharp. She took the top of her dress where it was raggie and cut it; it made a slit. A man came down the railway bank with a little girl with long blonde hair. He had a red checked shirt on and blue denim jeans. I walked away. She hid the razor blade under a big, square concrete block. She left the scissors beside him. She got out before me over the grass on to Scotswood Road. I couldn't run on the grass cos I just had my black slippers on. When we got along a bit she says,*

*"Mary, you shouldn't have done that cos you'll get into trouble,"*

*And I hadn't done nothing. I haven't got the guts. I couldn't kill a bird by the neck or throat or anything. It's horrible, that. We went up the steps and went home. I was nearly crying. I said,*

*"If Pat finds out, she'll kill you. Never mind killing Brian cos Pat's more like a tomboy. She's always climbing in the old buildings and that."*

*Later on, I was helping to look for Brian, and I was trying to let on to Pat that I knew where he was on the blocks, but Norma said,*

*"He'll not be over there; he never goes ther," and she convinced Pat he wasn't there.*

*I got shouted in about half past seven, and I stayed in. I got woke up about half past eleven, and we stood at the door as Brian had been found: The other day, Norma wanted to get put in a home. She says will you run away with us, and I said no. She says if you get put in a home and you feed the little ones and murder them then run away again.*

*I have read the above statement, and I have been told that I can correct, alter or add anything I wish, this statement is true. I have made it of my own free will.*

*Mary Flora Bell (signed at 6:55 pm)*

On the 8th of August, the Police formally charged Norma Bell and Mary Bell with the murder of Brian Howe. Both girls were detained in custody in small jail cells at the police station.

As news of the arrests of the eleven-year-old and thirteen-year-old girls hit the papers, it electrified the country.

Despite Mary's denials, the evidence against Mary was beginning to stack up. The police, by this time, had reopened Martin Brown's case file, as there were many similarities between his death and that of Brian Howe's, and they were now treating it as murder.

Eric Foster, Mary's teacher at Delaval Road Junior School on hearing of Mary's arrest, re-read her school notebooks and handed them into the police. The police were particularly interested in her news-story drawing about Martin Brown's death. The tablets next to Martin's body had never been disclosed to anyone. To the police, it was evidence that Mary had been at the scene of Martin's death.

The first night in their tiny prison cells in the police station, Norma and Mary were restless. They continually shouted to each other through the doors. Mary, who had always been a chronic bed wetter, was petrified of going to sleep, afraid that she might wet her bed. Whenever she did so at home, her mother Betty would severely humiliate her by rubbing her face in the pool of urine and would then hang the mattress outside for the entire neighborhood to see. She was petrified of what punishment she would receive in police custody; she was only an eleven-year-old-child.

Mary, between her arrest and trial, was first sent to an assessment center near London and then to Seaham Remand Home closer to home in County Durham, which catered for girls aged between fourteen and eighteen and was run by the prison department.

Many of the people who cared for Mary in the lead up to the trial became fond of the vivacious, intelligent, little girl that was in such deep trouble. They believed that Mary had no idea of the enormity of what she had done. She fretted about whether her mother would have to pay a fine and hoped her mother wouldn't be 'too upset'. Betty Bell did not visit her daughter for over a week after her arrest and then only to yell at her for the shame she had brought upon her. Mary told a police officer that Brian Howe didn't have a mother, so he wouldn't be missed. At some point one, of her guards asked whether she knew how it would feel to be strangled. Mary replied,

"Why? If you're dead, you're dead. It doesn't matter then."

During her trial Mary told one policewoman,

"Murder isn't that bad. We all die sometime anyway."

Norma, thanks to her barrister, R. P. Smith, QC, within days of her arrest had persuaded a judge in chambers in London that she should spend the period before the trial as a patient at a nearby mental hospital, the Prudhoe Monkton, being "observed" by nurses and doctors.

## The Trial

The trial of Regina v. Mary Flora Bell and Norma Joyce Bell for the murders of Martin Brown and Brian Howe began on December 5th, 1968 at the Newcastle Assizes in Court Two in front of Judge, Mr. Justice Cusack. It was a trial that fascinated, and at the same time horrified, a nation. Many people felt that the Crown Court was the wrong place to deal with such young children but in England the age of criminal responsibility is ten and so Mary and Norma were tried as adults.

However, to make it less intimidating for the girls, the Judge ruled that their lawyers could sit with them.

The Prosecutor Mr. Rudolph Lyons began the trial by indicating that whoever murdered Brian Howe also killed Martin Brown. He told the court that the two young girls had murdered "solely for the pleasure and excitement of killing." Rudolf Lyons then proceeded to methodically recount the suspicious behavior of Mary and Norma; how they had harassed the mourning family with their gruesome questions, and Mary's and Norma's smiling and asking if she could see little Martin Brown in his coffin, and how they maliciously vandalized the Woodlands Nursery leaving notes that amounted to a confession.

Handwriting experts were called into the court who said that the notes were written in both girls' handwriting. Forensic pathologists testified that gray fibers from one of Mary's dresses were found on the bodies of both Martin and Brian and that fibers from one of Norma's skirts were discovered on Brian's shoes. Altogether, the prosecution produced thirty-nine witnesses.

Taken all together, the prosecution had a strong case against both Norma and Mary. Both girls pleaded not guilty and blamed each other for the murders.

The two girls were scrutinized heavily by the public and media in court. Norma looked like a terrified frightened little girl, totally overawed by the court proceedings, and frequently breaking into tears. Behind her in the courtroom, she was surrounded by a solid protective loving family, who would frequently comfort her.

Mary, in contrast, showed no emotion and appeared defiant. And although her step-father, mother, aunts, and uncles sat behind her, never did they touch or demonstrate any physical comfort towards her. Mary, unlike Norma, appeared very alone. Mary's mother Betty did not help her case. She frequently disrupted the court proceedings with dramatic sobbing and wailing as her long blond wig would slide off her head, revealing her dark brown hair. On some occasions, she stormed out of the courtroom clumping on high heels during the trial and then would dramatically reappear just minutes later. Her stepfather Billy sat quietly, head in hand, and ignored his wife's theatrics.

Though highly intelligent, Mary admitted later that she was bewildered by the proceedings. She had little understanding of what was happening to her. She was ignorant of knowing what a jury or a verdict was or what was meant by rules of evidence. No one had attempted to explain to the small girl the alien language and rituals of a trial.

Norma elicited compassion, while Mary only seemed to attract animosity. On the fourth day of the trial, Norma was called to the witness stand. Here, she frequently broke down crying and answered questions in stuttering whispers and gave the impression of a very insecure, emotionally fragile, frightened little girl. The judge was gentle with her and rather protective, giving her frequent breaks if he thought the cross examination was getting too much for her. Everything she blamed on Mary: the strangling, the razor blade initial, the stabbing with the scissors, and the mutilation of Brian's penis. She projected herself as innocent who had the misfortune of having an evil friend. The only thing she could not entirely blame on Mary was the notes written in both girls' handwriting.

A psychiatrist, Dr. Frazer, who had treated Norma at the Prudhoe Monkton Mental Hospital, described Norma as emotionally immature and of sub-normal intelligence, who did not have the capacity "to be a leader." He said that while at the hospital, intelligence tests showed she had the mental age of a child of eight or nine and during her time at the hospital had got on well with the other children and had shown no signs of physical aggression.

On the sixth day of the trial, Mary was called to the witness box. In complete contrast to Norma, she showed no fear or discomfiture but appeared assuredly self-confident as she bandied words and witty quips with the prosecutor, Mr. Rudolph Lyons.

Spectators in the courtroom watched Mary with horrified curiosity. For a child who was to be branded as manipulative and cunning, she appeared to know little about attracting sympathy.

After Mary's testimony, the defense lawyers called the psychiatrist, Dr. Robert Orton, who had examined Mary. He testified,

"I think that this girl must be regarded as suffering from psychopathic personality," demonstrated by "a lack of feeling quality to other humans," and "a liability to act on impulse and without forethought." And, "She showed no remorse whatsoever, no tears, and no anxiety. She was completely unemotional about the whole affair and merely resentful at her detention."

A Home Office psychiatrist, Dr. Westbury, said that Mary showed no evidence "of mental illness or severe abnormality or sub normality of intelligence," but had a "serious disorder of personality... which required medical treatment." He continued, "Manipulation of people is [her] primary aim."

On cross-examination by Norma's lawyer, Mr. Smith, Dr. Westbury agreed that Mary was "violent" and "very dangerous."

The following day the closing arguments began. The prosecutor, Mr. Rudolph Lyons, branded Mary as a fiend. He said that Norma was a victim of

"...an evil and compelling influence almost like that of the fictional Svengali" and continued by saying, "In Norma, you have a simple backward girl of subnormal intelligence. In Mary you have a most abnormal child, aggressive, vicious, cruel, and incapable of remorse; a girl moreover possessed of a dominating personality, with a somewhat unusual intelligence, and a degree of cunning that is almost terrifying."

Norma's lawyer, Mr.Smith, said in his closing speech that Norma had been "an innocent bystander" who had told childish lies to get herself out of trouble.

In an attempt to rescue Mary from being cast off as a devilish "bad seed," Mary's barrister asked broader questions: Why did this happen? What made Mary do it? Mr. Harvey Robson declared,

"It is... very easy to revile a little girl, to liken her to Svengali without pausing for a moment to ponder how the whole sorry situation has come about..."

On the night of December 16th, eleven-year-old Mary knew that the following day the jury would decide her fate. She said to the policewoman guarding her,

"What would be the worst that could happen to me? Would they hang me?"

The jury, which consisted of five women and seven men, took less than four hours to return a verdict. Mary Bell was found "guilty of Manslaughter in Martin Brown's and Brian Howe's murders because of Diminished Responsibility."

Norma Bell was acquitted, as she was deemed by the jury as a passive slow-witted partner who had been led astray by the evil and devious Mary Bell.

Mary broke down and cried as she heard the jury's verdicts. Sitting on the benches behind her, her relatives also wept. However, it was only her young solicitor, David Bryson, who put a comforting arm around Mary.

## The Sentencing

In Judge Justice Cusack's sentencing he said,

"It is a most unhappy thing that in all the resources of this country it appears there is no hospital available which is suitable for the accommodation of this girl."

He continued, "It is an appalling thing that with a child as young as this one, one has to take into consideration such matters. I am not entirely unsympathetic but anxious, as I am to do everything for her benefit; my primary duty is to protect other people."

"There is a very grave risk to other children if she is not closely watched and every conceivable step taken to see that she doesn't do again what she has been found guilty of. In the case of a child of this age, no question of imprisonment arises. I have power to order a sentence of detention, and it seems to me that no other method of dealing with her in the circumstances is suitable."

"I, therefore, have to turn to what length of detention should be imposed. I say at once that if an undeterminate period is imposed, as in the case of a life sentence of imprisonment, that does not mean that the person concerned is kept in custody indefinitely or for the rest of their natural lives. It means that the position can be considered from time to time and, if it becomes safe to release that person, that person can be released. For that reason, the sentence of the court concurrently in respect of these two matters upon Mary Bell is a sentence of detention and the detention will be for life."

Norma Bell, for breaking and entering the Woodlands Crescent Nursery, was later given three years probation and placed under psychiatric care.

During all of Mary Bell's months in remand and during the trial no one had thought, or even seemed to care, what had made this extraordinarily pretty, blue-eyed, heart-shaped face girl commit these crimes. To the media and the British public, she was seen as a sweet-faced, chilling monster; a freak of nature, simply pure evil. She was described in the press under lurid headlines as a child who had been "born evil," a "demon," and "monster."

The detectives who had arrested Mary didn't see her in this light. They felt sorry for her and felt, given her upbringing, she had never stood a chance of being a normal child. The authorities in their dogged concern with determining Mary's guilt or innocence did not attempt to discover the truth about her horrendous home life.

Perhaps, if the whole truth of Mary's upbringing had been known, then the outcome of the trial may have been very different. Mary was a victim of abuse, appalling abuse, that was not uncovered for many years.

**Early Years**

Betty Bell (née McCrickett), was born in 1940, in Glasgow. Betty's mother described her as a profoundly religious child who she thought would grow up to be a nun. Her sister said she was always drawing nuns, altars, graves, and cemeteries.

Betty Bell gave birth to Mary when she was seventeen-years-old on May 26th, 1957 in Gateshead, a large urban town that sits on the south bank of the River Tyne opposite Newcastle upon Tyne.

It is unknown who Mary's biological father was. The first thing Betty said when Mary was placed into her arms by her mother shortly after giving birth was,

"Take the thing away from me!"

She rejected her daughter and frequently tried to kill her.

It is in Gitta Sereny's book *The Case of Mary Bell,* first published in 1972, where one learns about Mary's early years. Mary's maternal grandmother, uncles, Aunt Isa, and Aunt Cathy co-operated with Ms. Sereny in the hope that the public knowing about Mary's early life, might make them more sympathetic to Mary and show that she was a damaged traumatized little girl and not an evil monster. As told to Ms. Sereny by Mary's relatives and friends, Mary's childhood was a nightmare of abandonment and drug overdoses.

A few months after Mary was born, Betty met Billy Bell and married him in March of 1958. A few months later in the autumn of 1958, Betty gave birth to Billy's son. At the time, they were living with Betty's mother and sister Isa in Gateshead.

When Mary was aged one she somehow managed to get hold of her grandmother's medication, which she kept hidden inside a gramophone that was placed high up on a chest of drawers. Despite the pills being in a bottle with a childproof cap, Mary succeeded in swallowing enough of the pills to almost kill her. Luckily, her grandmother found her and rushed her to hospital where she had her stomach pumped. Her grandmother suspected Betty of giving Mary the pills.

Shortly afterwards, Betty, Billy, and the two children moved out. In November of 1959, Betty wrote to her sister Cathy and said she had given Mary away to some family friends. Cathy immediately went to visit the friends and returned Mary to Betty. A few months later, Cathy went to visit her sister and took a packet each of sweets for Mary and her younger brother. Leaving the children munching their sweets in the living room, Mary and Cathy went to make a pot of tea in the kitchen. When Cathy returned to the living room, she was horrified to see mixed up with the sweets little triangular blue pills which she recognized as Betty's Drinamyl, amphetamines known as purple hearts. Cathy, before taking the children to hospital, made them drink hot water and salt making both children vomit in the sink, an act that may have saved their lives.

"They must have taken the bottle out of my handbag," was Betty's explanation, which her sister found hard to believe.

When Cathy returned home and told her husband Jack about the incident, he suggested that for Mary's safety they should offer her a home. Cathy wrote to Betty making her the offer, but Betty refused to give Mary up.

A few months later when Betty and Mary were visiting her mother, Betty held Mary up by the open window of the third floor kitchen sink for a pee (the bathroom was on the ground floor). Suddenly Betty's brother, Philip, saw Mary begin to fall out of the window; he leapt up and only just managed to prevent her plunging out the window. The family was getting extremely worried about Mary's safety.

A few days later Betty, secretly followed by Isa, took Mary to an adoption agency and handed her over to a distraught woman who was not allowed to adopt because of her age and other reasons.

"I brought this one in to be adopted. You have her," Betty said, shoving Mary into the stranger's arms.

Isa followed the woman and Mary and, noting down the address, handed it over to her mother. Mary was eventually returned home with new dresses the stranger had bought her.

Mary's next overdose was just a few months later when Mary took a load of "iron pills," apparently mistaking them for Smarties. She had collapsed unconscious and had been rushed to the hospital where she had her stomach pumped. Mary told doctors that her mother had given her the smarties; a fact that was corroborated by a friend of Mary's to her Aunt Cathy. For a developing child, overdoses can cause serious brain damage, a frequent trait amongst violent offenders.

After this incident, furious arguments occurred between Betty, her mother, and siblings which culminated in Betty telling them she never wanted to see them again, and she cut off all contact with them for over a year.

As if these abuses weren't bad enough, the real horror of Mary Bell's childhood was not to surface until many years after her release from prison.

## The Incarceration

As Mary Bell's case was unique, the United Kingdom, who had never before been presented with an eleven-year-old murderess, was unsure what to do with her. Prison was not an option for a child. The Mental health hospitals weren't equipped to take her, and she was considered too dangerous for facilities that housed troubled children.

Straight after sentencing and after a brief visit by her relatives, the terrified Mary had a blanket thrown over her head and was led out of court blinded. Mary thought she was being taken to the gallows but was taken to Low Newton, an adult prison, in County Durham. Here, she was stripped, searched, and hosed down in the same manner as adult prisoners. As there was no prison uniform small enough, she was allowed to wear her own clothes. She was then put in isolation in the hospital wing of the prison. As it was law that she must receive education whilst incarcerated due to her age, the woman governor of the prison spent an hour a day with Mary reading and writing. Mary liked the governor and mentioned her fear of being hanged. The governor assured her that no one was going to hang her.

While Mary was incarcerated in Low Newton, her mother and step-father were trying to sell her story to the tabloid press. For once, the tabloid press was sickened by such a mercenary act on the part of her parents that they refused to touch the story.

Mary spent about two weeks at Low Newton before being transferred, shortly before Christmas, to Cumberlow Lodge: a high-security, short-term remand home for girls aged fifteen to seventeen, while the government frantically searched for a solution as to where to house the eleven-year-old Mary, long-term.

In February of 1969, Mary was taken to Red Bank reform schools Special Unit in Lancashire. It was a school for boys, and Mary was the only girl among twenty-two boys in the special unit for nearly all the five years she was there. It wasn't ideal but was the best the government could come up with. Mr. Dixon, who ran the school, travelled down to London to pick Mary up with his wife. Mary immediately took a liking to James Dixon and over time came to love and respect him. He was an ex-Navy man known for his strong moral character. To Mary, he became a strong, benevolent, father figure who provided structure and discipline for Mary that had been so lacking in her life.

The special unit sat in the middle of the reform school, which catered for around 500 boys. The children in the special unit were not free to mix with the children in the reform school as they were children who required a high-degree of security and who were kept locked in at all times. Despite this, it was, according to Gitta Sereny, who visited the unit a few times, a pleasant environment. It was light and modern. On the ground floor, there was a library, sitting rooms with comfortable chairs, a pleasant dining room, and a number of classrooms where the children were taught in small groups, depending on age and ability. Outside was a garden, a greenhouse, and a shed for pets. The children in the special unit also had the use of the swimming pool in the main reform school for an hour a day in the summer and access to the extensive sports facilities.

Upstairs, were the dormitories. When it was decided Mary was to be sent to the special unit, an area had been sectioned off for girls. However, during the entire time Mary was there, only five other girls were housed there and only for short amounts of time, the longest being three months.

The schedule at Redbank was regimented. The children were to be up at 7 a.m sharp, then shower, make their beds, and be downstairs for fingernail and shoe inspection before breakfast at 8 a.m. Lessons were from 8 a.m. to 12:45. Lunch was served promptly at 1 p.m. followed by more lessons between 2 p.m. to 4 p.m. Between 4-5 p.m., they could choose to play draughts or chess. The last cooked meal of the day was at 5 p.m. In the summer, they then had swimming at 6 p.m., followed by athletics or football. At 8 p.m. they had showers and then hot cocoa and a sandwich. Occasionally, they would be allowed to watch television if something suitable was deemed to be on. Bedtime was from 8:30 to 9 p.m. and lights out was at 9:30 p.m. There was a house-mother, Miss Hemmings, who looked over the children, and who grew to adore Mary.

The philosophy of Red Bank was to focus on the present. James Dixon believed that dwelling on the past was detrimental. He was of the belief that love and proper care could conquer all. A visiting psychiatrist to Redbank, Dr Dewi Jones, disagreed. He thought Mary was blocking out her troubled past and was being discouraged from attempting to discover why she had killed the two little boys. He put in a request to treat Mary individually at Redbank and was granted permission to see her once a week for between 30-60 minutes. He realized rapidly that for a child as severely disturbed as Mary, it was an inadequate amount of time to give her the attention he believed she needed. He requested that she be brought to him two to three times a week at the local hospital psychiatric unit. His request was turned down, leaving Mary to continue denying her crimes and the reasons for them.

The first ten months that Mary was at Redbank her stepfather, Billy Bell, whom Mary loved, visited regularly. Mary, who was never allowed to be alone with visitors, would sit and chat in one of the sitting rooms accompanied by one of the Redbank staff. Mary looked forward to and enjoyed his visits and news of her young siblings whom she missed. During one of the visits, Billy told her that her mother had left home for good, and they were to divorce. Billy's visits came to an abrupt halt when he was arrested and imprisoned for robbery with assault. Billy's sister, Aubrey, took in Mary's three young siblings, as Betty had no contact with them and had abandoned them. Betty had taken up with a new man, George, ten years her junior.

Betty Bell first visited Mary at Redbank in December of 1969 and continued visiting once or twice a month until April of 1970. The staff noted that after each of Betty's visits, Mary would become unsettled, difficult to deal with, and aggressive towards the other children. Betty used her visits to Mary to sell tidbits of information of Mary's life to the tabloid press. Betty enjoyed making Mary feel guilty as to how much she suffered as the mother of an infamous child murderer.

"Jesus was only nailed to the cross, I'm being hammered," Betty would complain to Mary.

James Dixon pondered about stopping Betty's visits to Mary but in that era, to prevent a mother's access to her daughter was unthinkable. In the end, Mary herself asked James Dixon to stop allowing her mother to visit.

However, the visits by Betty began again in the spring of 1971.

In the spring of 1970, Mary told her female counselor that a housemaster on night duty had sexually assaulted her. She asked the counselor not to tell anyone but, as it was the counselor's job, she did. Mary was questioned about the incident, but her evidence was considered unreliable. However, from that point on, Mr. Dixon insisted that all night duties were to be carried out in pairs.

Of course, today we are all aware, far too frequently, of reading in the press about children being assaulted in the care of foster homes, of monsters, such as Sir Jimmy Saville, getting away for decades with sexually abusing children in hospitals and elsewhere, and none believing the children who were abused. Society was not geared to hear such unacceptable truths from a child at the expense of an adult, especially a child such as Mary Bell.

In July of 1971, the home office psychiatrist, Dr Westbury, visited Mary. At the trial, he had testified that Mary had a "serious disorder of personality," and that "Manipulation of people is [her] primary aim," and that she was "violent" and "very dangerous."

In his report to the home office after visiting Mary at Redbank, Dr. Westbury said he had "found her remarkably improved," and had lost "nearly all of her aggressive tendencies." He suggested that a release date when Mary was 18 in 1975 should be considered.

In 1973, Mary, aged 16, sat her O'Levels examinations. She passed them all. She and Mr. Dixon were hoping that she might be able to be moved to the reform school soon, still supervised by James Dixon, and be allowed out daily to take her 'A' Levels in the local college and then go on to university. Mary was beginning to see a future for herself far removed from her abusive deprived childhood.

This dream was shattered when she was informed in November of 1973, by an extremely disappointed and saddened Mr. Dixon, that she was to be moved to prison. Mary was stunned. Her years at Redbank had been relatively happy and secure. It had become her home. She had progressed greatly in her time there from the damaged child she had been when she had first arrived. Mr. Dixon said he had done everything he could to make the Home Office change its mind but to no avail. It was a traumatic decision, not just for Mary, but for the staff at Redbank as well, in particular Mr. Dixon, who felt he had let Mary down.

The following day, Mr. and Mrs. Dixon drove the terrified sixteen-year-old Mary to Styal Women's prison in Cheshire, a large oppressive Redbrick Victorian building, in which she would be the youngest inmate.

Gitta Sereny wrote in her book *Cries Unheard*,

"There can be little doubt that this transfer was destructive for Mary."

Mary had to adjust from a caring almost entirely male community at Red Bank to a full women's adult prison. She became rebellious and was frequently punished. Mary, as part of her rebellion, decided to go "butch." When Betty Bell heard this, she said,

"Jesus Christ, what next? You're a murderer and now you're a lesbian?"

While in Styal, Mary learned that Billy Bell was not her biological father. This created in her an acute identity crisis. She wondered just who was she? The next time her mother visited her, she asked her who her biological father was. Her mother refused to answer and abruptly ended the visit.

In June of 1977, Mary was transferred to an open prison, Moor Court in Staffordshire, a beautiful 17th century manor house with pleasant gardens set in the countryside. Mary, having been locked up for the last ten years of her life in institutionalized buildings, found it hard to deal with, especially as she had still not been given any kind of release date. Within three months, along with another girl, Annette Priest, a 21-year-old prostitute and thief, she escaped.

Two young men who were on their way to Blackpool, a holiday resort on the North-East English coast which is famous for its funfair, picked up the two girls. Mary, now aged 20, had never seen the sea nor had she been to a funfair, nor had she ever been to a nightclub or drank alcohol, and had never had vaginal sex. In the two days she was free, she experienced all of these things before the young man she was with turned her over to the authorities and later sold his story to the tabloids.

Once back in police custody, Mary was taken to Risley prison in Cheshire, known among prisoners as Grisly Risley due to its 'barbarous, squalid, dirty, and dilapidated conditions.' Mary remained here for three months before being sent back to Styal. After nine months back in Styal, she was informed in September that she was to be released in May of the following year.

Mary was then moved to another open prison, Askham Grange, near York. Askham Grange was built in 1886 as a country house and although now a prison, it still retains a country-house feel to it. The brickwork is mellow and the grounds immaculate. At Askham Grange an outside visitor, a student from York University, introduced Mary to the music and youth culture of the times. She was also visited weekly by a psychiatrist who, like Mary, became increasingly concerned about her abilities to readjust to the outside world.

After three months, she was moved to a hostel in the grounds of Askham House and was given employment in a local restaurant as a waitress and then in a factory in Leeds, assembling electrical equipment. To get there, she had a mile-long walk to the bus stop and then two bus journeys. She felt "anxious and shaky" in public and would often find comfort in the ladies' lavatory because she was "behind a locked door" again. Her constant fear was that she would be recognized and within two weeks Mary's fears were realized: the tabloid press had discovered her movements, possibly from Betty Bell, and published details with photographs of her. Mary, when informed by the prison, was deeply upset. She kept asking, "Why can't they leave me alone?"

While at Askham, she met a local married man who fell in love with her. On her first home leave, she went and stayed with her mother and her new husband George. Her mother plied her with drink and introduced her to her new friends as her cousin. She forbade Mary to tell anyone she was her daughter. The experience left her utterly confused. In the morning at her mother's house, she had gotten up and stacked the sheets on her bed as she had done in prison for twelve years. Mary has since admitted that it took her years to rid herself of routine prison habits.

On returning to Askham, Mary soon discovered she was pregnant by the married man who had been, according to Mary, determined to show her she wasn't a lesbian. She was in a terrible dilemma. She did not know what to do. On the one hand, she wanted to keep the baby but was unsure if she would be able to look after herself, let alone a baby, and in all likelihood the baby would be removed from her care. She talked to the probation officers at the hostal and feeling she had no choice had an abortion. She later said to the author Gitta Sereny,

"But if I think that almost the first thing I did after twelve years in prison for killing two babes was to kill the baby in me...." before breaking down in tears.

Prior to Mary's release from prison, she needed to be given a new identity in order for her to have a chance at leading a normal life without the press or the hating public hounding her. This was because she was a high-profile case, partly due to her mother constantly feeding news about Mary to the tabloids, and because of her horrific crimes.

Mary, on learning of her new identity, wondered how she would cope with pretending to be someone other than Mary.

### Release

Mary Bell was released May 14, 1980, at the age of 23. She spent her first night of freedom in the isolated rural home of her probation officer in Suffolk on the east coast of England where she laid low for two weeks. During this time, Mary was plagued by anxiety, sleeplessness, indecision, found everything "strange and alien," and missed the security of prison.

From Suffolk, she went and lived with a family in Yorkshire. Here, she found herself a job in a nursery school, but her probation officer said it was not appropriate for her to be working with children. She then took a series of jobs, mostly waitressing. She enjoyed living with the family but then at Christmas her mother Betty turned up with her husband George. Betty persuaded Mary to return home with them to Whitley Bay, a seaside town on the North Sea coast in North Tyneside. Mary, after two weeks with her mother, who was constantly drunk, moved out and went to live in York. Here, she enrolled into a college and studied psychology, philosophy, and English Literature. She began to harbor dreams of becoming a teacher or therapist, until her probation officer dashed her aspirations by telling her that because of her past crimes those careers were prohibited professions for her. Depressed, she dropped out of college and once again returned to her mother and George.

While staying with her mother, she met a young man who was several years younger than herself. He became her first proper boyfriend. After constant roughs with her mother, she finally moved in with him.

The young couple got married, and Mary gave birth to their daughter on May 25 1984 ironically, 16 years to the day she had killed Martin Brown.

Officials were greatly concerned over whether Mary, having murdered two children, should be allowed to keep her child, but Mary fought hard for the right to keep her daughter. The child was made a ward of court, but Mary was allowed to bring her up. News of the birth was leaked to the media, possibly by Betty Bell, but a High Court injunction protected the child from being identified until the age of eighteen.

All was well until a couple of years into the marriage. Her young husband started going out more and more and discussing Mary with his friends. He was also on occasion violent towards Mary. By May of 1988, the marriage was over.

Betty's marriage to George also ended. George told Mary he just couldn't handle Betty anymore but would always remain Mary's friend.

Mary then met a new partner, X, and they moved with her small daughter to a small village. Mary constantly lived in fear of being exposed and when the villagers discovered Mary's identity, they marched through the village street with "Murderer Out!" signs. The small family decided to relocate to a seaside town in the south of England. Here they lived happily, undisturbed for a number of years. They kept their address hidden from Betty whom Mary believed, with good reason, had leaked her address and whereabouts to the press before. Mary had not seen her mother for several years but invited her to spend two days with them over Christmas in 1994.

Ever since Mary had discovered that Billy Bell was not her real father, she had been tortured by the question of whom her real father was. She suspected that Betty's father, Mary's grandfather, had abused her mother and that she may have been the result of this abuse. When staying with her mother, she looked through a large scrapbook her mother kept and discovered love poems Betty had written to her father. Later in life, she asked her mother directly if this was the case.

Her mother replied quietly, "You are the devil's spawn," and refused to say more.

Her mother died at the beginning of January in 1995. The post mortem and inquest concluded that she had died of pneumonia.

Following Betty Bell's death, Gitta Sereny approached Mary about the idea of writing a book about her life. By this time, several foreign and British publications had over the years since her release approached Mary and offered her huge sums of money for her story, all of which she had turned down. Up to this point, the only one who had profited from Mary's story was Betty Bell, who had never given a penny to Mary. Moreover, as one was to learn from *Cries Unheard*, Betty prostituted Mary in every conceivable way.

Mary agreed to meet Gitta Sereny and eventually agreed to co-operate with her in the writing of *Cries Unheard*. Gitta Sereny felt that as the book would involve months of hard work on Mary's part, and the uncovering of painful buried memories, Mary should receive part of the advance she was to be paid. This would later, when the book became published in 1998, cause much controversy over criminals profiting from their deeds. Mary thought and hoped that if she told her story, the media would leave her alone. Her hope for the book was to "set the record straight."

In *Cries Unheard*, one learns more of the appalling abuse Mary suffered as a child from her mother, Betty Bell. With Betty's repeated attempts at ridding herself of Mary failing, Betty found a use for Mary when she was four-years-old. She forced her daughter to take part in prostitution by pimping her to pedophiles. Sometimes Mary would be blindfolded, her mother would say it was a game, "blind man's bluff," and as Betty held Mary's head back with one hand twisted into her hair and with the other hand pinioned her arms behind her back allowed her clients to ejaculate into her mouth. Mary would promptly vomit when they had finished with her. On some occasions, the men would have anal sex with her and sometimes Betty whipped Mary for the entertainment of her clients.

Her mother told her that if she ever told anyone, she would be locked up forever and that no one would believe what she said anyway. After the sessions, Betty would then reward Mary with treats and would treat her nicely for a bit, rather then shout, hit, and verbally abuse her, and Mary never told anyone until after her mother's death when she confessed, after much probing, to Gita Sereny.

What I find extraordinary is that before and during the trial and in the twelve years Mary was imprisoned, the system made no effort to understand the reasons for her offenses. The truth, uncovered by an author, only emerged thirty years after the offenses were committed.

The detective in charge of the investigation into the boys' murders, James Dobson, told Gitta Sereny,

"My function was to determine who had perpetrated the crime and how it was committed. In our system, it is not the business of the police to find out why crimes are committed. But as we have seen here, sadly, when the perpetrators are children, it doesn't appear that it is anyone's business."

To comprehend and explain Mary's crimes is not to justify or excuse her behavior. What she did was horrific and the suffering she caused Brian's and Martin's families horrendous.

Children who kill or maim need to be humanely detained for as long as they are a danger. But invariably children who kill are victims of extreme abuse themselves who, in my opinion, deserve compassion, not hysterical condemnation. In truth, how many of us can be sure that, with a childhood like Mary's, we wouldn't have done something equally depraved?

### Publication of Cries Unheard

When *Cries Unheard* was published in 1998, and it was learned that Mary had been paid £50,000 ($76,000) it infuriated the public, who still regarded Mary as a freak and evil monster, who was now profiting from her heinous crimes. The British tabloid headlines decried Mary Bell's "blood money" and "depraved story." Mary Bell was yet again branded as a monstrous incarnation of evil.

Even while the tabloids were denouncing Mary for taking money for a story that she had every right to tell, they were offering her far greater sums than she had been paid to cooperate with the book.

Tony Blair, then the British Prime Minister, publicly decried her pay. His home secretary, Jack Straw, criticized the payment to Mary in a published letter in the *British Sun* newspaper to the mothers of the murdered boys. He stated that Mary, by co-operating with the book, had forfeited her right to anonymity.

Within hours of the *Sun* newspaper publishing Jack Straw's condemnation of Mary, dozens of reporters descended on Mary's Victorian terraced house perched on a hillside in a south coast resort.

Mary was forced to phone the police who evacuated the family from their home where she had lived anonymously with her partner and 14-year-old daughter, with blankets over their heads to avoid the flash bulbs and shouts from the media. It was in this traumatic manner that Mary's 14-year-old daughter learned of her mother's past. They were taken into protective custody to a secret address.

Mary has since said that her daughter accepts her identity and forgives her and said to her,

"Mum, why didn't you tell me? You were just a kid, younger than I am now."

Gita Sereny, said that she paid Mary Bell because,

"If I hadn't done so, I would have made myself guilty of doing what has been done to her virtually since she was born: to USE her..."

Since Mary was released from prison, she has had three different identities and has had to move, after being identified, on at least five occasions. Mary, since her release, has led a law-abiding life and became a loving and caring mother to her straight-A student daughter when she could have very easily fallen into a life of repeated crime. She has succeeded in breaking the appalling cycle of abuse from which she as a child suffered.

But Mary lives with the guilt of her crimes and the suffering she caused every day of her life. A guilt she will never be free from, which is probably as it should be.

When Mary's daughter turned eighteen, the court order giving her and her daughter anonymity ran out. In May of 2003,

Mary won a High Court case to have her own anonymity and that of her daughter extended for life.

In 2009, Mary Bell became a grandmother. The High Court order protecting her was updated to include Mary's grandchild, who was referred to in court as 'Z.'

June Richardson, 64, whose four-year-old son Martin Brown was suffocated by Mary, on hearing the news of Mary's grandchild said,

"I will never see a grandchild from my son. I hope every time she looks at this baby she realizes what my family is missing out on because of what she has done."

# Chapter 5: Bloody Benders

## By Dane Ladwig

### *The "First Family" of Serial Killing*

"Good day, madam," greeted the stately gentleman as he approached the middle-aged woman. It was apparent from her indistinguishable response that she was a foreigner. *Perhaps of European, German, or Hungarian descent*, the man thought.

"I say. Are you the Innkeeper, ma'am?"

The woman mumbled incoherently under her breath.

A breathtaking young woman emerged from behind a canvas curtain. "Hello, my name is Kate. Momma don't take kindly to strangers at first, but when she gets to know you, she'll talk your wretched ear off."

"My name is Doctor William Henry York. Is this an Inn?"

"Why, yes it is," said the young Kate. "Pa ain't fixed the sign yet. It blew off when we had that big storm last week."

"I noticed the "Groceries" sign propped up against the building. Can I get a hot meal and a sleeping room, please? Perhaps some feed for my horse?" the man inquired.

"Sure, mister. Ma was just makin' dinner. The dining room is right through there," Kate explained pointing to a doorway separating the General Store from the living residence with a curtain cut from a wagon canvas.

"I'm sure you want to freshen up first, mister. There is fresh water in your room. It's the first door on the right." Kate pointed to the rear of the General Store past another canvas – the one she had previously been behind – separating the rear of the building from the store.

A chuckle from a young man staring through the doorway summoned Doctor York's attention.

"Oh, don't mind him, mister. That's John. He's my brother...and that's my Pa," Kate added, pointing to a stout, aging man walking about the store filling orders and pulling stock.

"Ma said dinner will be ready in ten minutes," Kate announced after "Ma" spoke to her in a hushed voice.

"Thank you," said Doctor York.

Nine minutes later...

"There's our guest!" Kate exclaimed exuberantly. "Hey, mister, you can sit here," she told him motioning to a chair beside her.

John began to chuckle uncontrollably. The doctor, reflecting superior refinement, attended dinner wearing his finest garments, and with his usual proper etiquette, stood by the side of his assigned seat awaiting the innkeepers and their children to be seated before he took his place.

Doctor York attempted to talk to Pa, who grumbled something in response, but the doctor couldn't make out what Pa was trying to say.

John continued to chuckle as they ate.

"This is perhaps one of the most delicious stews I have ever tasted, ma'am," said Doctor York, complimenting Ma's cooking.

John left the table abruptly, snickering and cackling.

"Ma'am," Doctor York addressed Ma, "Last winter a friend and his newborn daughter traveled through these parts. His name is George Newton Longcor – his daughter is Mary Ann. Since embarking on their travels to Iowa, they have not been seen or heard from. This road being the only one they could travel, I thought, perhaps you may recall seeing them?"

Ma and Pa locked eyes.

The doctor lifted another forkful of delectable stew to his mouth as he shifted his gaze toward Kate. Kate looked up at the doctor who now had the attention of Ma and Pa as well.

Kate could not contain her enthusiasm, "Why, Dr. York, I do believe I can help. See, I possess great powers... powers to connect with entities beyond the realm of human comprehension."

Doctor York was immediately enthralled with Kate's claim of supernatural abilities that could influence matters beyond the control of humanities reach.

Kate continued, "When I was born I was given a gift, the gift to see things and people who have passed on."

Just then, Doctor York heard a rustling sound behind him, but as he began to turn, it was too late; his reflexes failed him.

Had he not lost consciousness, Doctor York would have heard the wicked shrills of laughter as John pummeled his skull with the claw end of a hammer. There is no doubt, had the doctor not collapsed, he would have noticed the diabolical smirk on Mrs. Bender's face as she grabbed the carving knife from the table and slit the doctors throat. Had he seen Ma's hand wielding the blade, Doctor York would have surely noticed Pa moving an area rug, opening the hidden trap door behind the chair that led to the cellar beneath the foundation of the Inn. Here the family would rob the doctor of his belongings, disgrace his corpse, and commit unspeakable inhumane acts against his lifeless flesh.

Although Doctor York's only mission was to locate his close friend, George Newton Longcor, and Mr. Longcor's daughter Mary Ann, Doctor York met instead with a horrific death. However, Doctor York's two prestigious brothers, Colonel Ed York (a highly decorated Confederate) and Alexander M. York (a member of the Kansas State Senate) would soon unravel the Bender family's most heinous secrets because Dr. York's disappearance ignited a statewide investigation.

*\*\**

*The Bender Inn – Townsfolk relocating the cabin to expose the hidden pit below the cabin*

The above dialogue is a fictionalization. However, its truth has been established and inspired through the exploits of one of America's most fiendish families. I can only imagine the stunning accuracy of the scene, from the facts and details of one murder, in the mind-twisting case of the *Bloody Benders of Kansas*. Nevertheless, the reality and the ruthless nature of the Bender family slaughters clearly demonstrates the psychopathic behavior of a tightly-knit clan of serial killers similarly depicted in Rob Zombie's cult classic movie, *House of 1000 Corpses* (2003 Universal Studios / Lions Gate Films).

When we think of the state of Kansas, images of twisters and tornados may come to mind. Some of us get all warm and fuzzy when we recall of a petite country girl named Dorothy who is swept away in a Kansas tornado while trying to escape the clutches of the wicked Miss Almira Gulch. Ms. Gulch's mission; to euthanize Dorothy's pet puppy, the poor little Toto. Before Dorothy awakes in her bed surrounded by family and friends, she embarks on a mission. During the adventure, Dorothy befriends a Cowardly Lion, a Scarecrow, and a Tin Man, and then they all travel together to the mystical Land of OZ. Dorothy defeats the Wicked Witch of the West, and as a reward for her victory, she earns a return trip home. The Wizard leaves the Land of OZ prematurely in his hot air balloon, without Dorothy. However, Glinda the Good Witch of the South comes to her rescue and grants Dorothy's wish. Dorothy recites and repeats, "there's no place like home, there's no place like home" while tapping her ruby slippers together. Subsequently she returns from whence she came after learning a valuable life's lesson.

In 1939, when *The Wizard of OZ* (Metro-Goldwyn-Mayer) premiered, most of the inhabitants of Kansas had all but forgotten the dark past of its turn-of-the-century reputation. In fact, those who could remember the details of the grim history, connected to Kansas, were well on their way to advanced golden years. It wouldn't be long before the world would soon forget the dismal events in the chronicles of Kansas. L. Frank Baum, the creator of *The Wizard of OZ*, (knowingly or unknowingly) pro-active in leading Kansas out of the prejudiced biases, which oppressed Kansas as it bore the stigma of being the home of the first documented serial killer family in American history, prior to the innocent Dorothy's venture to the Emerald City.

Let's take a step back in time to when Kansas was no more than an unchartered territory. A point in history when settlers were eager to make a new life in the west. When clothes were handmade and those who could afford the luxury would prefer to travel by rail. The modern amenities were limited to oil lamps, candles, and wood burning stoves. Indoor plumbing had yet to make its way to rural America. They called it the dawn of the "Gilded Age." This era was far from prosperous or luxurious. Most folks worked hard, slept little, and ate just enough to sustain themselves. The deadly cholera virus was threatening the Midwest, killing at least 50,000 Americans (Cholera Outbreaks and Pandemics 2013).

Gunslingers, outlaws, and mayhem were a "staples" in the American Midwest. Violence on the dusty streets was expected from midday to sun up depending on which saloon you had the misfortune of visiting. Hardened men, criminals, road agents, and Indians were sure to confront anyone who dared to travel the trails unarmed and unprepared, and anyone who did meet up with one of these unsavory characters was surely never heard from again. The turbulent Midwest was the gateway to the Wild West.

\*\*\*

*Unbelief of the carnage as observers witness the butchery at the Benders Inn*

The year, 1870. Fresh in the minds of every man, woman, and teenager, were the scars left behind by the American Civil War. Just a few short years prior, in 1863, then President of the United States, Abraham Lincoln, passed a law proclaiming all enslaved people of color in Confederate territory liberated and free from the oppressive chains of indentured bondage. On April 15, 1865, just two years after the President passed the law; he met his fateful end and was assassinated.

In the Midwest, the war with the Native Indians continued, although it was nearing its blood-soaked end. Homesteaders across rural America settled on what was once Native American soil. In true cowboy fashion, the Native Indians were driven from their camps as the Government sold plots of the formerly Indian-occupied land to the colonists.

The Osage Indians were driven from their native environment in Labette County, Kansas. Five families originally settled in Labette County on the grounds where the Indians once dwelled. Of the five families, two families left Labette County because of the droughts, high winds, demanding climate and difficult living conditions. All five families however, were considered "spiritualists." In 1870, spiritualism usually referred to a belief that the living had the ability to communicate with the dead, and more often than not, this was accomplished with a formal séance.

A father and his son, John "Pa" Bender Sr. and John Bender Jr., were among the first to occupy Labette, County. John Sr. procured 160 acres of land adjacent to the Great Osage Trail – the only road leading through town to the great frontier out West. The 160-acre plot, which would become the Bender family's homestead, had the distinct honor of sharing its property line with the Osage Mission-Independence Trail, claiming the only road (approx. 100 miles long) leading from Independence to Fort Scott. The Bender's Inn was closest to Independence, located about 12 miles northeast. John Sr. and his son built a cabin, a barn with a corral, and a well.

It would be seven months before John Sr.'s wife Kate "Ma" Bender Sr., and her daughter Kate Jr., would join the Bender men in their new habitat. Coincidentally, nobody knew Kate Sr.'s name, and historians have simply attached the moniker Kate Sr., as it was widely accepted as her named based on historical record and crime investigation testimony from the Bender's neighbors. For ease of storytelling, from here on, I will refer to John Sr. as "Pa" or "Pa Bender" and Kate Sr. as "Ma" or "Ma Bender." Their children will simply be referred to by their given names: John and Kate.

In the fall of 1871, when Ma Bender and Kate joined Pa and John, they began renovating their cabin. Pa Bender viewed their move to the new location, adjacent to the only road connecting the east with the west, as a lucrative venture. They separated the living quarters and the smaller rooms in the rear of the cabin, which were designated as the Bender's living quarters. The front section of the cabin was converted into a General Store and a generous section was allocated as the dining quarters.

Pa Bender was quite the entrepreneur. Many travelers would venture through Labette, County on their way to California in search of unclaimed gold from the Great Gold Rush of 1848 –

1855. Although a substantial gold claim had not been reported in over fifteen years, it did not stop the miners and profiteers and their aspirations of striking it rich. Pa Bender knew travelers would require supplies, a good meal, and a comfortable bed for the night. That is exactly what Pa, Ma, John, and Kate Bender would provide.

The townsfolk reported Pa Bender to be about sixty years old, but no one was certain of his age, or from where the Bender clan originally hailed. Because of his lanky frame, and stature over six feet tall, his thick bushy eyebrows and piercing, sunken black eyes, the townsfolk imparted the moniker "Old Beetle-Browed John," to Pa Bender (Legends of America 2003 -2013). The settlers of Labette, County reported that when Pa Bender spoke he was nearly indistinguishable. He spoke little English and his speech was raspy, inarticulate, and very throaty.

Ma Bender was fifty-five years old, with noticeably wide hips. She claimed to have the power to communicate with the dead. In her kitchen, Ma would boil herbs and roots claiming them as fodder to cast charms and wicked spells. The neighbors clamored over the picket fence anxious to share their scandalous prattle, "Do you know the 'she-devil'? She's so pithy. I heard that her husband... that tall fella... well, he's so afraid of her, and I can't say as I blame him. She conjures up the dead, because she scares the hell out of the living," one neighbor gossiped to another.

John Jr. was about twenty-five years old, and his sister, Kate, was just a few years behind him at twenty-three, or so; that is what the town's people assumed. Ma Bender and Kate planted a two-acre apple orchard and vegetable garden on the farmland. Neighbors would offer assistance or encouraging words. Ma would retort with such a biting snarl, the kind-hearted neighbor's crossing her path would whisper "she-devil". They would murmur under their breath as to not be heard by Ma, or the young Kate who was sure to defend Ma's honor by all manner of bewitchment and incantation. They did not want the wrath of "conjuring spiritualists" on their trail. They would much rather consider battling Satan's hellhounds; at least then they would have the protection of the Word of God on their side. But out on the farmlands of the Kansas prairie, it would come down to Ma, Kate, and both John's against a defenseless woman. So be it. It proved beneficial to ignore the Bender clan altogether.

John Bender Jr. is said to have been quite the handsome fellow. He had auburn hair and a well-manicured mustache. He stood tall when addressed and he spoke proper English with a noticeable German accent. To John's misfortune, he was an incessant chuckler – he would laugh uncontrollably without provocation. For this, the homesteaders in Labette, County considered him doltish and an imbecilic fool.

To her credit, John's sister Kate was both beautiful and educated. She spoke the English language fluently with little trace of her traditional German dialect. However, she did not go unnoticed by the neighbors. She would visit neighboring farms and go into town to hand deliver the pamphlets she created proclaiming herself as a "Healer and Psychic Harnessing Extraordinary Supernatural Powers to Cure Ailments and Illness."

In addition to offering lectures on spiritualism, Kate claimed other powers such as being able to break the barriers between the earthly dimension and the hereafter. When word spread about Kate's "unique" gifts, her reputation for conjuring up the dearly departed became an attraction which drew not only the curious and the grieving (to Bender's Inn), but also those seeking a mystical séance with the legendary Ms. Kate Bender.

Although the term "serial killer" did not become attached to a murderer until 1886 (Herman Webster Mudgett a.k.a. Dr. H. H. Holmes), there is no doubt the Benders were indeed a family of serial killers before the moniker was discovered. In the developing county of Labette, Kansas where the Bender family staked a claim, there is little doubt that the Bender's acts were indeed premeditated, and orchestrated long before they sought a new life in the quiet Midwestern farmlands.

The beginning of the end of the Bender's savage reign of murder, like many crimes, should have come much sooner than it did. In 1871, the deceased body of a man named Jones was uncovered in Drum Creek – his throat was slashed and his skull crushed. In 1872, two more bodies turned up in the same location with the same injuries. By 1873, there were numerous reports of missing people that had passed through the Osage Trail in Kansas. People were attributing the disappearances and the bodies found in Drum Creek to horse thieves, villains, vigilantes, and Native American attacks.

It was not until the men in a search party (headed up by Doctor York's brother, Colonel York) began questioning residents in Labette County that they were able to connect the disappearances to the Benders. The men were now convinced the Benders were the culprits and they demanded an eye for an eye, vindication. Rants of "Hang them!" rang throughout the camp.

Due diligence and common sense prevailed. The town represented by seventy-five townsfolk and Colonel York and his men, held a trial. Pa Bender and John Jr. attended. The outcome: they agreed to issue search warrants to inspect the Bender's property.

Three days after the towns meeting, a neighbor of the Benders, Billy Tole was grazing his herd when he noticed something odd. As he approached the Bender's Inn, Mr. Tole was surprised to find the animals on the Bender property roaming freely and appearing severely malnourished. After rapping on the door several times and investigating the Inn for any signs of the Benders, Mr. Tole was convinced the Inn was abandoned and he immediately reported his findings.

When Colonel York, the town magistrate, and other townspeople appeared at the Bender's residence, what they found in the abandoned Inn settled any doubts they had. The cabinets in the General Store had been ravished and were left bare. Clothing and all the Bender's personal possessions were missing and there was a report of a "disturbing foul stench" as they entered the Inn.

Colonel York, not compelled to wasting time, had his men begin searching the property for "evidence." Colonel York's men noticed there were more than a dozen bullet holes adorning the roof and sidewalls of the cabin. This led them to believe some of the Bender's victims may have fought back and in turn were shot at random to insure their deaths, or perhaps the frightened captives took pot shots at the Benders. They began by raising the trap door, which had been nailed shut and as the door was lifted, it became noticeably apparent that the "disturbing foul stench" was emitted from the hole that served as a makeshift cellar. The area below the house was covered in clotted blood, and hence the smell. Colonel York's men and neighboring townsmen physically lifted the building and relocated it so they could gain access to what might be found below. As it turned out, there were no bodies buried below the Inn.

Colonel York, sitting stately in his horse drawn buggy, observed the terrain as the sun began to set and noticed a suspicious mound of dirt, which did not sit well with Colonel York. Shortly after issuing the command to dig where the odd mound of dirt was located, the body of Colonel York's brother, Doctor William Henry York, was exhumed. It had been buried in the garden just below the surface. As the darkness of the night stymied any further attempts of investigation, the ongoing search was postponed until daylight despite Colonel York's mixed feelings.

The following morning; however, an additional nine bodies were found, all reflecting the identical wounds, their heads had been smashed in with a hammer and their throats had been slashed. In addition, a young woman's body was found with no marks, or wounds, and it was presumed she had been buried alive.

As anyone might imagine, when news of these brutally horrifying crimes reached beyond the boundaries of Labette County, Kansas, reporters and curious onlookers flocked to the Bender Inn from miles around.

*The Bender Farm – Neighbors and onlookers aghast at the site of what was once the serene Kansas homestead in Labette County*

**Locating the Benders would prove to be a daunting task...**

So, what happened to the Benders? There were many dramatic accounts given by people who wished to step into the limelight capturing the nation's attention, even at the risk of their credibility. Several groups of vigilantes were desperately searching for the whereabouts of the Benders. One group claimed to have caught up with the macabre family of deranged butchers and shot each one dead, except for Kate. Because Kate's "supernatural" abilities were well known, the vigilantes – assigning themselves as the "Keepers of God's good will," allegedly tied Kate to a tree post and burned her alive, ridding humanity of all traces of Kate's evilness.

One thing we know for certain, Pinkerton Detectives were immediately called into the Bender case and, shortly after they were, the Pinkerton Detectives discovered the Bender's wagon. The wagon was abandoned and the horses were severely malnourished. The Pinkertons' confirmed that the Bender family bought train tickets in Thayer, Kansas. However, shortly after they departed the station, in Chanute, Kansas, John Jr., and Kate switched trains and headed to Texas, then headed to New Mexico, which at that time was part of Mexico and exempt from U.S. laws. Lawmen rarely ventured to New Mexico, as they would almost never return. One such lawman claimed he tracked John Jr. to the border of New Mexico where witnesses claimed John Jr. died of apoplexy (a bleeding out from bursting blood vessels in the brain impairing neurological function and often resulting in fatality – think cerebral hemorrhage). Apoplexy could also be caused by blunt force trauma to the cranial cavity (head), i.e. a rapid thrust of a clawed hammer to the head could result in apoplexy (for more on apoplexy visit http://www.thirdage.com/hc/c/what-is-apoplexy).

It is believed that Ma and Pa Bender headed north to Humboldt and then on to Kansas City, perhaps assuming new names and identities; and Pinkerton Deputies investigations revealed other startling facts. First, there was a question regarding John Jr.'s identity. As it turned out the name John Flickenger, a friend of John Sr., was in question as the true identity of John Jr. However, later in the investigation it was revealed the Flickenger name was that of Pa Sr. before he and Ma joined in common law union as a couple. Also, as the investigation intensified, there were many indicators to convince investigators and the Bender's neighbors in Labette County that John Jr. and Kate were brother and sister, and that perhaps Ma and Pa Bender may have actually been brother and sister.

This theory was dispelled as the investigation turned up evidence that John Jr.'s. given name was indeed John Gebhardt. The only true relation was that of Ma Bender and Kate, who were, in fact, mother and daughter.

You may recall the mention of John Jr.'s peculiar disposition and his sudden outbursts of uncontrolled laughter. His odd behavior segregated him from the townsfolk and he became a ridiculed outcast for his inability to restrain his emotional outbursts. According to historic accounts, the boy laughed at that which was clearly not laughable, such as somber moments or tragedy.

Today's medical advances afford us the benefit of assessing symptoms and disease with little effort and virtual accuracy, unlike any other time in history. Based on historical accounts of his erratic behavior, there may indeed be a medical diagnosis that explains his affliction. And the reason it is important to mention, is because it may lead to yet another layer of the Bender story never before considered.

A neurological disorder, such as "Pseudobulbar affect (PBA), emotional liability, labile affect or emotional incontinence," such as uncontrollable laughing or crying, stemming from a neurological disease or brain trauma will result in uncontrollable bouts of laughing or crying. According to the accounts of John Jr. and his incessant chuckling, and laughing uncontrollably without provocation, he certainly fits the description of an individual afflicted with PBA (Pseudobulbar Affect 2013).

However, if this is the case, if John Jr. was the victim of brain trauma, could it be possible that the young good-looking John Jr. had been an early victim of the elder John or Ma? Perhaps even the beautiful charismatic Kate Bender? Might the young man have survived an attempt against his life and pleaded for an opportunity to "serve" the Benders? Nothing can be left to chance, as the possibility does exist.

The horrid details of the Benders story spread quickly and along with it, the tale of a family of serial killers roaming the country free to kill again. Oft times, people would stop a wagon with two female occupants and inquire as to their identification and intentions. There was more than one account of mistaken identity like when an elderly woman and her daughter were detained and questioned and reportedly misjudged as being Ma and Kate Bender. This went on for fifty years, until the Bender's crimes were replaced by high-spirited new generations consumed with contemporary objectives of the day, and with dreadful realities of the latest serial killers roguery.

Coincidentally, in 1884 a report was filed that John Flickinger (recall, this was an alleged birth name of Pa Bender) had jumped into Lake Michigan and was swept away from land as the tide was receding, and the man clearly drowned by way of suicide. There were other accounts as well. Later that same year, a man was arrested near Salmon, Idaho on the charge that he had killed a man by crushing his skull with a hammer. It is said that the man committing the act fit the physical description of Pa Bender. However, by the time a deputy arrived to I.D. the body, it was so badly decomposed there was no way of making a comparison.

*Two men uncovered the burial site and mourn an innocent's demise*

# Timeline of Bender Murders

| | | |
|---|---|---|
| 1869 | Joe Sowers | Found with crushed skull and slashed throat (later not attributed to the Benders, however perpetrator behind cause of death never established). |
| May 1871 | Mr. Jones | Body found in Drum Creek – skull crushed and throat slashed. |
| 1871 /72 | Two – Unidentified | The bodies of two unidentified men found in the prairie – skulls crushed and throats slashed. |
| 1872 | Ben Brown | Ben Brown was a guest at the Bender's Inn, stopping over from Howard County Kansas. When his remains were recovered in the Bender's apple orchard, it was learned he was missing his purse with $2,600.00 (2014 – $47,000.00). |
| 1872 | W.F. McCrotty | W. F. McCrotty Co. D 123$^{rd}$ Infantry was a military man seeking an overnight stay at the Inn. He was carrying $38.00 ($685.00 – 2014) at the time of his disappearance, and a wagon and team of horses were missing. |
| Dec. 1872 | Henry McKenzie | Passed through stopping at the Benders Inn as he was relocating from Hamilton County, Indiana to Independence. At the time of his disappearance, the victim was carrying $36.00 ($670.00 – 2014) and had a matched team of horses. |
| 1872 | Johnny Boyle | Boyle was from Howard County, Kansas. When he went missing, he was carrying $10.00. He had a pacing mare which was mounted by an $850.00 saddle ($15,000.00 – 2014). The saddle was later located in the Benders well. |
| Dec. 1872 | George Newton Longcor | Stopped at the Benders Inn on way to visit/relocation to parent's home in Lee County, Iowa, after his wife Mary Jane died giving birth to daughter Mary Ann, and infant son Robert died due to pneumonia. Mr. Longcor was robbed of $1,900.00 ($34,000.00 – 2014). |
| Dec. 1872 | Mary Ann Longcor (Infant child -18 months.) | Since there were no apparent wounds found on the infant child's body, it is believed she was buried alive. The Benders buried the infant alive in the same grave with her father George Newton |

| | | |
|---|---|---|
| | | Longcor's corpse. |
| May 1873 | Dr. William York | Dr. William York, longtime friend of George Newton Longcor, met his finality while on a quest to locate his friend. He stopped off at the Bender's Inn and later his brother found his body buried in the apple orchard. Missing was Dr. York's horse and $2,000.00 ($36,000.00 – 2014). |
| ? | John Greary | The body of John Greary found buried in the apple orchard, was identified by his family through examination of his clothing, dental records, and other distinguishing marks. |
| ? | Unidentified Male | Buried in the apple orchard. |
| ? | Unidentified Female | Buried in the apple orchard. |
| ? | Four – Various | Various body parts were found buried throughout the apple orchard and the vegetable garden. These body parts were separate from the remains of other victims found on the grounds and they total a "body part" count equal to four distinct and separate, but related victims of the Benders. |
| 1873 | Four Unidentified Males | Drum Creek turned up four male bodies, their skulls crushed with a hammer and their throats slashed. One of the victims was thought to be a former acquaintance of the Benders, Jack Bogart, who claimed his horse was purchased from a friend through the Benders; the man who purchased the horse and the horse allegedly went missing… again! |

*The Pit located under the house. The house was physically moved,*
*by brute force (men), to uncover the pit*
**Images used by permission from the Kansas Historic Society.**

In all, twenty-one murders are attributed to the Bloody Benders. However, unaccounted for missing persons might be added to that number. As for the bodies or remains recovered, they were buried in a graveyard 1-mile southeast of the Benders orchard in Cherryvale, Kansas.

The question one must consider is: how does a "family" arrive at the point of abandoning all sense of morality to embark on a life of serial murder? Some experts will try to convince you that there are "shared" experiences serial killers exhibit: "alcohol and substance abuse, psychological abuse during childhood, sexually stressful events in childhood, bed-wetting, growing up lonely and isolated, fantasies, preferring auto-erotic activities, developing voyeurism and fetishism in adulthood, acting out fantasies on animals, physical injuries (10 Most Common Traits of Potential Serial Killers 2013)."

In my years consisting of thousands of hours of comprehensive research, I have come to the conclusion that there really is no "common" thread linking serial killers when you are referring to the most diabolical and cunning murderers in history. Sure, there are "likenesses" and similarities, which are entirely different from what I am talking about. For instance, because an infant endures child abuse, wets the bed, "experiments" on small animals, has fantasies and then grows up an isolated adult who drinks too much and is addicted to drugs, that does not necessarily suggest that the child, or adult, will become a serial murderer. Throughout history, there have been many outgoing individuals with loving, healthy family histories, who have turned to the life of a serial killer. But, that is the great deception; some of them can blend into society so well, you would never suspect them to be anything other than a normal, emotionally healthy, and well-adjusted individual. Therefore, how do you know if Uncle Bob, Aunt Marie, or the checkout clerk at the local grocery store is a serial killer? You don't! The Benders, despite all of their peculiarities, blended into society (for the most part), and that is how they were able to commit their crimes and how they were able to escape with relative ease.

The Bloody Benders were never captured – they simply moved on. Many unsolved murders in the years that followed had earmarks of the Bloody Benders. Perhaps with the technology available today the Benders would never stand a chance of evading the authorities. However, they would still be able to carry out their crimes until they were apprehended just as today's serial killers. Today, the case files on the Bloody Benders remains an unsolved crime and for the most part a mystery filed away with thousands of unresolved "cold case" files.

# Chapter 6: Manuel Pardo, Jr.

## By Michael Newton

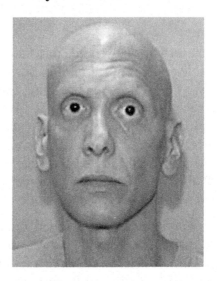

## "I Accomplished My Mission"

Manuel Pardo Jr. seemed to lead a charmed life for his first twenty-three years. Born in New York on September 24, 1956, he was an Eagle Scout who joined the U.S. Marine Corps at age eighteen and served four years in uniform, winning medals for good conduct and marksmanship. Honorably discharged in February 1978, he moved south, worked briefly as a bank clerk, then was accepted to the Florida Highway Patrol Training Academy in Tallahassee before year's end. Pardo graduated in 1979 as class valedictorian and was assigned to patrol Dade County, surrounding Miami.

The future looked bright, but all that glitters in Miami is not golden. In January 1980, less than a year after his triumphant passage through the FHP academy, Pardo was out. Caught up in a ticket-fixing scandal, personally accused of falsifying more than one hundred traffic warnings and correction notices, he was allowed to resign in lieu of being fired and prosecuted. That technicality, while minor, proved to be his saving grace. Barely two months after his stark humiliation, in March 1980, Pardo found another law enforcement job, patrolling the Miami suburb of Sweetwater.

Once again, fortune had smiled on Pardo. His superiors praised his work ethic and decorated him for performing CPR on a two-month-old boy who had stopped breathing, saving the infant's life. Pardo went back to school, earning a two-year associate's degree in criminal justice from a local community college. (Some later media reports also credit him with a master's degree in business management.) In 1981, when the state attorney general's office charged Pardo and three other Sweetwater cops with brutality, a local prosecutor intervened to scuttle the case.

Even then, Pardo might have saved himself, but Miami lured him to his doom. The city's "cocaine cowboy" era had arrived, overrun with Cubans, Colombians, and homegrown soldiers of fortune, all battling for turf and access to the multibillion-dollar drug trade, striving to be like Scarface on the silver screen. Pardo befriended several dealers, and when one of them—an ex-Sweetwater cop—was jailed for smuggling in the Bahamas, Pardo risked everything to help him out. Flying in for the trial, Pardo perjured himself on the witness stand, claiming that he and the defendant were international undercover agents waging war against drug cartels. Back home in Sweetwater, that indiscretion—formalized in charges citing "lack of good judgment and a habit of lying"—ended his police career for good on January 21, 1985.

Unemployed once more, Pardo took stock of his situation and decided it was time to alter his approach. Since fame and fortune had eluded him in law enforcement, he would try a life of crime. As he would later tell Miami newsman Gary Nelson, "It was my New Year's resolution for 1986."

* * *

Accounts of Pardo's criminal career vary widely. From prison, in 1990, he would tell Gary Nelson that he acted solely as a high-minded vigilante, purging the "scum of the earth" from Miami's mean streets. His plan, Pardo said, was to "systematically eliminate as many as I could before they finally caught me or killed me." And, while Nelson heard "conviction in his voice," state prosecutors took a very different view, describing Pardo as a trigger-happy drug dealer in his own right, robbing dozens of cocaine traffickers, killing six—and three allegedly innocent victims—for the sheer hell of it. Testimony from Pardo's accomplice in the crime spree, 23-year-old Rolando Garcia, supported the latter view.

According to Garcia—a laborer who met Pardo through his brother-in-law—he and Pardo worked directly for Ramon Alvero Cruz, a 40-year-old cocaine smuggler known to the underworld as "El Negro." It was on Alvero's behalf, Garcia said, that he and Pardo started robbing rival dealers of their merchandise, until Alvero stiffed them on a deal or two and thereby earned his own death sentence.

The pair staged their first hit on January 22, 1986, at the North Miami-Dade home of Mario Amador, a 33-year-old civil engineer who sold drugs on the side, operating with 28-year-old partner Roberto Alfonso. Amador had two kilos of cocaine for sale, but Pardo and Garcia decided it was better to save money and simply steal the drugs. To that end, Pardo brought along a .22-caliber Ruger semiautomatic pistol, equipped with a silencer, shooting both victims numerous times in their heads and torsos.

The slayings did not faze Pardo; in fact, he seemed to revel in them. In 1990, Gary Nelson asked Pardo how he felt after killing. "Fantastic," Pardo replied. "I would go home and go to sleep. Inside I felt great. I was proud of myself." How often, Nelson asked, had Pardo shot each victim? Casually, Pardo answered, "Well, as many as I felt that was necessary. I felt good doing it so, if I ran out of bullets, I put another clip in my gun."

Pardo felt good again on January 28, 1986, when he executed Michael Millot, a 43-year-old gunsmith from Haiti. Known around Miami as a vocal opponent of President Jean-Claude "Baby Doc" Duvalier's crumbling Haitian dictatorship, Millot sold several silencers to Pardo and Garcia, before Pardo discovered Millot's secret life as a federal informant. Fearing a potential setup, Pardo borrowed his wife's car and took Millot for a one-way ride, shooting him in the head with a 9mm pistol. Afterward, Pardo and Garcia dumped Millot's corpse in a rural area, then had the car cleaned and reupholstered to eliminate forensic evidence. Still worried about getting busted, Pardo later sank the car in a canal.

On February 27, 1986, Alvero sent Pardo and Garcia to buy three kilos of cocaine from 37-year-old Luis Robledo. Determined once again to steal the drugs, rather than paying for them, they visited Robledo's West Miami-Dade apartment, finding him there with Ulpiano Ledo, a 39-year-old welder and Santeria priest. In a virtual replay of the Amador-Alfonso double killing, Pardo excused himself to use the toilet, then returned with his .22-caliber silenced automatic, blazing away at both men from close range, shooting each multiple times in the head and body.

The next double murder, at least by Garcia's account, was a personal matter. As Garcia told the story, he had stolen Luis Robledo's credit card, asking two young women—Sara Musa, 30, and Fara Quintero, 28—to purchase several videocassette recorders. Arriving at the women's home on April 22, 1986, Pardo and Garcia found no VCRs awaiting them. Instead, Quintero picked a fight with Garcia over a ring he had pawned for fifty dollars, neglecting to give her the money as promised. As the quarrel heated up, Pardo allegedly saw Quintero typing "8888" on her pager, interpreting the numbers as a "Santeria death sign." Furious, he pulled his trusty .22 and shot both women until the gun jammed. To clear it, he pounded Quintero's skull with the weapon, the reloaded for another round of close-range shots.

Next, Pardo and Garcia turned on El Negro himself. Alvero had angered his gunmen by stiffing them on two high-ticket drug buys, then dropping out of sight. Pardo and Garcia found Alvero on April 23, 1986, in company with his girlfriend Daisy Ricard, 38-year-old owner of a medical lab, described by police as an innocent victim of circumstance. Ricard's actual knowledge of Alvero's drug dealing is anyone's guess—her relatives staunchly defend her innocence to this day—but she was clearly in the wrong place, at the wrong time. Pardo and Garcia emptied two pistols into the couple, with Pardo's Ruger jamming again. This time, while pounding it on Ricard's skull, he accidentally shot himself in the foot.

Police found Ricard's corpse later that day, in a field outside Hialeah, missing one shoe. Her watch lay nearby, bearing one of Pardo's fingerprints. On April 24, construction workers found Alvero's car a mile away from Daisy's final resting place, his body in the trunk. Beside him lay two shell casings from Pardo's pistol, and Ricard's missing shoe. Some accounts, perhaps confused, report that Pardo also left a fingerprint on El Negro's wristwatch.

When the search began for Pardo, he was in New York City. He and Garcia had flown from Miami on the night of April 26, seeking medical care for Pardo's festering foot wound. All states presently require physicians to report suspected bullet wounds, but Pardo had an angle, claiming that he had been shot after arriving in New York. Stranger things have happened in the Big Apple, and doctors accepted his report at face value—but they also kept the slug extracted from his foot, as evidence.

Whether Pardo knew it or not, his time was swiftly running out.

\*\*\*

Back in Miami, homicide investigators caught another break when one of Pardo's shady friends, fearing he might be marked for death next, fingered Pardo as one of South Florida's busiest hit men. He had bragged about the killings, witness Carlo Manuel Ribera said, and backed his boasts with photos taken of the bloody corpses where they fell. Researching Pardo's recent movements, the police traced him to Manhattan and retrieved the slug extracted from his foot. It matched one of the weapons used to kill six local victims in the past three months.

Police arrested Pardo at his home on May 7, 1986. A search of the premises turned up the rumored crime scene photos, newspaper clippings on various murders, a shell casing identical to those found in Ramon Alvero's car, and a date book filled with meticulous notes describing each of Pardo's homicides. Pardo's private arsenal, as listed in court documents, included "bazookas, submachine guns, a torpedo shooter, grenade launchers, mach-12s [sic] and 45s, as well as a variety of military fatigues and police uniforms, false police identification documents, police radios and walkie-talkies." Officers also turned up a cache of Nazi memorabilia, including a framed photo of Adolf Hitler and a Nazi flag—plus Pardo's pet Doberman pinscher, with a swastika tattooed on one of its legs. Receipts from stolen credit cards provided evidence that Pardo had robbed his victims of more than cocaine.

In custody, Pardo seemed proud of his crimes and eager to talk. He fingered Rolando Garcia as his accomplice, prompting Garcia's arrest on May 23. Confronted with photos of their various victims, Garcia also admitted his guilt, telling detectives, "We took care of all these people."

While confessing, Pardo insisted that his murders were vigilante slayings, targeting drug smugglers who "have no right to live." Pardo extended that verdict to Jews and African Americans, as well, declaring boundless admiration for Hitler's genocidal Third Reich. Miami Metro-Dade detective Ted MacArthur took another view, in statements to the press. Pardo's crimes, he said, "were drug rip-offs, and quantities of cocaine were taken from the scene[s]."

Another detective, John Allickson, later told Miami Herald reporter David Ovalle that he found interviews with Pardo a daunting experience. "I don't know if it's because he was in law enforcement that made it such a nasty, chilling case," Allickson said, "but I spent over nineteen years in homicide and this one always sticks out. In sitting there, talking to him, he was Ted Bundy-esque."

Pardo and Garcia initially faced nineteen felony charges, including six counts of first-degree murder (for victims Amador, Alfonso, Robledo, Ledo, Musa and Quintero), six counts of unlawful possession of a firearm while engaged in a criminal offense, six counts of credit card forgery, two counts of robbery, and two counts of second-degree grand theft. A later amended indictment added two more counts of first-degree murder (victims Alvero and Ricard), two more firearms charges, six more counts of credit card forgery, two more counts of robbery, and two more of second-degree grand theft. Pardo filed a not-guilty plea on March 11, 1987, but in jail he told a different story to his cellmates, boasting of murder victims still unidentified, who were never added to his formal tally.

***

Prosecution of Pardo and Garcia proceeded by fits and starts. Dade County Circuit Judge Philip Knight initially ordered that the defendants be tried separately, saying that Pardo's insanity plea might hamper Garcia's defense, then Knight reversed himself and ruled that both must face a single jury. Prosecutors, pleased with that order, led off on March 31, 1988, with key witness Carlo Ribera, a criminal acquaintance of both defendants. Ribera described meeting Garcia in 1985, and later asking him for a job unloading illegal drug shipments. Garcia had referred Ribera to Pardo, whom he later met at a family gathering. They were friendly enough for Pardo to boast of his murders, Ribera said, and to brag about bombing a Sweetwater police car.

The latter statement brought strenuous objections from defense attorneys Ronald Guralnick, representing Pardo, and Bill

Surowiec, speaking for Garcia. Both complained that the bombing allegation, nowhere mentioned in the state's indictments, would unfairly prejudice the jury picked to hear an already complex and convoluted case. Judge Knight agreed, declaring a mistrial and granting Surowiec's renewed motion to sever Garcia's trial from Pardo's. Garcia shook Pardo's hand and wished him well, while Knight announced selection of a new jury in Pardo's case, beginning the same afternoon.

At Pardo's second trial, in April 1986, lawyer Guralnick persevered with his insanity defense, telling reporters, "The man is crazy. All you have to do is listen to him to know he's totally out of his mind." A clinical psychologist, Dr. Syvil Marquit, supported that view in more technical terms: Pardo understood the physical consequence of his actions, Marquit said, "but he doesn't know right from wrong." Two other court-appointed analysts found Pardo sane within the definition established by law. All three analysts agreed that Pardo was competent for trial, with Dr. Leonard Haber branding him "sane, but evil." That statement probably influenced Pardo's view of all psychologists in general. "They're whores," he said. "Pay them enough money and they'll say anything."

As in the first abbreviated trial, the state led off with Carlo Ribera as its key witness. He described Pardo as a "killing machine," proud of his murders, who had shown Ribera crime scene photos, newspaper clippings, even entries from his detailed diary of death. Most of Pardo's victims were selected, said Ribera, "to rip them off and get the cocaine and sell it for money." Victims Musa and Quintero had been shot to gain "respect," and to cancel out Rolando Garcia's fifty-dollar debt to Quintero. Garcia, cast by Ribera as "the brains" of the two-man drug operation, was still in thrall to Pardo, refusing to make a move without his homicidal partner's approval.

Against advice from his attorney, Pardo took the witness stand to plead his case on April 13, 1988. Far from denying any crimes, he told the court, "Instead of nine, I wish I could have been up here for ninety-nine. I enjoyed what I was doing. I enjoyed shooting them. They're parasites and they're leeches, and they have no right to be alive. Somebody had to kill these people." He continued shooting victims after they were dead to "punish" them for crimes they had committed, Pardo testified. By photographing them in death, then burning selected photos in an alabaster ashtray, "I sent their souls to the eternal fires of damnation of hell for the misery they caused."

Senior prosecutor David Waksman, sharing duties at the trial with colleague Sally Weintraub, pounced on Pardo during cross-examination, branding him a mercenary felon who had killed drug dealers after robbing them, murdering informer Michael Millot to protect himself, slaying Sara Musa and Fara Quintero because they had welshed on the VCR purchase. Pardo fired back, calling the state's theory "ludicrous" and "ridiculous." When Waksman cited $50,000 Pardo earned from selling two kilos of stolen cocaine, dutifully recorded in his diary, Pardo answered that he'd kept only $2,000 for himself—a mere stipend, to purchase guns and ammunition for his personal crusade.

Waksman asked how much the bullets cost him. Pardo answered that the .22s he used sold for a dime apiece. So, had it only cost $1.30 when he shot two of his victims thirteen times? Smiling, Pardo replied, "That's a pretty good investment, isn't it?"

The jury failed to share his sense of humor, and its members—including two Jews and five African Americans—were undoubtedly put off by Pardo's racist and anti-Semitic ideas. Adolf Hitler was "a great man," Pardo said, whose efforts to sanitize the human race inspired Pardo to read more than five hundred books on Nazism. The panel deliberated for six hours on April 15, then returned a guilty verdict on all sixteen remaining counts.

Court reconvened on April 20, for the penalty phase of Pardo's trial. Attorney Guralnick and Pardo's parents pleaded for leniency, citing his deranged mental state, while prosecutor Waksman argued the reverse. "He was weird, weird, weird," Waksman said, "but he was not insane." Pardo, as in the guilt phase of his case, insisted on speaking up for himself. "I'm ridding the community of this vermin and technically it is not murder because they are not human beings," he declared. "I am a soldier. I accomplished my mission and I humbly ask you to give me the glory of ending my life and not let me spend the rest of my days in the state prison."

The jury agreed, recommending execution on each of eight first-degree murder counts by margins of eight to four (victims Amador and Alfonso), nine to three (for victims Robledo, Ledo and Musa), and ten to two (for Alvero and Ricard). Unlike most other states, Florida does not require a unanimous verdict to ratify execution. Judge Knight accepted those recommendations, condemning Pardo for each of the eight homicides, then tacked on superfluous concurrent terms of fifteen years for each of Pardo's eight noncapital offenses. On April 21, Knight reconsidered those terms and amended Pardo's sentence, imposing three-year mandatory sentences to run concurrently, on each of four robbery counts, while the prior sentences on four counts of firearms violations were suspended.

In Florida, America's fourth most active state for executions—after Texas, Virginia, and Oklahoma—Pardo's hope of ever leaving prison while alive was virtually nil.

\*\*\*

Rolando Garcia, meanwhile, had legal problems of his own. Severance of his case from Pardo's spared him from trial on the Musa-Quintero murders, but charges remained in the Amador-Alfonso, Robledo-Ledo, and Alvaro-Ricard homicides. (Prosecutors listed Michael Millot's murder as a separate case.) At trial, on December 8, 1988, jurors convicted Garcia of the Amador-Alfonso and Alvaro-Ricard murders, while acquitting him in the Robledo-Ledo case. He also stood convicted on two counts of armed robbery and four counts of credit card forgery. The panel recommended execution on all four murder counts, and Garcia's judge agreed.

Garcia appealed his sentence to Florida's Supreme Court, which overturned his capital sentences in 1990. In its ruling, the court found that the six murders and related charges had been improperly joined for trial, declaring that "each pair of homicides and related offenses tried in this case involved different victims at different dates and in different places stretching across a three-month period. The first pair of murders occurred about five weeks before the second, and the second pair of murders occurred two months before the final murders. There was no temporal or geographical connection to link these crimes in an episodic sense. The only clear similarity is that they were similar types of offenses and allegedly they were committed by the same two people, either for money, drugs, or both." Accordingly, the Supreme Court directed that Garcia be retried separately for the murders of Amador and Alfonso, which arose out of one episode, and the murders of Alvaro and Ricard, which arose from a separate episode.

Subsequently, separate juries acquitted Garcia of the Alvero-Ricard slayings and Michael Millot's murder, leaving only the Amador-Alfonso killings and related charges. At Garcia's second trial for those homicides, the judge ruled Pardo's prior confession, which exonerated Garcia as a shooter, inadmissible in court. Jurors proceeded to convict Garcia on two counts of first-degree murder, one count of robbery with a firearm, and one count of possessing a firearm while engaged in a criminal offense.

At the penalty phase of that trial, Garcia barred his relatives from the courtroom and took the stand to tell the jury, "Good morning. First of all, I would like to thank you for your effort and consideration in this case even though you found me guilty and I am not. Number two, although you found me guilty, I would like to say that I need for your recommendation to be death because it is the only way that a proper Court will hear what you weren't allowed to hear in this case. And number four [sic], I would like to thank my attorneys for the hell of a job that they did for me in trying to fight for my life.

That is it."

As in Pardo's case, jurors took Garcia at his word, recommending death by margins of ten to two (for Amador) and seven to five (for Alfonso). The judge concurred, and again sentenced Garcia to die.

On his next appeal to Florida's Supreme Court, Garcia raised six issues concerning the guilt phase of his trial, and four concerning the penalty phase. His guilt phase objections included the court's failure to allow Garcia to impeach Carlo Ribera with his prior inconsistent statements; allowing the lead detective and prosecutor to improperly vouch for Ribera's credibility; failure to admit Pardo's exculpatory testimony; admitting evidence from Pardo's diary; admitting hearsay statements by the victim and others that they were afraid of Garcia and did not trust him; and the cumulative effect of the trial errors. Penalty phase objections included failure to let the jury to consider Pardo's former testimony; failure to consider any of the mitigating circumstances raised by defense counsel (Garcia's age, lack of prior criminal history, relatively minor participation in another defendant's capital crime, his loving family, and so on); and alleged unconstitutionality of Florida's death penalty statute.

Once again, on April 18, 2002, the Supreme Court reversed Garcia's conviction and sentence, remanding the case for retrial. From available public records, it appears that the state gave up on retrying Garcia. The Web site maintained by the Florida Department of Corrections indicates that Garcia was released from prison on September 5, 2002, after spending sixteen years in custody.

*** 

Meanwhile, despite his expressed wish to die, Manuel Pardo was busy pursuing appeals of his own. His first, to Florida's Supreme Court, was filed on May 13, 1988, raising five legal issues: that the trial court erred in not ordering a competency hearing; that the state did not carry its burden of proving he was sane when he committed the crimes; that prosecutorial misconduct in the closing argument necessitated a mistrial; that none of the aggravating circumstances was proved, thereby justifying execution; and that the trial court erred in declining to find the statutory mitigator that Pardo could not appreciate the criminality of his conduct or was seriously impaired in his ability to conform his conduct to the requirements of the law. The court rejected all of Pardo's claims on May 31, 1990, and denied a rehearing on July 27 of that year.

Next, on October 26, 1990, Pardo petitioned the U.S. Supreme Court for a writ of certiorari, demanding a record of his case for federal review. The nation's highest court denied that petition routinely, on May 13, 1991.

On May 26, 1992, Pardo filed a "3.850 motion" with the state circuit court, seeking to vacate his conviction and death sentence based on alleged ineffective assistance by counsel. Under Florida law, 3.850 motions must normally be filed within two years of conviction, but an exception was granted in Pardo's case because Rolando Garcia's appeals and retrials rendered certain public records unavailable. In fact, more than eleven years would pass before the circuit court denied Pardo's motion on August 26, 2003.

On November 22, 2004, Pardo petitioned Florida's Supreme Court for a writ of habeas corpus, once again claiming ineffective representation by counsel during his direct appeal from 1988. Specifically, Pardo accused his lawyer of failing to challenge the trial court's error in precluding cross-examination of Carlo Ribera on prior crimes he admitted committing but was not charged with, and the court's perceived errors in rulings on several evidentiary issues. The Supreme Court denied that petition on June 29, 2006.

On November 2, 2007, Pardo filed another petition for a writ of habeas corpus, this one before Miami's U.S. District Court for the Southern District of Florida. That court denied his petition on April 23, 2008—the twenty-second anniversary of the Alvero-Ricard murders—but Pardo was persistent. He filed a motion to alter judgment on May 7, 2008 (denied on June 10), then filed yet another for certificate of appealability on July 8, 2008 (rejected in turn on the following day). Undeterred by that roadblock, Pardo filed a habeas appeal on September 29, 2008, before the Eleventh Circuit U.S. Court of Appeals (denied on November 10, 2009).

Undaunted by failure, Pardo filed a new petition for a writ of certiorari with the U.S. Supreme Court on April 5, 2010, denied on May 24 of that year. His petition for rehearing, filed on June 16, 2010, likewise went nowhere.

It was all a game for Pardo, conducted at public expense, but serial appeals were not his only form of entertainment. As the decades passed, he also found a way to wound and rob new victims from his death row cell.

***

It was a well-known racket for convicts, trolling newspaper lonely-hearts columns in search of gullible prey. The Globe and other supermarket tabloids charged an average twenty-five dollars per week to run personal ads like Pardo's, which read:

FLA. 116-156 CORRECTIONAL INSTITUTE INMATE. Ex-cop Vietnam vet. Took law into own hands and ended up on Death Row. He needs letters from sensitive/understanding female, for real/honest relationship.

Pardo's ads first went to press in July 1994, and bore immediate results. Reporter Martin Merzer, writing for the Seattle Times on April 7, 1996, cited prison records showing that thirty-two persons—twenty-six of them women unrelated to Pardo—had sent money to Florida's "Death Row Romeo" since January 1995, inflating his prison account to $3,530.08 at one point. One of those contributors was Barbara Ford of Findlay, Ohio, a house-cleaner earning some $7,500 per year in 1995, who first saw Pardo's ad in April of that year. Over the next seven months, she sent Pardo $430 in money orders, ranging from ten to fifty dollars at a time.

All she expected in return was love, and Pardo seemed to deliver. His first letter to Ford, dated April 26, 1995, read:

Dear Barb,

Hi and thank you for your sweet letter. I received 3 responses to the ad.... Those [other] two "ladies" are not what I wanted or need in my life.

Your response was the 3rd and only normal one. I am not into ads, but my neighbor, who is the only other person I speak to in this place, put it in for me....

I wish they let us work like other prisoners to make a few bucks a week for personal items like stamps, paper, shampoo, etc. But we are not allowed to work. We stay locked up. I am telling you this because as pathetic as it may sound it's true and at times I have trouble coming up with a simple thing as a stamp....

Yours, Manny

Ford read between the lines and began shelling out from her meager income, to keep Pardo's letters coming. "I want one special lady in my life," he wrote. "I don't play emotional games cause I hate emotional games. I also hate liars and users. I believe in honesty and I've laid all my cards on the table."

Or not.

Ten months before receiving Ford's first letter, Pardo had already hooked another pen pal, Betty Ihem, an impoverished part-time Wal-Mart employee from Chickasaw, Oklahoma. He snared her on July 11, 1994, with a letter reading:

Dear Betty,

Hi, I hope this letter finds you in good health. I received your sweet letter and pretty pictures today. Thank you! Do you know you have been the only one to answer my ad as of yet? I guess ex-cops are not popular ....

The last time I saw my daughter, she made me cry in the visiting parlor. She said, "Daddy, when I'm older and able to work, I will buy you a radio so you can listen to music...and I will send you money from my weekly check so you can buy coffee, shampoo and your other needs..."

Call me Manny. Take care and write soon.


Pardo's repeated pleas for shampoo were ironic, considering the fact that he had shaved his head in prison, while a nervous condition compelled him to pluck his eyebrows and eyelashes. In 1990, reporter Gary Nelson noted—and prison mug shots confirmed—"There was not a hair anywhere on his head."

By the time Barbara Ford read Pardo's ad in The Globe, he and Ihem were writing to one another as "husband" and "wife." Pardo had sent Ihem 275 letters by autumn 1995, receiving $1,200 by mail in return for his vows of eternal loyalty. "You will see I'm very direct, open, honest," he told Ihem, "and I do not play games or play with anyone's feelings."

Which, naturally, is exactly what he did.

In July 1995, Pardo mailed identical letters to Ford ("My Dearest Barb") and Ihem ("My Dearest Betty"). The carbon-copy notes read:

Hi sweetheart, how is the love of my life doing today? I hope this letter finds you in the best of health. I am NOT DOING WELL AT ALL!! I had a visit from my attorney today and he brought news that broke my heart....

The solution, of course, was more money.

Perhaps a breakdown in the system was inevitable. On October 12, 1995, Pardo inadvertently sent one of his "Dear Barb" letters to Betty Ihem, telling her—that is, Ford—"You are all I want and need. I am not a dream and if my love interests you, well then it's yours. I love you, Manny." Predictably furious, Ihem sent the letter on to Ford, with her own explanatory note penned on the back. Eight days later, Ford wrote to Pardo, addressing him as "Thief of Hearts" and enclosing photocopies of the money orders she had previously sent him. "You received the money under false pretenses," she wrote, "which makes you a fake and not the 'Man of Honor' which you professed to be. Needless to say, you are a liar and a hypocrite—the very things you said you hated in people. If you choose not to return the money, I will be your very worst nightmare and expose you for the hypocrite you truly are. I'm not a very patient person so I hope you respond to my request immediately. The choice is yours."

Pardo replied on November 2, 1995, with all the arrogance of a condemned prisoner who knows he is effectively untouchable.


Barb,

I hope you are in good health. I am reading your letter and am amazed you think your threats would affect me at all! You and your troubled life will also be exposed. In addition, my attorney will have a field day with you and that will be your nightmare lawsuit for slander, etc. You are a bitter and vindictive woman.

God bless,

Manny


Ford took her case to Florida governor Lawton Chiles on November 18, asking, "What kind of people are you in Florida? You have a guy on Death Row, and he still hurts people." Her reply came from Judy Belcher at the Florida Department of Corrections on November 29, advising Ford that no law forbade prisoners from placing personal ads or soliciting gifts from gullible pen pals. "On the contrary," Belcher wrote, "Florida Statutes have ruled it illegal to deny inmates that privilege because doing so would deny inmates access to the outside world. Many inmates, both male and female, have accumulated considerable amounts of money this way. They are convicts and some are experts at 'conning' honest people out of their hard earned dollars. Often, when we advise a person that an inmate is not being honest, the person will still choose to believe the inmate."

Questioned by journalist Martin Merzer in April 1996, DOC spokesperson Debbie Buchanan admitted official knowledge of Pardo's ongoing scam—including cash deposits from as many as four different women on a single day—but repeated Judy Belcher's statement that inmate mail, while routinely examined for breaches of prison security, could not be halted unless evidence of criminal activity was found. "I know it sounds cruel," she told Merzer, "but basically our hands are tied. He has broken no rules."

Curiously, even with her hopes of romance dashed, Betty Ihem was not bitter. She told Merzer, "As awful as it was, I don't know what I would have done if I hadn't had those letters. I might have gone over the edge. I guess I got my money's worth, if you want to look at it that way, because of the sexual stuff, the romance and the support, but it was just a dream. It was like reading a novel because the real person was not there."

*\*\**

In 1988, when Pardo asked jurors to give him the "glorious end" of a soldier, Florida had used an electric chair—dubbed "Old Sparky"—to execute condemned inmates. Over the next decade, however, Old Sparky had performed poorly on a number of occasions, setting Jesse Tafero's hair afire in May 1990, producing more flames and an acrid stench with Pedro Medina in March 1997, and scorching Allen Lee Davis from scalp to ankles in July 1999. By the time cop-killer Terry Sims went to his reward in February 2000, the state had switched over to lethal injection, but the revamped system offered Pardo one more opportunity to duck the very death he claimed to crave.

On October 30, 2012, Governor Rick Scott signed Pardo's death warrant, setting the date for December 11. That, in turn, prompted yet another appeal to Florida's Supreme Court, Pardo complaining that the state's lethal injection protocol was unconstitutional, that the circuit court erred in denying him various public records, that he was incompetent to stand trial in 1988, and —the kicker—that his twenty-four years on death row, protracted by his own appeals, constituted cruel and unusual punishment. On December 4, 2012, the court denied him any further hearings.

Pardo's only consolation in his final days came from correspondence with Dr. Ken Craven of Sparta, Tennessee, founding father of the Desert Prison Ministry, self-described on its Internet Web site as "a private, unrecognized, unauthorized, unsanctioned Catholic ministry to prisoners." Visiting prison inmates is the sixth Corporal Work of Mercy outlined in Roman Catholic doctrine, and Dr. Craven takes it very seriously. As to Pardo's level of devotion, we may only speculate. His final "Dear Ken" letter, dated December 11 and also posted on the DPM's Web site, thanked all concerned for their friendship and reported that "Brother Dale" Recinella—attorney and Catholic lay minister, author of Now I Walk on Death Row: A Wall Street Finance Lawyer Stumbles into the Arms of A Loving God (2011)—would accompany Pardo on his last walk "to God's Eternal Kingdom."

In parting, Pardo wrote: "At least tomorrow after the first two hours when I have my last meal...they will give me a one hour of contact visit...when I'll be able to kiss and hug my daughter, sister, godson, nephews, etc. So thank God I will be able to have closure with them...I've made my peace with God, have him in my heart, and pray hard to protect Michi [Pardo's daughter] and give her strength to carry on and have a long, healthy, happy life!"

Florida prison regulations specify that ingredients for a condemned inmate's last meal must be purchased locally for forty dollars or less, and must be prepared in the prison's kitchen. That rules out any gourmet feast, though Allen Lee Davis went to Old Sparky in 1999 after a meal including one lobster tail, a half pound of fried shrimp, six ounces of fried clams, fried potatoes, half a loaf of garlic bread, and thirty-two ounces of root beer. Pardo's menu was somewhat more modest: red beans and rice, roasted pork, plantains, avocado, tomatoes and olive oil, with pumpkin pie for dessert, all washed down with eggnog and Cuban coffee.

End game attorney William McKinley Hennis III fought for Pardo's life to the eleventh hour, appealing one last time to Florida's Supreme Court with a claim that failure to disclose the ingredients of his client's final drug cocktail rendered death by lethal injection a form of "cruel and unusual punishment." The court rejected that argument on December 8, 2012, declaring that Pardo's alleged fears of a painful death were based solely on "pure speculation and conjecture." Still, Hennis complained to reporters that Pardo suffered from longstanding hyperthyroidism, a condition whose effects include nervousness, irritability, a racing heartbeat, hand tremors, anxiety, difficulty sleeping, thinning of the skin, fine brittle hair, and muscular weakness, among other symptoms. On December 8, Hennis told David Ovalle of the Miami Herald, "He's never been allowed to put on an expert about hyperthyroidism and the impact it had on his crimes and his competency at trial."

And now, he never would.

Pardo's execution proceeded as scheduled on December 11, 2012. Strapped to a gurney, with a white sheet pulled up to his chin and covering the IV lines inserted in both arms, Pardo muttered parting words that were inaudible to witnesses, and was officially pronounced dead sixteen minutes after the lethal cocktail entered his system, at 7:47 P.M. Prison spokesmen later told reporters that he last words had been "Airborne forever. I love you, Michi baby."

Another parting message, penned in his cell on December 11, sounded like the same old Manny Pardo. In that letter, he staunchly denied slaying any women, but accepted "full responsibility for killing six men. I never harmed those 3 women or any female. I took the blame as I knew I was doomed and it made no difference to me, at this time, having 6 or 9 death sentences. I don't want this hanging over my head, especially these last few minutes of life, because my war was against men who were trafficing [sic] in narcotics and no one else!" To the kin he left behind, Pardo wrote, "You all are so loving and wonderful, not deserving of this nightmare. Remember Michi you are Airborne and hardcore...No tears!" Digressing toward the end, he added, "On a lighter note, as a New Yorker and loyal fan, I was happy to see my Yankees and Giants win so many championships during my lifetime." And finally, he scolded Spanish politicians for their recent waffling on the cruel and controversial "sport" of bullfighting. Pardo admonished them never to give up that "part of our culture and heritage. And if they do, I'm glad I won't be alive to see such a travesty!"

Indeed, he would not. And that, for the survivors of his victims, was at least some small relief.

# Chapter 7: **Anthony Sowell**

## By RJ Parker

## Cleveland Strangler

From 2007 through 2009 at least 11 women were raped and killed by Anthony Sowell. There could very well be more victims, perhaps even some as far away from his home in Cleveland,

Anthony was in the Marines from 1978 to 1985. Stationed in North Carolina , California and Okinawa, Japan; he received a Good Conduct Medal with one service star, a Sea Service Deployment Ribbon, a Certificate of Commendation, a Meritorious Mast, and two Letters of Appreciation. He received an Honorable Discharge, despite a two month period when he disappeared.

His daughter was born in 1978, only nine months after he joined the Marine Corps at the age of 19. People describe him as a guy who liked to help others in his neighborhood. He would shovel the snow, fix a broken sink, borrow them a few dollars. He liked to have cookouts and chess games. He stopped by the local store twice a day to buy a 40 oz. King Cobra beer or cheap smokes. He pushed his shopping cart around the neighborhoods looking for scrap metal to turn in at the local scrap yard for a few dollars. Everybody knew who he was and he knew most of them too.

\*\*\*

He was 50 years old at the time of his arrest on Halloween day, 2009. Only two days before, police came to his house with a search warrant to look for evidence in regards to a rape and attack he was accused of committing back in September that same year.

The stench surrounding the house, in fact choking the whole neighborhood, was nothing new. The police that entered the house must have smelled it as soon as they exited their vehicles. Anthony was not at home, but when they entered the house the officers became physically ill at the strong odor. Soon they found the first two bodies in a room located on the third floor of the house.

Some had assumed the foul smell was from the sewers or even Ray's Sausage Company, which was right next door to the Sowell house. There had been a report to City Hall by a woman who lived across the street on June 29th, 2007 about a foul odor in the neighborhood, which she said smelled like a dead person or animal. Some sources have indicated that there may have been reports on the odor as far back as 2006. Replacement of a sewer line and grease traps at Ray's didn't help. Workers in the offices above Ray's kept the windows closed.

It is this smell that emanated off Anthony Sowell wherever he went, so much so that most people avoided him and became ill when he entered businesses. Anthony slept, ate and lived only a few feet away from the bodies of the women he raped, strangled to death and then kept around as they decayed. But not every woman he raped and attacked died.

We may never know the full extent of Anthony's crimes or who all of his victims were. The FBI launched an investigation searching for leads across the globe.

***

August 19th, 1959 Anthony Edward Sowell was born to Claudia Garrison. His father never was a factor in his life and his mother had six other children. They lived in Cleveland and later East Cleveland, along with seven other children belonging to Anthony's sister after she died. Claudia Garrison physically abused the children while other children watched from other rooms and would beat them with switches and extension cords. Sometimes she would wake them up from a dead sleep to give them a good beating. Anthony's niece was forced to strip naked in front of the other kids and whipped with electrical cords until she was bleeding. When the niece was 10, her 11 year old uncle, Anthony started raping her on a daily basis. He also told a mental health professional, who testified at his trial for the defense in 2009, that when he would mimic performing lewd sex acts on a doll and rubbed the doll with feces.

Anthony claims he witnessed his older sister being sexually abused by one of their older nephews, and that the nephew also sexually molested him until he bit him. He was about 5 or six years old at the time. He said this nephew also forced some of the kids to perform sex acts on each other.

He says his mother never showed love or caring and it was not until he married his wife Kim, also a Marine when they were both stationed in Japan, that he could allow someone to touch him affectionately. They returned to the States and were married in North Carolina in September 1981. When Anthony's vehicle overheated and he got hot steam into his eyes, burning and blinding him for over three months, Kim helped take care of him. They got divorced in 1985 because of his heavy drinking and he left the military shortly thereafter.

When Anthony got drunk, he got mean and very angry. He was 25 years old when he moved back to East Cleveland. He admitted in 2005 during an psychological evaluation that during this time he started drinking when he woke up and continued throughout the day; always having at least six drinks and sometimes got to the point when he would black out.

From 1986 to 1989 he had numerous arrests for disorderly conduct, DUI and public drunkenness. In 1988 he was arrested on a charge of domestic violence and served eight days in jail. Also in 1988 he was arrested on a charge of possessing a dangerous substance. It does not mention what drug this was.

In May of 1988 a woman's body was found in her home near where Anthony was living. Rosalind Garner was only 36 when she was strangled to death.

February 27th, 1989 Carmella Karen Prater was found in an abandoned home, dead at age 27. She was a suspected drug user and also found near where Anthony was living.

Mary Thomas, also 27 and a suspected drug user, was found strangled to death with the red ribbon still around her neck near an abandoned building in the same neighborhood on

March 28th, 1989.

These three women's cases have never been solved even though police reopened the cases after Anthony's arrest in 2009. No definitive link could be made, but this would not be the last time these type of killings occurred around where Anthony lived.

*** 

In July of 1989 Anthony met a 21 year old woman at a local motel. She was three months pregnant and when police showed up at the motel she was afraid they would arrest her as she had a previous criminal record of drug use. Anthony told her that her boyfriend was waiting for her at his house.

Her boyfriend was not at Anthony's house but he lured her to the bedroom, threw her onto the bed and proceeded to choke and rape her repeatedly.

When she tried to leave, Anthony tied her hands with a necktie, bound her feet with a belt and stuffed a rag in her mouth. He was drunk and he fell asleep, giving her a chance to wiggle free and escape out a window.

Anthony was indicted by the Grand Jury but he did not show for his court date. A warrant was issued for his arrest, but he was not found just yet.

On June 24th 1990 about 4 miles away Anthony was drinking and a 31 year old woman sat down next to him and started drinking too. Anthony, according to the police report, got up, came up behind her and started choking her. He told her a bunch of obscene sexual acts he would be doing to her and told her "she was his bitch, and she had better learn to like it."

He then dragged her upstairs by her neck and raped her orally, vaginally and anally. She tried to tell him she was five months pregnant and begged him to stop but he made her say "Yes, sir, I like it." He went to sleep and she left and brought police back. He was still sleeping when they came and arrested him.

Charges were not filed in the case because police said the woman could not be found to testify, but Anthony found himself in jail waiting for the trial on the 1989 rape.

He pled guilty to a lesser charge of attempted rape and was sentenced to 15 years in prison on September 12th, 1990.

While in Prison he tried to sign up for sex-offender treatment but was denied because he would not admit he was a sex offender. He also took courses for GED, "Living Without Violence", "Cage Your Rage", and other self help courses.

***

On June 20th, 2005 Anthony left prison clean and sober, at age 45, and was deemed unlikely to rape again.

He registered with the Cuyahoga County Sheriff's Department as a sex offender and reported to them once a year until 2008, when federal law passed that required every 90 days.

He moved in with his stepmother who owned the three level home on Imperial Avenue. She stayed on the first floor, which was immaculate even after her disabilities forced her to move into a nursing home in 2007 and Anthony was arrested in 2009.

He started smoking crack cocaine shortly after his release and started using it as a way to lure women back to his place to hang out with him and get high. He also set up a profile on an alternative lifestyle website looking for submissive women he could be master to. He listed his stats as 5' 10", 160lbs. and as having a distinctive facial scar. Said he liked to party and was a people person.

He met Lori Frazier, the niece of the mayor and they started dating in 2005. She was also a crack smoker and she moved into the house on Imperial with Anthony and lived with him until 2007 when they broke up. He says he helped her to get clean and then she quit coming around. Finally on his birthday, which she had forgotten, he went up town to find her and tell her they were through. She says that Anthony took good care of her but got nasty when he smoked crack and sometimes hit her, although she says she was shocked at the news of his arrest in the murders. She later said he told her he "got rid of them" and she saw blood on his carpet and saw him digging in his backyard. She knew Crystal Dozier, one of the women whose body was found in the house. She was the first of the known victims to go missing in May of 2007 Sowell didn't break with Lori until some time around his birthday August 19th, 2007. Lori had been in and out of the house at some point in 2007, so it is possible she was in the house only a short distance away from her friend's body.

*** 

Anthony claims something in him broke after he broke it off with Lori. He definitely seemed to need more and more victims to fulfill his need to rape and strangle women. Most of his victims were suspected or known drug addicts that he lured to his house with the promise of a good time of smoking crack or getting drunk. He says that women who became crack whores and had children fueled his rage, but some say he chose these women because they were easy pickings.

Listening to testimony and reading the reports of the women who came forward about their experiences with Anthony gives a picture of what probably happened to the women who didn't get away. He usually struck up a friendly conversation with a woman and offered to help her out with getting high or just having a good time back at his place getting drunk.

Then he would walk back with them to his house, unlock the door and lead them up to the third floor, where he lived in squalor and used rags for toilet paper. Sometimes he would cook a meal for them in his tiny kitchenette (where he had a box of raw chicken and food in a box on the table rotting), more often he led them straight to his bedroom. There they would sit on the edge of the bottom of the bed next to each other and have a casual conversation about a variety of topics. He liked to talk about food, ask them if they had family and happenings in the neighborhood.

Then they would get drunk or high and that is when the real Anthony came out. He would hit them hard in the face or get his hands around their neck, choking them, sometimes until they passed out, sometimes using his hands other times an extension cord. Sometimes he would talk about his ex-girlfriend or other women. Usually he then raped them repeatedly after describing in detail what he was going to do to them.

He would make them perform oral sex on him and sometimes make them say they liked it, under threats of locking them in a closet and forgetting about them for days. He told them no one would hear them scream and he would rape them both vaginally and anally, usually multiple times.

If they talked right or begged enough, they might be lucky and he would let them go. One victim described walking down the hall of the third floor and there was a sheet of plastic covering one of the doorways. On a walk back by it she glanced in and saw a body with no head... a woman's body propped up, with no head on it and wrapped in plastic. He escorted her all the way back down to his door and out to the steps. She described that walk as being extremely painful as her face was injured, her female organs were injured and later she lost control of her bowels. When she called police to report it, they told her she would have to come in all the way down to the station.

Some women he bound and gagged after beating them or raping them. A couple women escaped when he fell asleep or passed out drunk and they jumped out a window.

He told them that no one would miss them if they were gone, and it seemed that way when more and more women went missing and nothing seemed to be really happening to stop it. Some families were told filing a missing person's report would be useless; to just wait until the drugs ran out and they would come back home, as is often the case with drug addicts. This is the kind of jaded attitude that helped Anthony to keep killing women.

He kept and used a variety of cords and items that he would use to strangle his victims with. Removed from the necks of the women recovered from Anthony's property were belts, shoestrings, socks, cell phone charger cords and coaxial cables.

At some point he decapitated some of them and then stuck them in a heavy duty garbage bag or sheet of plastic. He buried five in the backyard. Some were stuck in a crawl space or the basement. One was under the stairs covered in dirt and wood from a broken table. A couple were just left in that room that once had the plastic sheet hung up over it. Later he stuffed towels along the bottom of the doorway.

Also found in the basement was a bucket containing the head of a woman. Her body was never recovered.

There has been speculation that Anthony is a necrophiliac, that he had sex with dead bodies, but this has never been confirmed by him, although he was charged and convicted with abuse of a corpse.

Some of the other evidence gathered from Anthony's property paint a picture of a man who subjected his victims to even more brutality than beating and raping them, such as a sex toy found in a tool box on the third floor. It tested positive for blood. He had a large quantity of pornography, pounds of magazines and many VHS tapes.

Some neighbors recalled seeing Anthony dragging large garbage bags down the street to dumpsters and that the dumpster behind his house smelled of that same odor that permeated the neighborhood.

He also kept numerous articles of clothing, jewelry and hair extensions from his victims. His DNA was matched on a bra belonging to one of the women. None of his fingerprints were recovered for the plastic, bags or tape used in the disposing of the bodies, but it makes sense that he wore gloves when doing this if he was dumping some bodies in dumpsters, which could have been discovered and checked.

***

After his arrest, Anthony was interrogated by detectives from the sex crimes unit as well as homicide and he admitted to the crimes. He blamed the voices in his head, that he was like two people in one and said he really didn't recall committing the acts, but must have because no one else could have committed them. He said he had blackouts and nightmares in which he saw himself hurting women with his hands. He also said the voices told him not to look behind the locked door on the third floor. He claimed he didn't notice anything unusual in his house. His boots found at the scene were caked with dead maggots.

During his entire trial Anthony showed no emotion during crime scene photos, survivor and witness accounts or expert testimony. After a lengthy trial jurors deliberated for 7 hours and came back with a verdict of guilty and recommended the death penalty. Anthony Sowell was sentenced to death in August 2011. He is currently on death row.

# Chapter 8: Martha Hasel Wise

## By Sylvia Perrini

### The Funeral Hobbyist

Martha Wise, nee Hasel, was born in 1884. She was born to modest farmer parents, Wilhelm and Sophie Gienke Hasel, in Hardscrabble which is located in Medina County, Ohio. Although it is only twenty-three miles from the large bustling city of Cleveland, Hardscrabble was a world apart: just a small hamlet of modestly-sized farms. Newspapers of the era categorized it as a "forsaken mud and slime crossroads."

As a small child, Martha was slow and sickly. She suffered from an acute bout of spinal meningitis. A serious illness today, it was particularly serious around the turn of the 20th century when medical care was not as advanced as it is today. Her spinal meningitis may well have resulted in her learning disabilities and brain damage. Her teacher, Mrs. Elma Reisenger, said she had found Martha clearly mentally retarded. She said,

"She couldn't learn. She was queer and erratic. She was not a normal child."

Martha was also suspected of suffering from undiagnosed epilepsy. While most people associate epilepsy with severe seizures where people fall, shake, froth at the mouth, and bite their tongues another eighty percent of patients only suffer from mild seizures that are harder to spot; thus, often making a diagnosis of epilepsy impossible. These characteristics and illnesses made Martha particularly vulnerable to contempt and bullying in the community and in particular from her family. To add to this, Martha was also unfortunate in her looks with sunken eyes and a pinched face. By the time she was an adolescent in 1898, she had developed hypochondria and was frequently running to the local doctor, Henry John Abele, with a whole host of imaginary ailments.

Martha left school when she was fourteen, which was not uncommon for a farm girl in those days. Martha then spent some years working as a kitchen girl in various local homes. Oddly, Martha's favorite entertainment was attending funerals. This may have been because there was not much other entertainment to offer in the small rural community. Martha loved funerals since there was music, flowers, singing, a gathering of people, and plentiful supplies of food, pies, cakes, and homemade jars of pickles and relishes that adorned the tables. Martha attended every funeral within reach, whether she had known the deceased or not, and by 1924 was notorious as one who had not missed a local funeral for twenty years. What she particularly enjoyed was the wailing and weeping to which she would abandon herself, too, with complete gusto. Perhaps this was her way of letting go of the anguish she felt from all of the bullying she received, especially because people would think she was crying for the deceased and, thus, would not tease her.

In 1906 Martha was twenty-four. She was still single and living with her parents with little prospect of marriage in sight. She often attended a "box social," an old, quaint tradition in which young single ladies demonstrated their culinary skills for potential beaus. Here, she met a substantially older local farmer, Albert Wise, who was supposedly so impressed with Martha's chicken sandwiches that he soon proposed, and the two were married before the year's end.

It is not known exactly why Albert married Martha. He even refused to buy her a wedding ring. It was obvious he had not married her for her looks, intelligence, or money. Many speculated that he just needed a free housekeeper and another worker on his 100 acre farm, as during their fifteen years of marriage he used her as a common field hand even when pregnant with the five children the marriage produced. The first child, Albert, failed to survive infancy; fortunately, four others: Everett, Gertrude, Kenneth, and Lester did survive. Martha was the only white woman in the area who was made to slop out the hogs and do field work that most men found hard to do like the plowing while still expected to perform the usual household chores of baking, washing, taking care of the children, and cleaning. Albert, in addition to treating her like a slave, would also beat her.

In 1923, Albert Wise died, leaving Martha a 40-year-old widow with four children left to raise. Because of later events, it is suspected that Martha poisoned him with arsenic. However, at the time of his death, no one suspected that Martha would murder her own husband. Following Albert's death, the local people soon found that Martha became even queerer as she began displaying increasingly bizarre behavior. She would be seen roaming the countryside at night. Sometimes it was said that she was foaming at the mouth with her eyes rolling madly or even (it was rumored) barking like a dog. She told her family that she had frequent hallucinations and was visited by angels and white doves. She also started attending even more funerals, often traveling out of town to be a "guest" at funerals of people she did not even know! Also at around this period, a spate of mysterious fires began in the area and jewelry and farm tools disappeared. She later said by reason of an "explanation",

"Some of the fires I started at night. Some of them I started in the daytime after the devil had told me at night to do it. I was afraid to at night. I always saw him when I did light the fires, and he always told me something new to do. I didn't think about the fires killing anybody at first but later I knew they might; that's when I started out to set them at night, so I could surprise people. I never stayed at the fires; I slipped away to a hiding place and watched them blaze and crackle and burn."

Despite not being all that attractive, nor being considered a "catch", Martha also began to have a few lovers, which set the local tongues wagging. One in particular was Walter Johns, who worked as a farmhand on a property close to her farm. Martha was particularly smitten with Walter and wanted to marry him, even though he was much younger than she. Her family disapproved, ridiculing Martha for "cradle-robbing." Her mother Sophie and uncle Fred Gienke took a particularly strong stand against the relationship and disliked all the gossip about Martha in the small, ultra conservative, close-knit community. They put their foot down and forbade Martha to marry Walter. Her mother, Sophie, delivered an ultimatum to Martha that she would cut her out of her will and publicly disown her if she should marry him. No matter how much Martha ranted, raved, and threatened her family, her mother and Uncle would not give in. The relationship ended and Walter soon moved to Cleveland and eventually the couple lost contact. Martha was furious. Her family's words and ridicule played in her mind repeatedly. She walked aimlessly around her house, muttering words under her breath.

On November 24th, 1924 Martha visited the local Medina pharmacy and bought two ounces of arsenic, which she signed for in her own name in the poison register as required by law. She told the pharmacist, Mr. Weber, that she needed it to kill rats. Several days later, she went to her mother's house for Thanksgiving Dinner. Sometime during this family dinner, Martha slipped into her mother's water bucket a potent pinch of arsenic. Everyone, including Martha, who had dinner at Sophie's house that night complained the following day of stomach pains. Everyone eventually recovered, but Sophie continued to worsen.

A couple of days later, Martha returned to the chemist and bought another ounce of arsenic. She then returned to her mother's house and again put it in her mother's water bucket. Sophie Hazel then began suffering from appalling abdominal pains and weakness in her legs. After a few days of excruciating pain, she died on December 13, 1924. The doctors put down the cause of death as "influenza and inflammation of the stomach."

At her mother's funeral, Martha sobbed and shook in an extreme outburst of grief – more so than she had at any of the other funerals she had attended - and sung her mother's favorite hymn "All the way my savior leads me."

Two days later at the wake held for Sophie's mother at her Brother Fred's house, Fred, his wife, his son Edwin, and two other relatives, Paul and Henry Hasel, became violently ill after drinking coffee. Despite this, no foul play was suspected. It was thought to be just a stomach bug.

One of the reasons arsenic was especially popular as a murdering tool in the 19th and early part of the 20th centuries was because it was almost tasteless, and its slightly sweet and metallic taste was simply cloaked by the food to which it was added. In addition, if administrated in small doses over a certain amount of time, the symptoms (such as diarrhea, vomiting, and stomach pains) were comparable to those of other diseases such as cholera, dysentery, and Gastroenteritis. As gastro-intestinal illnesses were so widespread, doctors in countless cases failed to spot the signs of arsenic poisoning.

On New Year's Day at a family gathering at her Uncle Fred's house, within twenty minutes of having a glass of coffee Fred Ganske, his wife Lillian, his daughter Marie, and his sons Fred Jr., Rudolph, and Walter, as well as Martha's brother Fred and his son Edwin were all violently ill. Martha also claimed to be ill. Martha's children were all fine, as they had been told quietly by their mother not to drink the water or the coffee. Several of the family members had to be hospitalized. Most recovered; however,

Lillian Gienke writhed in agony for three days before dying on January 4<sup>th</sup>, 1925.

The symptoms of poisoning by arsenic differ depending on the dose, but the common symptoms are diarrhea and vomiting, progressing to tingling and numbness of the feet, followed by muscular cramps, intense thirst, exhaustion, and collapse. The doctor who attended Lillian was suspicious and contacted the Medina County Coroner, E.L.Crum, who unfortunately decided Lillian's death didn't warrant an investigation. The other members of the family slowly began to recover.

On January 16<sup>th</sup> of 1925, Martha struck again. This time around, Fred Gienke and his children: Rudolph, Marie, Herman, and Richard as well as Lillian's sister Rose were all once again stricken with the most agonizing stomach pains. Martha also claimed that she was suffering, too. It was thought at the time the illness was caused by ptomaine poisoning. "Ptomaine Poisoning" was a misconstrued, vague, and inaccurate term used before the actual causes of food poisoning were known. The family continued to be ill throughout the rest of January of 1925.

In early February of 1925, Fred Gienke, Lillian, Rudolph, and Marie were all hospitalized, and a nurse who had been employed to nurse the patients at the Gienke house became ill after making a cup of coffee; however, she quickly recovered. Lillian succumbed to her illness, and Fred Gienke soon followed her, dying in the hospital on February 8<sup>th</sup>, 1925 in agony. The official cause of death for both was noted as "inflammation of the stomach."

Meanwhile the doctors at the hospital were increasingly concerned about Rudolph and Marie Gienke. Doctors ran thorough tests on them and discovered a quantity of unexplained arsenic in their bodies. Four of the children had become partially paralyzed from their as yet unidentified illness. The doctors alerted the Medina County Prosecutor, Joseph Seymour.

Cleveland Newspapers soon picked up on the story and sensationalized stories appeared in the press as to who the mysterious poisoner might be and where he or she might strike next. Three dead and fourteen sick said the papers. Virtually every theory and some neigh impossible ones were played out on the front pages of competing newspapers.

In the *Cleveland Press* one journalist wrote,

"The ghost of a series of wanton murders, apparently directed at the extermination of a peace-loving and industrious family, today arose from the mud and slime of Hardscrabble to add its ghostly name to Ohio's record of crime."

Another headline read,

"Super-Killer Hunted in Medina County." ("A Super-Killer is a murderer who kills for the mere joy of killing.")

In the meantime, the police investigating had already found Martha's name in the local pharmacy poison register. Not only were the police and, in particular, Sheriff Fred Robson, suspicious of Martha so also were her cousins Richard and Fred Gienke. Richard went so far as to give an interview to the Press on March 16th, 1925:

"This woman threatened to get us. We heard about that but did not pay attention to it. After mother and dad died, we began to wonder about the poison but did not think of the threats. However, when the rest of us kept getting sick, we remembered them."

The Sheriff also received an anonymous letter,

"I just want to make a suggestion. See if you can find out if there was any ill feeling between Martha Wise and Lilly Gienke. She claims to have been sick, too, but that may be a lie."

No one ever did determine from whom the letter was sent.

On Wednesday, March the 18th of 1925, the body of Lillian Gienke was exhumed from Myrtle Hill cemetery and was taken to Elyria Memorial Hospital for a postmortem. The coroners discovered in Lillian's digestive track and throughout her body enough arsenic to kill three people.

On Wednesday March 18th, Martha was arrested by Sheriff Fred Roshon while attending the Fairview Park Hospital in Cleveland where she was having an arm infection treated.

On the way back to Medina, Martha, with tears streaming down her cheeks, said of the victims,

"My heart bleeds for them. It must have been a monster that would kill them, and my poor, innocent old mother, why did they kill her? It was terrible. I sometimes think they were poisoned by accident because I cannot imagine anyone being so terrible."

Once back in Medina, Sheriff Fred Roshon took Martha to the Prosecutor, Mr. Joseph Seymour's, office for an official interrogation. Also present at the interrogation were the Coroner and Roshon's wife, Ethel, along with a stenographer.

Martha denied the charges for hours insisting that she knew nothing; that the arsenic had been purchased to kill rats.

"We know you did it, Martha," Joseph Seymour said.

"Why not confess and get it off your conscience?" He continued.

"You are wrong, Mr. Seymour. I would never have done such a thing," replied Martha shaking her head in stony-faced denial.

It then began to rain, and the prosecutor's office was filled with the sounds of the falling rain. It was then that Ethel Roshon said softly to Martha,

"Listen, Martha. The rain - it is God's Voice. It is saying, 'You did, you did, you did.'"

Martha listened in silence before shrieking,

"Oh, God! Yes I did it. The Devil told me to."

Martha then made a full confession admitting to first poisoning her mother's drinking water on Thanksgiving Day and then at her brother's and Uncle's houses. All told, she admitted to poisoning seventeen people.

She said to anyone that would listen,

"It was the devil who told me to do it. He came to me while I was in the kitchen baking bread. He came to me while I was working in the fields. He followed me everywhere."

She also admitted to numerous burglaries and arson incidents. She explained her reason for committing these acts by stating,

"I like fires. They were red and bright, and I loved to see the flames shooting up into the sky."

In explanation as to why she had targeted her own family, she said it was because her family had told her that she,

"Had no business wantin' to get married again. Said I was old and ugly. They laughed at me. I hated them, and the Devil said: 'Kill them!' And I did."

On March 23, 1925 in front of a grand jury, Martha, despite her confession, pleaded not guilty to the murder of Lily Gienke. She testified to the grand jury that she was addicted to attending funerals, and if there was a shortage of funerals in the area, she would create them by murder. On April 7, 1925, Martha was indicted on a charge of the first-degree murder of Lillian Gienke

## Trial

Martha's trial began on May 4, 1925. A jury of seven women and five men were selected. The prosecution was led by Joseph Seymour and assisted by Arthur Van Epps. Martha was defended by Joseph Pritchard.

The trial attracted a great deal of media attention, and there were long lines for seating in the public gallery. All eyes were on Martha as she was led into the courtroom by Ethel Roshon. A

231

newspaper article of the day described Martha in the following manner:

"Her face was drawn, her eyes downcast. There were lines about her eyes and mouth, testifying to the mental suffering thru which she has passed during the months that she has been in jail. Her hair was combed straight back from her wrinkled and yellow forehead. Her eyes were weird, dark caverns, deep-sunk behind her steel-rimmed glasses. When she was arrested, her hair showed few traces of gray. Today, it is thickly streaked with white. The woman walked like one who was very tired. Her shoulders sagged. Her head dropped on a sunken chest. Her clothes were clean but ill-fitting over her gaunt form. Her hands hung listlessly at her sides, one clutching claw-like a small blue handkerchief."

From the beginning, Joseph Seymour announced he was not seeking the death penalty. Joseph Pritchard's, Martha's defense attorney, defense strategy was that Martha was criminally insane. He even alleged that Martha was told to poison her relatives by Walter Johns, her former lover. The prosecution called many witnesses which included the pharmacist who had sold her the arsenic, a still partially paralyzed Fred Gienke Jr. who limped into the courtroom, his sister Marie, who was brought by stretcher from the hospital crippled for life, and Martha's other cousin Herman Gienke who hobbled into court on a cane. Martha's son, Lester, also gave evidence for the prosecution.

Defense lawyer Joseph Pritchard called fifty-two witnesses who all described Martha as a half-wit, a pathetic village idiot, an arsonist, a thief, a hypochondriac, and a moron. Her former lover, Walter Johns, testified that she barked like a dog when he was making love to her and foamed at the mouth. However, the defense, was plagued by a number of setbacks which included the suicide on May 6 of Edith Hasel, Martha's sister-in-law, followed by the collapse of Fred Hasel, Edith's husband. Both Edith and Fred had been prepared to testify for the defense.

Another defense witness, Frank Metzger, told the prosecution on cross-examination that the defense team had requested him to perjure himself to support Martha's claims that she was insane; and Martha's decision to take to the witness stand on her own behalf which is often never a good choice when one is on trial.

In his summation, Joseph Pritchard said Martha was an incredibly sick and deeply distressed woman. He said,

"Pyromania, plus kleptomania, plus epilepsy, plus spinal meningitis equals insanity."

The prosecutor, Joseph Seymour told the jury,

"Slipping into the Gienke home when no one was watching, putting arsenic into their water and coffee buckets, returning twice to add more poison is not the manner in which insane people kill. She bought enough arsenic to kill the population of Hardscrabble where she lived. She visited the Gienkes when they were all ill and told their doctor she thought their illness was influenza. That is not the act of an insane woman."

The jury took slightly less than an hour to find her guilty of murder in the first degree. They recommended mercy, which meant a life sentence.

The judge sentenced Martha, at the age of forty-one, to a life sentence in Marysville Prison, and said she could only be set free by executive clemency.

The press labeled her the "Borgia of America."

Martha settled into life in prison and seemed to enjoy mundane chores such as doing laundry and caring for the chickens. During her time spent in prison, Martha displayed nothing less than good behavior.

Due to her good behavior, in 1962, the then Ohio governor Michael DiSalle commuted Martha's sentence to second-degree murder, and at the age of seventy-nine she was granted parole.

Martha was old and sick and was released into a world completely foreign to her. What was left of her family refused to give her a home and a number of rest homes, catering  for the elderly refused her residency.

With nowhere else to go, Martha had no choice but to voluntarily return to prison where the commutation of her sentence and her parole were revoked. Martha died in prison on June the 28th, 1971. Her body was buried in the prison, as no one came forward to claim it.

# Chapter 9: Erzsébet (Elizabeth) Báthory
## By Michael Newton

"Cruelties Unheard of Since the World Began"

Count György Thurzó was deeply troubled in December 1610. The previous year, he had been appointed as Palatine of Hungary, second highest-ranking official in the realm after King Matthias II. In fact, as a son of Hungary's richest family, Thurzó possessed more treasure and a larger army than the king himself. His family was vulnerable, though, to any taint of scandal—and none was more deadly in that Early Modern era, marked by witch trials and religious warfare, than allegations of trafficking in the Black Arts.

The very charges lodged against a cousin of the Palatine himself.

Thurzó, an ardent Lutheran who had erected churches on his lands and earlier in 1610 had issued a decree of *Cuius regio, eius religio* (literally, "Whose realm, his religion," dictating the creed of his serfs), could scarcely ignore the allegations made against a member of his family—and, some said, his occasional lover. Worse yet, the target of those charges was a lofty noble in her own right, the Countess Erzsébet Báthory.

Before he took irrevocable steps, Thurzó knew that he must investigate the claims, then learn if there was adequate support for an unprecedented move against a member of the royal family who was, for all intents and purposes, above the law.

***

Erzsébet (Elizabeth) Báthory was born on August 7, 1560, at her family's estate in Nyìrbátor. Her parents, Baron and Baroness George and Anna Báthory, ranked among the richest Protestants in Hungary, related by blood before their marriage born of political strife. George Báthory sprang from the Ecsed branch of the clan, which had supported Archduke Ferdinand I (later Holy Roman Emperor) in his claim to the Hungarian throne, while Anna's side —the Somlyòis—had backed John Zápolya, *voivode* of Transylvania. Those rivals clashed at the Battle of Mohács in August 1526, resulting in division of the kingdom. Ferdinand was then recognized as king in the north and west of Hungary, while Zápolya ruled central Hungary and Transylvania until his death in July 1540. Transylvania became a semi-independent principality in 1570, but tension remained between rival branches of the rising Báthory family, resolved—at least in theory—by the marriage of George and Anna.

Erzsébet was thus related to some of Hungary's and Eastern Europe's most prestigious and powerful figures. Her kinsmen included Sigismund Báthory, Prince of Transylvania; Stephen VII Báthory, Palatine of Hungary; Stephen Báthory, King of Poland; and Andrew Báthory, whose offices included those of Roman Catholic cardinal, Prince-Bishop of Warmia, and Grand Master of the Order of the Dragon, created to defend Hungarian Christianity against the Ottoman Turks.

On the darker side, Erzsébet's closest relatives also included brother Stephen, an alcoholic lecher; Uncle Gábor, a reputed Satan-worshiper; and Aunt Klara, a sadistic lesbian and practicing witch who introduced young Erzsébet to the pleasures of inflicting pain. Habitual inbreeding among European royals left many leading families prone to a wide range of mental and physical defects, aggravated by their sense of divine entitlement and virtual immunity from prosecution in their dealings with peasants.

The full extent of Erzsébet's childhood corruption is impossible to measure, shrouded as her story has become in myth and legend. Various tales suggest an early fondness for boy's clothing and sexual experimentation with serfs, allegedly resulting in Erzsébet's pregnancy at age thirteen or fourteen, bearing a daughter who was foisted off on peasant parents and forgotten. Perhaps significantly, that story did not surface until 1894, with publication of German author R. von Elsberg's *Die Blutgräfin* [*The Blood Countess*] *Elisabeth Bathory*. Other tales, published long after the fact, claim that Erzsébet witnessed the execution of a Gypsy, bound and sewn inside a rotting horse's carcass on a charge of selling children to the Turks. In 1995, novelist Alexandrei Codrescu altered that scene to depict the murder of Elizabeth's two sisters by rebellious peasants.

Stories persist that Erzsébet was deranged from childhood, as evidenced by periodic "fits" and rages, diagnosed by some biographers, generations after the fact, as evidence of epilepsy. Contrasted with those tales are reports of her advanced education. In an age when many royals—and virtually all serfs—were illiterate, Erzsébet was fluent in Hungarian, German, Greek, and Latin. Her letters, written in adulthood and preserved in state archives, reveal a polished elegance but give no hint of any brooding madness.

What historians *do* know about Erzsébet is that in 1571—at the age of eleven, three years before her supposed first pregnancy —she was engaged to marry sixteen-year-old Count Ferencz Nádasdy, in a union arranged by Nádasdy's mother, Baroness Ursula Kanizsay de Kanizsa. Barely literate in Hungarian, Nádasdy spoke German and Latin well enough to negotiate battlefield treaties, but otherwise, in his own mother's estimation, Ferencz was "no scholar."

Some modern accounts say that Nádasdy learned of his fiancée's pregnancy and punished the infant's father—named as László Bende, a servant at the Bathory family's Castle Sárvár—by having him castrated and fed alive to a pack of dogs. If true, that act would not have been out of character for Nádasdy, recognized in later years as a ruthless and sadistic warlord in the style of Wallachian predecessor Vlad the Impaler.

By most accounts, Nádasdy's union with Erzsébet would be a match made in Hell.

***

Erzsébet and Ferencz were married on May 8, 1575, at Sárvár (literally "mud castle"), the Nádasdy family seat in the western Hungarian county of Vas. Erzsébet quickly settled in as mistress of the estate, also residing at various times in other castles and homes maintained by her family and Nádasdy's at Beckov, Bratislava and Čachtice (all now in Slovakia), and in Vienna, Austria. Ferencz, meanwhile, immersed himself in the life of a warrior, ranging far and wide to battle troops of the Ottoman Empire that had captured Belgrade in 1521 and occupied most of central and southern Hungary over the next two decades. In the process, Ferencz earned recognition as the "Black Knight of Hungary"—and loaned large sums to Kings Rudolf II and Matthias II, to bankroll their endless wars against the Turks.

No definitive catalog of Nádasdy's military campaigns exists, but we know that he helped liberate a series of castles and cities held by Ottoman invaders. Those campaigns included the siege and capture of Esztergom and Visegrád in 1595, the conquest of Vác in 1597, the liberation of Székesfehérvár in 1598, and the brief occupation of Győr in 1601. Other forays probably included the Battle of Sisak in June 1593, aiding Michael the Brave in raids along the Lower Danube during 1594, participation in the Battle of Călugăreni (August 1595), the Battle of Keresztes (October 1596), and the Battle of Guruslău (August 1601). Prince Sigismund Báthory of Transylvania also played a key role in planning those campaigns.

Nádasdy's frequent absences from home may help explain the fact that he and Erzsébet produced no children during their first decade of marriage. Daughter Anna was born in 1585, followed in turn by Ursula (named for Nádasdy's mother), son Andrew, and daughter Katalin. The second and third Nádasdy children died young, but not before Erzsébet wrote to Ferencz in May 1596, saying: "I can write to your lordship of Anna and Ursula that they are in good health. But Kate is in misery with her mouth because that rot has appeared, and the rot is even in the bone of her jaw. The barber-surgeon went in with his iron up to the middle of her tooth, and says that she will be fortunate if she does not lose some teeth. Of myself, I can say that I am better than formerly."

Katalin would survive the "rot," joined by brother Paul—another survivor—in 1598. Ferencz saw little of them, but Erzsébet apparently remained an attentive mother and spouse, signing most of her letters to Nádasdy "your loving wife" or "your servant." As befit her royal station, of course, Erzsébet delegated many child-rearing duties to servants, chiefly her own childhood nurse, Helena Jo (often rendered as "Ilona Joo"). Other members of the household, later notorious, were Anna Darvulia of Sárvár (described in some accounts as Erzsébet's lesbian lover), and a dwarf named Janos Ujváry, nicknamed "Ficzko."

It was a motley crew, at best. Stories, spread after the fact, depict Helena Jo as a witch in the mold of Erzsébet's Aunt Klara, prone to sacrificing young children. Another member of Erzsébet's household, Dorothea "Dorka" Szentes, also is described as a witch possessed of unusual physical strength. French author Valentine Penrose, writing in 1962, claimed that Erzsébet carried a parchment made from the caul of a newborn infant, inscribed with a protection spell that read in part: "When I am in danger, send ninety-nine cats. I order you to do so because you are the supreme commander of cats...Order ninety-nine cats to come with speed and bite the heart of King Matthias...And keep Erzsébet safe from harm."

Nine years later, in his book *True Vampires of History,* American writer Donald Glut quoted an alleged letter from Erzsébet to her husband, describing a newly learned black magic ritual. According to Glut, she wrote, "Thurko has taught me a lovely new one. Catch a black hen and beat it to death with a white cane. Keep the blood and smear some on your enemy. If you get no chance to smear it on his body, obtain one of his garments and smear it." If true, this seems to be the only letter ever written by Erzsébet containing any reference to blood.

Glut also joined the chorus of modern authors describing Erzsébet's habit of entertaining both male and female lovers in Nádasdy's absence. Glut describes one such visitor as a pale, long-haired nobleman with a penchant for drinking blood, who supposedly taught the technique to his hostess. Penrose, curiously, disagreed on one point, suggesting that the still unidentified guest was a woman dressed as a man.

Published accounts of Erzsébet's years at Sárvár disagree concerning Ferencz Nádasdy's participation in torture of household servants. No historian disputes his cruelty toward prisoners of war, including execution by impalement, but some claim that he only tolerated Erzsébet's sadism on the home front, while others cast him as her mentor in torment, schooling her in new techniques and even sending her black magic spells from distant lands to try at home. One victim reportedly slain on Nádasdy's order was a sibling of Helena Jo. As described in sworn testimony at trial—

His Lordship had the younger sister undressed until stark naked, while his Lordship looked on with his own eyes; the girl was then covered over with honey and made to stand throughout a day and a night, so that she, due to the great pain she was forced to endure, got the falling sickness. She fell to the ground. His Lordship taught the countess that in such a case one must place pieces of paper dipped in oil between the toes of the girl and set them on fire; even if she was already half dead, she would jump up.

The hotfoot technique was dubbed "kicking stars," from the sparks it produced, while biting insects were employed to torture girls coated with honey. A variation on that theme, reserved for winter, was to douse a bound victim in water and observe her as she froze to death. Over time, Erzsébet developed her own brutal repertoire, employing needles, heated keys and coins, clubs and whips with barbed lashes, among other tools.

Whatever Nádasdy's role in his wife's abuse of female servants, Erzsébet would not hit her stride until after his death—another event shrouded in controversy. Most accounts agree that Ferencz died on or about January 4, 1604, but the cause of death is widely disputed, ranging from wounds suffered in battle to poisoning by his wife. One version claims Nádasdy "fell ill" in 1601 and was bedridden until his passing; another dates the onset of his sickness from December 1603. One attribution of his death to an infected wound blames the injury on a prostitute, enraged when Ferencz failed to pay for her services.

In any case, one day before his death, Nádasdy wrote to Lord Palatine György Thurzó, admonishing him to watch over Erzsébet and their children after Nádasdy was gone. The Black Knight of Hungary could scarcely have predicted where that stewardship would ultimately lead.

\*\*\*

Erzsébet Báthory mourned her husband for all of four weeks, then shocked royal sensibilities by moving to Vienna, where she could enjoy the social whirl of high society. Over the years to come, she would drift back and forth between her castles at Beckov and Čachtice (also known as Csejthe), where she had more privacy for pleasures of the flesh. Meanwhile, she grappled with the Herculean task of managing the Nádasdy estates and guarding them against rapacious neighbors.

One such was Count George Bánffy, a Transylvanian nobleman who had the temerity to usurp one of Erzsébet's smaller properties in January 1606. On February 3, Erzsébet fired off the following letter from her late mother-in-law's castle at Kapuvár.

*Magnifice Domine Nobis Observandissime*

God give you all the best. I must write to you on the following matter: My servant János Csimber arrived home yesterday evening, and he reported to me that you have occupied my estate at Lindva. I do not understand, why have you done this thing? Just do not think, George Bánffy, that I am another Widow Bánffy! Believe me that I will not keep silent, I will let no one take my property. I wanted only to let you know this.

*Ex arce nobis Kapu 3 Feb. 1606.*

*Elizabeta Comittissa de Báthor*

P.S. I know, my good lord, that you have done this thing, have occupied my small estate because you are poor, but do not think that I shall leave you to enjoy it. You will find a man in me.


No record survives of that dispute's resolution, but Erzsébet's reference to the widow of another Bánffy, dispossessed of her property after husband Gáspar Bánffy's death in the 1580s, demonstrates her knowledge of contemporary scandals.

While defending her own estates, Erzsébet pursued King Rudolf II and successor Matthias II with demands for repayment of her husband's loans to the crown of 17,408 *gulden* ($11.5 million today), made to support their wars against the Turks. Both monarchs stalled interminably, pleading for more time, nursing their grudge against the widow who behaved so badly out of character for women of her era. Erzsébet moved to strengthen her position by marrying off daughters Anna and Katalin to Counts Miklos Zrínyi and György Homonnay Drugeth, respectively, but the fate of her fortune rested on young son Paul, who spent most of his time with tutor Imre Megyery (tellingly nicknamed "Imre the Red") at Sárvár. Gábor Báthory's elevation to Prince of Transylvania, in 1608, failed to benefit his niece. Erzsébet had already been forced to sell off her castle at Bratislava, in 1607, followed by another at Beckov in 1609.

Those embarrassing losses probably fueled the rage that Erzsébet directed toward hapless young women. She focused first on female servants, imposing sadistic penalties for the slightest infraction, real or imagined. A maid who fell short of pressing the countess's clothes to perfection might have her face seared with the iron. Inadequate performance of some other simple task, such as sewing or binding straw, demanded repetition performed in the nude, with a jeering audience of male lackeys. Outdoor torture with honey and freezing water persisted, while other victims were beaten or stabbed with hot needles. In once case, Erzsébet reportedly set a maid's pubic hair on fire with a candle. On other occasions, Erzsébet bit the girls in rabid fits of rage, leaving deep wounds.

The worst crime any servant of the countess could commit was trying to escape. The punishment for that offense was always death; the mode of execution was dependent on the time and place. During winter of 1607, one girl fled while Erzsébet was attending the wedding of Count Thurzó's daughter at Bytča. When captured, the fugitive received an ice-water bath that left her frozen stiff. Another, twelve-year-old Pola, escaped from Čachtice castle and was likewise caught. Her fate involved a hanging spherical cage, two small to comfortably sit or stand in, its interior lined with sharp spikes. While Pola was suspended from the rafters, Ficzko swung the ropes and jostled her until her punctured body drained of blood.

Over time, it seems that peasant girls recruited for domestic service were consigned directly to the dungeons of various Báthory castles, specifically as objects of Erzsébet's sadistic amusement. Wherever the countess was staying, Erzsébet's accomplices—Anna Darvulia, Ficzko, Helena Jo, and Dorothea Szentes—roamed through the countryside and nearby villages, offering jobs to any available girls. Some victims were delivered by their parents, as when Mrs. György Szabo of Čachtice sent her two daughters to serve the countess. Other identified procurers included Mrs. Janoz Szabos of Sárvár, who gave up her own daughter, then recruited other girls; Mrs. Istvan Szabo of Vep, who brought in "a great many" victims; Mrs. Janos Barsony of Gyöngös, who also brought "many"; Mrs. Janos Liptay, who furnished "two or three" in full knowledge of their impending fate; Mrs. Janos Szilay of Köcs; Mrs. Miklos Kardos; and an unnamed Croatian woman from Sárvár.

Methods of torture varied according to Erzsébet's whim. She was known to stab servants with needles as they rode in her carriage, to sew their lips shut, burn and cut them, bite them in animalistic rages, force them to eat strips of their own flesh, and starve them to the point of death. Savage beatings claimed the most lives, with Erzsébet demanding that her cronies join in when her arms grew tired or her clothing was blood-soaked. Some victims had their fingers cut or torn off with scissors and pincers, a game particularly favored by Dorothea Szentes. Early victims received Christian burials, until Pastor Janos Ponikenusz balked at their increasing numbers and refused to officiate at any further services. Thereafter, corpses were hidden under beds and floorboards, buried in fields and orchards, or dumped in rivers and canals. Inevitably, some were found, and while no law protected peasant girls from royal slayers, Erzsébet's reputation made it increasingly difficult to obtain willing recruits.

In 1609, a convergence of events laid the groundwork for Erzsébet's eventual downfall. Anna Darvulia sickened and died, depriving Erzsébet of her most ardent accomplice and rumored lesbian lover. Her replacement in both roles, Erzsi Majorova, was the widow of a tenant farmer from Miava, who conveniently shared Erzsébet's sadistic inclinations. She also suggested a new means of obtaining victims, urging Erzsébet to open a "finishing school" at Čachtice for the daughters of lesser nobles, pretending to instruct them in the fine points of courtly etiquette. Some two dozen families lined up to take advantage of the service, little realizing that their daughters would, indeed, be "finished" by the ghoul squad at Čachtice.

During that same year, Erzsébet's cousin by marriage, György Thurzó, ascended to his post as Palatine of Hungary. He owed that promotion to the House of Habsburg, represented by King Matthias II of Hungary and his predecessor, Rudolf II, who had ceded the Hungarian throne but remained in overall command as Holy Roman Emperor, presiding over most of central Europe. The Habsburgs were staunch Roman Catholics, although Matthias tolerated wealthy Protestant families such as the Báthorys. Count Thurzó, despite his blood relationship to Erzsébet and their rumored sexual dalliance, was forced to walk the fine line of religious dissent between Matthias and Rudolf, always judging who could serve him best.

Inevitably, Erzsébet's charm school students fell prey to her murderous rage. When her first boarder died, Erzsébet staged the death to resemble a suicide, but by then she was losing control. In Vienna, while residing at her home on Augustinian Street, Erzsébet heard neighbors praise the talents of young Ilona Harczy, star singer in the choir at the Church of Holy Mary. The countess summoned Harczy for a private performance, but on arrival, the girl developed stage fright in the presence of her infamous hostess. Furious, Erzsébet declared that if Harczy could not sing for her, she would sing for no one. The girl became another victim, slaughtered on the spot.

Other victims died in groups. During summer of 1609, Erzsébet planned to visit Piešťany and enjoy the healing waters of its famous spa. In preparation for that journey, she demanded that the servants who would travel with her undertake an eight-day fast, bathing in cold water and standing nude in the Čachtice castle courtyard overnight to prevent them from sneaking food or drink.

On the day of her departure, Erzsébet found five of the six maids too frail to travel, whereupon she railed at Dorothea Szentes for "carrying things too far." Erzsébet and Szentes then beat five of the girls to death. The sixth survived to reach Piešťany, but died on the return journey, either from starvation or maltreatment suffered at the spa.

At last, with younger noble women added to the list of dead and missing, time was running out.

***

Reports of Erzsébet Báthory torturing young women at her finishing school had reached the royal court by early 1610. Count Thurzó, though reluctant to involve himself, felt pressure from King Matthias and naturally chose to place his family's broader interests above those of one demented cousin-in-law. On March 5, he ordered an official inquiry into Erzsébet's alleged crimes, with testimony commencing on March 22. Over the next three months, thirty-four witnesses from the counties of Bratislava, Gyor, Nitra, Trencin and Veszprem told their stories to chief notary Andrei de Keresztur. The notary's final report, dated September 19, 1610, summarized the charges against Erzsébet by saying that "many young girls and virgins and other women were killed in various ways."

While that inquiry was in progress, on June 7, Báthory sons-in-law Miklos Zrínyi and György Homonnay Drugeth met privately with Count Thurzó, seeking some way to prevent the scandal from touching their families. Thurzó suggested snatching Erzsébet and depositing her in convent, which pleased all concerned, but before that plan could be put into action, Imre Megyery surprised the conspirators, filing a formal complaint against Erzsébet before Hungary's Parliament. Historians account for that move in various ways. Some describe longstanding animosity between Megyery and his employer (who, in turn, may have resented his seeming domination of son Paul Báthory). Others are more charitable, claiming that Megyery simply sought to protect his student's best interests when the nightmare of Erzsébet's madness was finally revealed.

In any case, Megyery's end run forced Count Thurzó to take official notice of Erzsébet's alleged indiscretions. A court of inquiry was held before Judge Antonii Moysis Cziráky de Dienes-falva on October 27, 1610, with testimony implicating several of Erzsébet's retainers at Sárvár.

The ongoing investigation, while theoretically secret, did not escape Erzsébet's notice. On August 19, 1610, she traveled with a widowed noblewoman named Hernath to the court at Vasvár-Szombathel, to testify concerning the death of Madame Hernath's daughter while in Erzsébet's care. Despite allegations that the girl in question had been murdered, Erzsébet convinced the court that she died from natural causes, and her case was not included in Erzsébet's final list of charges.

It was a victory of sorts, but only transitory. Some accounts claim that Erzsébet dictated her last will and testament on September 3, 1610, leaving all of her property and possessions to son Paul, but if so, that document has vanished from the historical record, supplanted by a later will. In October, Erzsébet ordered her jewelry packed up and shipped from Sárvár to Čachtice, which would henceforth be her base of operations as she marshaled her defenses. On November 4, Erzsébet wrote to Prince Gábor Báthory, requesting legal documents detailing her possessions.

Whatever happened next, Erzsébet was not prepared to surrender. That winter, at Čachtice, she still felt confident enough to have the corpses of four recent victims pitched over the castle walls as food for prowling wolves. Local villagers witnessed those dumpings and passed word on to Count Thurzó. Countess Báthory, meanwhile, accustomed now to killing on the slightest whim, prepared to slay her scheming enemies en masse.

The plan, as sketched in testimony at a subsequent trial, was somewhat bizarre. Although Erzsébet was reputedly adept at mixing poisons in small doses, based on observations from accomplice Ficzko, for top-flight assassination she turned to Erszi Majorova, widow of a tenant farmer from Myjava who had joined Erzsébet inner circle following her husband's death. On command from her mistress, Majorova prepared a lethal potion for inclusion in a coffee cake. Prior to baking, Erzsébet reportedly bathed in the mixture, then discarded half the bath water and took another dip in the remainder. The final product was intended for King Matthias and Count Thurzó, during a scheduled visit to Čachtice, but first, Erzsébet tested the cake on several servants. When all survived with nothing worse than bellyaches, she abandoned the plan.

As luck would have it, she had missed her final chance.

\*\*\*

On December 27, 1610, Count Thurzó set out from Bratislava to Čachtice, accompanied by Erzsébet's two sons-in-law, Imre Megyery, and a troop of soldiers. They reached Erzsébet's castle on the evening of December 29, and entered without difficulty, despite the melodramatic accounts set forth in various latter-day novels. Outside the main door, they found the corpse of a servant called Doricza, beaten and stabbed to death for the crime of stealing a pear from Erzsébet's larder. Inside, the raiders found bodies of two more young women. Subsequent tales of a midnight invasion with torture in progress, mass graves, and Count Thurzó cornering Erzsébet in a reeking dungeon are merely fiction. Author Raymond McNally notes that 17th century Calvinist preacher Elias Laszlo, renowned for his detailed diaries, barely mentioned the raid in passing: "1610. 29 December. Elizabeth Bathory was put in the tower behind four walls, because in her rage she killed some of her female servants."

Erzsébet was not the only one arrested. Thurzó's party also bagged Janos Ujváry, Ilona Jo, Dorothea Szentes, and a third suspected accomplice, Katarina Benecsky. Erszi Majorova slipped through the net but was traced and arrested soon after the raid on Čachtice. When Count Thurzó and company left with their prisoners, Erzsébet alone remained in the castle, under guard.

But what was to be done with her?

On January 2, 1611, Thurzó convened the first trial of Erzsébet's accomplices at Bytča, before three local officials: Daniel Eördeögh, Kaspar Kardos, and Kaspar Nagy-Najaky. The proceedings were relatively brief, including testimony from defendants Benecsky, Jo, Szentes and Ujváry, plus that of thirteen locals who had knowledge of young women killed or missing around Čachtice. The four accused confessed their roles in the long killing spree, more or less corroborating each other's testimony with variations. No record has survived of any testimony gleaned from Erszi Majorova. Erzsébet was not present in court, and thus could not refute the charges blaming her for "an unbelievable number of murders." The panel condemned Jo, Szentes and Ujváry, but found insufficient evidence to order Benecsky's execution, decreeing instead that she should be imprisoned pending further judicial action.

A second trial convened on January 7, 1611, with Supreme Court Judge Theodaz Szimma of Szülö presiding over a panel of fifteen jurists. Despite allegations of sorcery and black magic, church authorities declined to try the case or question any witnesses. King Matthias tried repeatedly to place Erzsébet herself on trial, but Count Thurzó doggedly resisted, saying, "As long as I am Lord Palatine in Hungary, this will not come to pass. The families which have won such high honors on the battlefield shall not be disgraced in the eyes of the nation by the murky shadow of this bestial female...In the interest of future generations of Nadasdys everything is to be done in secret. For if a court were to try her, the whole of Hungary would learn of her murders, and it would seem to contravene our laws to spare her life. However, having seen her crimes with my own eyes, I have had to abandon my plan to place her in a convent for the rest of her life."

Witnesses at the second, somewhat longer trial included Count Thurzó, Erzsébet's sons-in-law, Imre Megyery, several visitors to Castle Čachtice, and a rare survivor of Erzsébet's household staff, identified only as "the maiden Zusanna." Aside from describing tortures inflicted by defendants Jo, Szentes and Ujváry, while begging mercy for Katarina Benecsky, Zusanna dropped a bombshell on the court, stating that Jacob Silvassy of Čachtice had found a list of victims in Erzsébet's own handwriting, numbering 650. During her four years of service to the countess, Zusanna testified, at least eighty servants had died under torture at Čachtice to her personal knowledge.

The second court confirmed death sentences for Helena Jo, Dorothea Szentes and Janos Ujváry, citing their "voluntary confessions" and "the ones made under torture," plus the fact that none denied the allegations made against them by other witnesses. Jo and Szentes were sentenced to have the fingers ripped from their guilty hands with red-hot pincers, then to be burned alive. Ujváry, based on his relative youth and participation in fewer slayings, would be mercifully beheaded, then drained of blood before his corpse was cremated. Zusanna's plea for mercy, coupled with an ongoing dearth of evidence, spared Katarina Benecsky from any further punishment. Erszi Majorova, belatedly captured, joined the list of those condemned and executed on January 24, 1611.

Meanwhile, King Matthias continued his agitation for Erzsébet's trial. On January 14, 1611, he ordered Thurzó to begin a new investigation of "the guilty woman responsible for the death of three hundred girls and women born into noble and peasant families." It commenced in February, interrogating 224 new witnesses, and Thurzó delivered his report to Matthias on April 17, recommending that Erzsébet be sentenced to life under house arrest at Castle Čachtice. Matthias countersigned that order, then almost immediately felt the wrath of Hungary's Parliament, pressed by the Catholic Habsburgs to make an example of Erzsébet Báthory. Passing the buck, Matthias sought opinions from his *curia regis* (king's court), and received that body's advice on July 26, 1611. Those learned attorneys wrote:

It is left to Your Majesty's pleasure whether further proceedings should be instituted against the above named Lady with a view towards decapitation, or the present sentence of life imprisonment be left standing and be confirmed, the latter being recommended by the useful and faithful service of her Ladyship's deceased husband, and their daughters' service to Your Majesty, one of whom is married to Miklos Zrinyi, the other to György Homonnay, both Barons of the Realm and faithful and useful servants of Your Majesty.

Finally, after one last hearing on December 17, 1611, Matthias abandoned his efforts to execute Erzsébet and seize her property for the crown. He confirmed the life sentence, formally pronounced to Erzsébet by Count Thurzó at Čachtice, where he told her, "You, Elizabeth, are like a wild animal. You are in the last months of your life. You do not deserve to breathe the air on earth, nor to see the light of the Lord. You shall disappear from this world and shall never reappear in it again. The shadows will envelop you and you will find time to repent your bestial life. I condemn you, Lady of Čachtice, to lifelong imprisonment in your own castle."

Nor would Erzsébet have free run of the place where so many had died. In fact, she was confined within a small room in the castle's tower, its windows bricked over, its only door walled up with the exception of a slot for passing food trays back and forth.

Captivity did not break Erzsébet Báthory's spirit. From her cell, she continued to proclaim her innocence, while greedy relatives picked over her estate. Son Paul and Imre Megyery took control of her castle Sárvár, effectively blocking prosecution of their servants for complicity in any homicides committed there. Erzsébet's sons-in-law seized other Báthory lands, and even Count Thurzó's wife joined in the looting. During January 1613, Baroness

Erzsébet Czobor visited Čachtice and stole items of jewelry, which she sold to finance one of her daughters' lavish weddings. That relatively petty theft inspired Hungary's highest judge, Lord Chief Justice Zsigmond Forgách, to write Thurzó on February 16, 1613, urging him to curb his wife's rapacious appetite.

On July 31, 1614, Countess Báthory summoned two priests from the Esztergom bishopric, Imre Agriensy and Andreas Kerpelich, to witness the signing of her last will and testament. They stood outside her bricked-up cell, under guard, while Erzsébet dictated that her remaining properties should be divided equally among her children, while opposing further administration of her estates by son-in-law György Homonnay Drugeth. That document was formally signed during the feast of Saint Peter in Chains, on August 3, 1614.

Just under three weeks later, on August 21, a guard peered through the feeding slot in Erzsébet's door and saw her sprawled facedown on the floor. Dead at age fifty-four, Erzsébet was reportedly buried in a vault beneath the main church in Čachtice, then exhumed three years later and moved to the Nádasdy family crypt at Nyírbátor. An expedition to locate her corpse found nothing in the Čachtice crypt, when it was opened on July 7, 1938. Likewise, when Erzsébet's supposed grave at Nyírbátor was opened in 1995, it proved to be empty.

Erzsébet Báthory outlived her uncle Gábor, assassinated at Oradea on October 27, 1613, by two Balkan outlaws, reportedly paid to kill him by political rival András Ghiczy. King Matthias succeeded Rudolf as Holy Roman Emperor in July 1612, ruling until his death at Vienna in March 1619. György Thurzó survived his infamous cousin-in-law by two years and four months, dying in Bytča at age forty-nine, on Christmas Eve 1616.

*** 

The court judgment of January 7, 1611, referred to "the satanic terror against Christian blood and horrifying cruelties unheard of among the female sex since the world began, which Elizabeth

Bathory, widow of the much-esteemed and highly-considered Ferenc Nadasdy, perpetrated upon her serving maids, other women and innocent souls, whom she extirpated from this world in almost unbelievable numbers." But how many victims, finally, died at her hands and those of her accomplices?

No trace of the murder diary listing 300, 612 or 650 victims survives today. Purported quotes from that diary—including a reference to Erzsébet's disappointment when one maid died quickly under torture, noting that "she was too small"—appear in various histories without supporting documents. In 2009, a spokesman for Hungary's National Archives denied any knowledge of the diary, but confirmed that reports of its possession by a private collector in Nagyszombat (now Trnava, Slovakia) were merely idle gossip.

We are left, then, with the testimony of Count Thurzó and his raiding party, who discovered three fresh corpses in December 1610, and the admissions of Erzsébet's accomplices, some extracted under torture, as to how many servants were slain in their presence. At trial, Janos Ujváry claimed that "some thirty-seven" girls were killed during his sixteen years of service with the countess. Dorothea Szentes recalled the deaths of thirty-six, while Helena Jo had counted "fifty-one, perhaps more." Katarina Benecsky kept no tally of murders, but guessed that fifty girls were slain during her time in the Báthory household. Witness Zusanna, meanwhile, remembered at least eighty victims killed during her four years of service to the countess.

How are such relatively modest tallies reconciled with the much higher numbers reported by various authors? Raymond McNally, writing in 1983, suggested one possible answer.

Did the culprits deliberately underestimate the number in order to soften the blow? Not at all! The reason is simple: most previous experts assumed that Elizabeth began torturing and killing servant girls only in the year 1604 when she became a widow. This would have meant one hundred deaths per year—certainly a rather high number, even in those days of badly treated servants. But from the evidence available today it is clear that Elizabeth was torturing and killing girls from her adolescence onward, and continued unhampered until stopped by Count Thurzo, late in her life.

Conversely, some latter-day defenders of Erzsébet Báthory deny that any murders occurred. In that scenario, the Protestant Erzsébet was marked for a frame-up by Catholic monarchs who coveted her property and owed her a fortune in debts they would never repay, once she was safely walled up at Čachtice. Similar defenses have been mounted on behalf of 15th-century child killer Gilles de Rais, and with greater credibility for the Knights Templar, bankers for the early Roman church, executed en masse on charges of idolatry and sorcery, in 1307. Even Raymond McNally, who pronounced Erzsébet guilty of hundreds of murders, suggests that the trials of 1611 were manipulated by "the secret conspiracy that had been formed among Imre Megyery at Sarvar, \ relatives, and Count Thurzo." The latter group, presumably, hoped to save Erzsébet's treasure for themselves, rather than see it lost to the Habsburg Empire.

*\*\**

From those murky and contradictory sources, a chilling gothic legend has emerged over successive centuries. Today, Erzsébet Báthory is known primarily from tales spun long after her death, including an embellishment not raised by any witnesses at trial. According to those stories, Erzsébet despaired at growing old and sought to halt the march of time by bathing in the blood of slaughtered virgins. Some accounts, tinged with the supernatural, claim that she slashed a young maid's face one day and noticed, while wiping the blood from her hands, that it made her skin appear more youthful. From then on, the spinners of fiction maintain, Erzsébet was hell-bent on a regimen of bloodbaths to preserve her beauty.

That fable first surfaced 115 years after Erzsébet's death, in 1729, when Jesuit scholar László Turóczi examined Erzsébet's case in his *Tragica Historia*. Matthias Bel quoted Turóczi in his four-volume *Notitia Hungariae novae historico geographica* (1742), but questioned details of the priest's account. Verbatim testimony from the Hungarian trials resurfaced in 1765, published for the first time in Prague, during June and July 1817, and while those transcripts contained no mention of bloodbaths, the legend endured. British author John Paget devoted a chapter to Erzsébet's crimes in his *Hungary and Transylvania* (1839), followed by a treatment in Rev. Sabine Baring-Gould's *The Book of Werewolves* (1854). Writing in an era when women were deemed incapable of killing for sadistic pleasure, those writers reduced Erzsébet's actions to a case of female vanity run amok.

One tenuous link between Countess Báthory and vampirism lies in reports of her family's association with Vlad Tepes (1431-76), the real-life model for Bram Stoker's *Dracula*. Better known to history as Vlad the Impaler, Tepes belonged to the House of Drăculeşti, which used the patronymic "Dracul"—Dragon—derived from the Order of the Dragon, founded in 1408 to battle Ottoman Turks and other enemies of Christianity. A patent of nobility granted to the House of Drăculeşti by Holy Roman Emperor Ferdinand I, in January 1535, describes the clan's ancient symbol as identical to that of the Báthory family, a sword covering three wolf's teeth.

Beyond that document, history notes that a cousin of Erzsébet's, Stephen Báthory of Ecsed (1430-93), led 8,000 infantry and 13,000 cavalry in a 1476 campaign that helped Vlad Tepes capture Târgovişte, the capital of Wallachia. In November of that year, Vlad and Stephen pledged eternal loyalty to one another in their war against the Turks, but Vlad's end of that bargain fell through a month later, with his death in battle outside Bucharest.

Most modern authors dealing with Erzsébet's life and crimes have produced works of fiction, including Jozo Niznansky's *The Lady of Čachtice* (1932); Kálmán Vándor's *Báthory Erzsébet* (1940); *La Comtesse sanglante,* by Valentine Penrose (1962), Alejandra Pizarnik's *Acerca's de la Contessa sangrienta* (1968); *Comtesse de Sang,* by Maurice Périsset (1975); Andrei Codrescu's *The Blood Countess* (1995); *Ella, Drácula,* by Javier García Sanchez (2002); Alisa Libby's *The Blood Confession* (2006); Alexandre Heredia's *O Legado de Báthory* (2007); *The Countess,* by Rebecca Johns (2010); Maria Szabó's *Én, Báthory Erzsébet* (2010); and *The Blood Countess* by Tara Moss (2012).

Erzsébet's case was also a natural for dramatic presentation, spawning at least ten stage plays between 1865 and 2010. On movie screens, Britain's Hammer Films premiered with *Countess Dracula* in 1970, followed by *Necropolis* (1970), *Daughters of Darkness* (1971), *Blood Castle* (1973), *Thirst* (1979), *The Bloody Lady* (1980), *Bloodbath* (1999), *Báthory* (2000), *Eternal* (2004), *Báthory* (2008), *The Countess* (2009), and *The Bloody Countess* (2011). None of those productions should be mistaken for straightforward history, but they teach us a valuable lesson.

**Legends are more durable than flesh and blood.**

# Meet the Authors

## Peter Vronsky

**Peter Vronsky, Ph.D.** is a criminal justice historian, filmmaker and the author of two bestselling histories of serial homicide, _Serial Killers: The Method and Madness of Monsters_ and _Female Serial Killers: How and Why Women Become Monsters_.

"Serial Killer Zombie Apocalypse" is a preview from his forthcoming book for Berkley Books at Penguin Random House, on the history of serial killing since 2001, **_Serial Killer Chronicles: A New History of Serial Murder Today_**. Peter Vronsky teaches in the history department of Ryerson University in Toronto where he lectures on the history of terrorism and espionage in international relations.

**Peter Vronsky books can be found on** www.petervronsky.com
**Websites** www.petervronsky.org **and** www.SerialKillerChronicles.com
**Facebook** www.facebook.com/killersbypetervronsky

# Dane Ladwig

**Dane Ladwig** resides in DuPage County, Illinois USA. He holds degrees in English, Philosophy, and Theology. He is an Ordained Chaplain and a member of the American Legion Robert E. Coulter, Jr. Post 1941 Legion Riders. Dane Ladwig is also a member in good standing of the prestigious Chicago Writer's Association. Dane is an accomplished author who has confronted society's most heinous criminals. His riveting interviews and intensive research exposes compelling aspects of killers seldom considered by devotees or experts of criminal justice.

His new book, *Dr. H. H. Holmes and the Whitechapel Ripper*, postulates a convincing and irrefutable link between two nineteenth-century serial killers; Herman Webster Mudgett a.k.a. Dr. H. H. Holmes and Jack the Ripper. An innovative newcomer to the true-crime scene, Dane Ladwig has been the recipient of critical acclaim from the General Assembly for his literary successes.

**Website**  http://www.daneladwig.com/
**Blog**  http://daneladwig.wordpress.com/

**Facebook** https://www.facebook.com/AuthorDaneAllenLadwig

# Sylvia Perrini

**Sylvia Perrini** is an author, historian, wife and mother to two sons and two daughters. Sylvia, studied history and law at Manchester University and developed a particular interest in women who live outside the common boundaries of society.

Sylvia divides her time between the New Forest, Hampshire, UK. and the Mediterranean island of Mallorca, Spain. Here she spends her time reading, writing and painting.

Sylvia is the queen of true crime writers as it relates to female serial killers with thirty books written, which include:

*I don't like Mondays: Female Rampage Killers*

*Women Serial Killers Through The Time*

*Women Serial Killers of The 20th Century*

**Author Page** http://www.amazon.com/SYLVIA-PERRINI/e/B007WRWEI0

**Facebook** https://www.facebook.com/AuthorSylviaPerrini

**Website** http://sylviaperrini.goldmineguides.com/

# Michael Newton

**Michael Newton, Ph.D.** has published 215 books under his own name and various pseudonyms since 1977. He began writing professionally as a "ghost" for author Don Pendleton on the best-selling Executioner series and continues his work on that series today. With 104 episodes published to date, Newton has nearly tripled the number of Mack Bolan novels completed by creator Pendleton himself. While 156 of Newton's published books have been novels--including westerns, political thrillers and psychological suspense--he is best known for nonfiction, primarily true crime and reference books. He has written many books on serial killers including:

*The Encyclopedia of Serial Killers (Facts on File Crime Library)*

*The Encyclopedia of Unsolved Crimes (Facts on File Crime Library*

*The Encyclopedia of Crime Scene Investigation*

**Website** http://michaelnewton.homestead.com/

**Author Page** http://www.amazon.com/Michael-Newton/e/B001IXMYNO

**Facebook** https://www.facebook.com/MichaelNewtonAuthor

# RJ Parker

**RJ Parker, P.Mgr.,CIM,** is most well known for his books, *TOP CASES of The FBI* (Winner of the World Book Awards 2012), *Cold Blooded Killers* and *Serial Killers Case Files*.

Born and raised in Newfoundland, he now resides in Oshawa and St. John's, Canada. To date, RJ has donated over 1,800 books to allied troops serving overseas and to our wounded warriors recovering in Naval and Army hospitals all over the world. He also donates a percentage of royalties to Victims of Violent Crimes. He's a proud dad to two daughters and two twin sons, two grandsons and a granddaughter on the way. RJ's books are available on all book markets in eBook, Paperback and Audio.

**Facebook** http://www.facebook.com/AuthorRJParker

**Website** - www.RJParker.Net

**Amazon Author's Page** -
http://www.amazon.com/author/rjparkertruecrime

**A special Thank You to our beta readers and loyal fans:**

Andrea Carver

Angela Vangelisto

Claire Woodman

JoAnn Brown

Mary Daniels

Shelly Little

Sue Ann Sipin

Susan Barclay

Thank you for purchasing and reading the first annual SERIAL KILLERS TRUE CRIME ANTHOLOGY 2014. If you enjoyed this book, please take a moment and leave a review. Your consideration would be much appreciated. Thanks again for your support.

*Michael Newton*

*Sylvia Perrini*

*RJ Parker*

*Peter Vronsky*

# References

**Timothy Wayne [McBride] "T.K." Krajcir**
    Campbell, Jessica. Lynn, Samantha. McCarthy, Ryan. 2011.
Department of Psychology Radford University. 11 14. Accessed 2013.
http://semissourian.com/images/misc/solved/1983-letter.pdf.

    Encyclopedia, Wikipedia the free. 2013. Oedipus Complex. July 2.
Accessed July 9, 2013. http://en.wikipedia.org/wiki/Oedipus_complex.

    Estrada, Ismael. 2007. CNN.com/US How serial killer stumped cops
for decades. December 17. Accessed June 25, 2013.
http://www.cnn.com/2007/US/12/17/serial.killer/.

    Images

    Image one – Krajcir

    1979 photo – St. Louis Post-Dispatch

    stltoday.com St. Louis, MO. Police Handout. Accessed 7-29-2013

    http://www.stltoday.com/news/multimedia/timothy-krajcir/image_3588dcfd-86f4-5ec8-8bfa-595eb365916b.html

    Image two – Krajcir

    2007 photo – St. Louis Post-Dispatch

    stltoday.com St. Louis, MO. Police Handout. Accessed 7-29-2013

    http://www.stltoday.com/news/multimedia/timothy-krajcir/image_56a3807a-cf06-537e-bb49-cdcbf720e299.html

    Image three – four – Pontiac

    Photographic Images of Pontiac Correctional

    Proeber, David. The Pentagraph. Used by permission.

    Pentagraph.com. Accessed 6-24-2013

    http://www.pantagraph.com/news/local/media-takes-look-inside-pontiac-correctional-center/article_7a7472d4-98ca-11e2-b8e5-0019bb2963f4.html

    Image five – six (Letter)

    Letter from Paul M. Gross M.D.

Jessica Campbell, Samantha Lynn, & Ryan McCarthy

Department of Psychology

Radford University

Radford, VA 24142-6946

http://maamodt.asp.radford.edu/Psyc%20405/serial%20killers/Krajcir,%20Timothy.pdf

Image – (Victims)

Montage of Victims –

Murderpedia.org

http://www.murderpedia.org/male.K/k/krajcir-timothy-victims.htm

## Erzsébet Báthory

Kimberly L. Craft, *Infamous Lady: The True Story of Countess Erzsébet Báthory*. CreateSpace, 2009.

Kimberly L. Craft, *The Private Letters of Countess Erzsébet Báthory*. CreateSpace, 2011.

Donald F. Glut, *True Vampires of History*. Castle, 1971.

Raymond T. McNally, *Dracula Was a Woman: In Search of the Blood Countess of Transylvania*. McGraw Hill, 1983.

Valentine Penrose and Alexander Trocchi, *The Bloody Countess: Atrocities of Erzsebet Bathory*. Solar Books, 2006.

## Manuel Pardo, Jr.

Gary Nelson, "Confessions Of A Serial Killer: A First Person Account." CBS Miami, Dec. 10, 2012, http://miami.cbslocal.com/2012/12/10/confessions-of-a-serial-killer-a-first-person-account (accessed June 25, 2013).

David Ovalle, "Manuel Pardo: The saga of a Sweetwater ex-cop convicted of mass murder, now set for execution," *Miami Herald,* Dec. 8, 2012.

cop.html#storylink=cpy

*Pardo v. State*, 563 So.2d 77 (Fla. 1990).

*Pardo v. State*, 941 So.2d 1057 (Fla. 2006).

*Pardo v. Secretary, Florida Dept. of Corrections*, 587 F.3d 1093 (11th Cir. 2009).

*Rolando Garcia v. State of Florida*, No. SC95136 (Fla. 2002).


## Frank Spisak

Brief of Respondent for Smith v Spisak, 08-724, http://www.americanbar.org/content/dam/aba/publishing/preview/publiced_prev iew_briefs_pdfs_07_08_08_724_Respondent.authcheckdam.pdf (accessed June 2, 2013).

"Frank G. Spisak Jr.," http://www.clarkprosecutor.org/html/death/US/spisak1241.htm (accessed June 25, 2013).

John Hyduk, "The Long Goodbye." *Cleveland Magazine* (May 2007), https://www.clevelandmagazine.com/ME2/dirmod.asp? sid=586CA122EB394032BD4AA3B686FF03D9&nm=Editorial&type=Publishi ng&mod=Publications%3A %3AArticle&mid=1578600D80804596A222593669321019&tier=4&id=15F50 389F2414857B385B36F667F136D (accessed June 25, 2013).

Jared Klaus. "Cheating Death: A cross-dressing Nazi murdered a prosecutor's dad 25 years ago. He's back." *Cleveland Scene*. Dec. 6, 2006.


## Robert Pickton

RCMP
    http://www.rcmp-grc.gc.ca/index-eng.htm

Missing Women Commission Of Inquiry
    http://www.missingwomeninquiry.ca/obtain-report/

The Pig Farm: Robert Pickton Serial Killer Documentary

http://www.youtube.com/watch?v=eyr1stchTZI&feature=c4-overview&playnext=1&list=TLKKnH_I1scTs

National Post newspaper
    http://www.nationalpost.com/index.html


## Mary Beth

Cries Unheard: Why Children Kill: The Story of Mary Bell

Gitta Sereny

Publisher:Picador; 1st edition (April 15, 2000)


Documentary; The Mary Bell Case

Blakeway Productions for the BBC


The Telegraph

09 Jan 2009

http://www.trutv.com/library/crime/notorious_murders/famous/bell/index_1.html

Shirley Lynn Scott

The Guardian

30 April 1998

BBC NEWS

http://news.bbc.co.uk/2/hi/uk_news/3043567.stm


## Bloody Benders

2013. 10 Most Common Traits of Potential Serial Killers. May 14. http://listverse.com/2013/01/02/10-most-common-traits-of-potential-serial-killers/.

2013. Cholera Outbreaks and Pandemics. May 2. http://en.wikipedia.org/wiki/Cholera_outbreaks_and_pandemics.

2003 -2013. Legends of America. http://www.legendsofamerica.com/ks-benders.html.

2013. Pseudobulbar Affect. May 7. http://en.wikipedia.org/wiki/Pseudobulbar_affect.


## Anthony Sowell

http://blog.cleveland.com/metro/2009/11/neighbors_wonder_how_stench_of.html

http://www.cnn.com/2009/CRIME/11/04/ohio.cleveland.bodies/

http://www.cbsnews.com/8301-504083_162-5495923-504083.html

http://www.cleveland.com/anthony-sowell/index.ssf/2011/07/anthony_sowells_interrogation_by_police_transcript.html

http://birminghamtimesonline.com/index.php?option=com_content&view=article&id=5973%3Aex-girlfriend-slayings-suspect-often-bled&catid=36%3Anational-news-headlines&Itemid=96&showall=1

http://www.wkyc.com/news/specials/imperialmurders/

http://www.youtube.com/watch?v=KA1uFpfzfTk

http://www.cleveland.com/metro/index.ssf/2012/09/sowell_opens_up_to_psychologis.html

**Martha Wise**

Murderpedia

http://murderpedia.org/female.W/w/wise-martha.htm

Find a Death

http://www.findadeath.com/forum/showthread.php?13139-Martha-Wise

http://www.crimezzz.net/serialkillers/W/WISE_martha.php

The Unknown History of MISANDRY

http://unknownmisandry.blogspot.com.es/2011/09/martha-wise-ohio-serial-killer-murdered.html

Women Behaving Badly: True Tales of Cleveland's Most Ferocious Female Killers

By John Stark Bellamy,

Publisher:Gray & Company Publishers (31 Oct 2005)

\*\*\*

# Endnotes

[1]   Edmund Kemper interview in *Killing of America*, directed by Sheldon Renan and Leonard Schrader, Filmlink International - Towa Productions: 90 min, 1982.

[2]   Brian Meehan, "Son of Cain or Son of Sam? The Monster as Serial Killer in Beowulf", *Connecticut Review,* Connecticut State University, Fall issue, 1994;  Dirk C. Gibson, *Legends, Monsters, or Serial Murderers?  The Real Story behind and Ancient Crime,* Santa Barbara, CA:  Praeger, 2012.

[3]   M.A. Farber, "Leading the Hunt in Atlanta's Murders', *New York Times*, 3 May 1981.

[4]   On the coining of the term "serial killer" see: Peter Vronsky, *Serial Killers: The Method and Madness of Monsters,* New York: Berkley-Penguin Group, 2004.  pp. 327-329. www.petervronsky.com

[5]   On the serial killer "epidemic" Ginger Strand, *Killer on the Road: Violence and the American Interstate*, Austin, TX: University of Texas Press, 2012.  (Kindle Locations 1459-1470). Kindle Edition; and Peter Vronsky, *Serial Killers*, pp. 23-27

[6]   Janet McClellan, *Erotophonophilia: Investigating Lust Murder,* Amherst, NY:  Cambria Press, 2010. (Kindle Location 85). Kindle Edition.

[7]

http://www.ucrdatatool.gov/Search/Crime/State/RunCrimeStat ebyState.cfm  For claims serial murder is declining, see for example: James Alan Fox and Jack Levin, *Extreme Killing: Understanding Serial and Mass Murder,* Sake Publications, 2011

[8]   Eric W. Hickey, *Serial Murderers and Their Victims,* Sixth Edition, Belmont, CA: Wadsworth, 2013.  p.221.

[9]   Hickey (2013), p. 11.

[10]   Uniform Crime Reports (UCR), FBI. http://www.fbi.gov/about-us/cjis/ucr/

[11] Ginger Strand, (Kindle Locations 1706-1707); Hickey (2013), p. 239

[12] Eric W. Hickey, *Serial Murderers and Their Victims,* Fifth Edition, Belmont, CA: Wadsworth, 2010. p.187

[13] Paul D. MacLean, *The Triune Brain in Evolution: Role in Paleocerebral Functions*, New York: Plenum, 1990.

[14] Paul D. MacLean, "New findings relevant to the evolution of psycho-sexual functions

of the brain", *Journal of Nervous and Mental Disease*, Volume 135, Issue 4, 1962. pp. 289–301.

[15] J. Money, "Forensic sexology: Paraphilic Serial Rape (Biastophilia) and Lust Murder (erotophonophilia)", *American Journal of Psychotherapy*, (Jan 1990), Volume 44, pp. 26–36.

[16] L. Miller, "The Predator's Brain: Neuropsychodynamics of Serial Killing," in Louis B. Schlesinger (Ed.), *Serial Offenders: Current Thought, Recent Findings* (pp. 135–166). Boca Raton, FL: CRC Press, (2000). p. 158

[17] Quoted in Peter Vronsky, *Serial Killers,* p. 267

[18] On the DNA evidence for interbreeding between *homo sapien* and *homo Neanderthal* see http://www.eva.mpg.de/neandertal/draft-neandertal-genome.html

[19] Akop P. Nazaretyan, "Western and Russian Traditions of Big History: A Philosophical Insight", *Journal for General Philosophy of Science,* (2005) Vol. 36, pp. 63-80 and "Fear of the Dead as a Factor in Social Self-Organization", *Journal for the Theory of Social Behaviour*, Vol. 35, Issue 2, 2005, pp. 155-169

[20] M.A. Farber, "Leading the Hunt in Atlanta's Murders', *New York Times*, 3 May 1981, *New York Times* online, Proquest search, 31 December 2012.

[21] Vronsky, *Serial Killers,* pp. ix-xx.

22   Robert D. Keppel and Richard Walter, "Profiling Killers: A Revised Classification Model for Understanding Sexual Murder", *International Journal of Offender Therapy and Comparative Criminology*, 43(4), (1999) pp. 417-437.  p. 435

23   Interview with Fezzani, in Barbara Necek, *Serial Killers*, documentary film, Patrick Spica Productions, 2009.

24   *New York Times Online,* Proquest searches, 31 December 2012.

25   See photo at: http://en.wikipedia.org/wiki/File:Johnwaynegacyrosalynncarter.jpg

26   Derf Backderf, *My Friend Dahmer,* New York: Abrams, 2012.  pp. 96-97

27   Stephen Singular, *Unholy Messenger: The Life and Crimes of the BTK Killer*, New York: Simon & Schuster, 2006. pp. 101-102

28   Peter Vronsky, *Female Serial Killers: How and Why Women Become Monsters,* New York: Berkley-Penguin Group, 2007. p. 4, 15.

29   Federal Bureau of Investigation (FBI), *Serial Murder: Multidisciplinary Perspectives for Investigators,* Behavioral Analysis Unit, National Center for Analysis of Violent Crime (NCAVC), Department of Justice, Washington DC: 2008.  pp. 4-9

30   Hickey (2010), p. 27

31   Hickey (2013), p. 221.

32   Catherine Purcell & Bruce A. Arrigo, *The Psychology of Lust Murder: Paraphilia, Sexual Killing, and Serial Homicide*, New York: Elsevier Press, 2006. Kindle Edition. p.26; Robert K. Ressler, Ann W. Burgess, and John E. Douglas, *Sexual Homicide: Patterns and Motives,* Lexington, MA: Lexington Books, 1988. Free Press Kindle Edition. (Kindle Locations 1048-1049).

[33] American Psychiatric Association, *Diagnostic and Statistical Manual of Mental Disorders,* Fifth Edition, *(DSM-5),* American Psychiatric Publishing, 2013.

[34] Hickey (2013), p. 157

[35] Janet McClellan, *Erotophonophilia: Investigating Lust Murder,* Amherst, NY: Cambria Press, 2010. (Kindle Locations 173-178). Kindle Edition.

[36] Vronsky, *Serial Killers,* p. 169.

[37] Vronsky, *Serial Killers,* p. 164.

[38] Quoted in Donald T. Lunde, *Murder and Madness,* New York: Walker, 1976. p. 90.

[39] Vronsky, *Serial Killers,* p. 244

[40] Vronsky, *Serial Killers,* p. 32

[41] C. Crepault and M. Couture, "Men's Erotic Fantasies", *Archives of Sexual Behavior,* Vol. 9, Issue 6, 1980. pp. 565-581

[42] Craig S. Neumann and Robert D.Hare , "Psychopathic traits in a large community sample: Links to violence, alcohol use, and intelligence", *Journal of Consulting and Clinical Psychology*, Vol 76, Issue 5, 2008. pp 893–9.

[43] J. Coid, M. Yang, S. Ullrich, and R. Hare "Prevalence and correlates of psychopathic traits in the household population of Great Britain", *International Journal of Law and Psychiatry*, Volume 32, Issue 2, 2009. pp 65–73.

[44] Hickey (2013), p. 224; 292.

[45] Lee Mellor, *Cold North Killers: Canadian Serial Murder,* Toronto: Dundurn Press, 2012.

[46] Robert K. Ressler, Ann W. Burgess, and John E. Douglas, *Sexual Homicide: Patterns and Motives,* Lexington, MA: Lexington Books, 1988.

[47] Vronsky, *Serial Killers,* p. 110

[48]  R. Langevin, "A study of the psychosexual characteristics of sex killers: Can we identify them before it is too late?", *International Journal of Offender Therapy and Comparative Criminology*, Vol 47, Issue 4, 2003. pp 366–382. p. 368

[49]  Ian Brady, *The Gates of Janus: Serial Killing and Its Analysis*, Los Angeles: Feral House, 2001, pp. 87–88.

[50]  Hickey (2013), p. 226

[51]  Hans Dollinger, *The Decline and Fall of Nazi Germany and Imperial Japan,* New York: Bonanza Books, 1965. p. 422

[52]  http://www.spiegel.de/international/germany/crystal-meth-origins-link-back-to-nazi-germany-and-world-war-ii-a-901755.html

[53]  For the debate on the role of women as spousal enablers of genocidal killers in the Third Reich see: Claudia Koonz, *Mothers in the Fatherland: Women, the Family and Nazi Politics,* London: Jonathan Cape, 1987; Atina Grossmann, "Feminist Debates about Women and National Socialism," *Gender and History* 3:3 (1991), pp. 350-58; Adelheird von Saldern, "Victims or Perpetrators? Controversies about the Role of Women in the Nazi State," in David Crew (ed.), *Nazism and German Society 1933-1945*, London: Routledge, 1994, pp. 141-64; Gisela Bock, "Ordinary Women in Nazi Germany: Perpetrators, Victims, Followers, and Bystanders," in *Women in the Holocaust*, Dalia Ofer and Lenore J. Weitzman (eds.), New Haven: Yale University Press, 1998, pp. 85-100; Vandana Joshi, "The Private Becomes Public: Wives as Denouncers in the Third Reich," *Journal of Contemporary History*, Vol. 37, No. 3 (July 2002), pp. 419-435. On "gendered performativity" and social construction in war crime prosecutions of female Nazi perpetrators, see: Peter Vronsky, *Female Serial Killers: How and Why Women Become Monsters,* New York: Berkley-Penguin Books, 2007, pp. 378-394; Alexandra Przyrembel, "Transfixed by an Image: Ilse Koch, the 'Kommandeuse of Buchenwald,'" *German History,* Vol. 19, No.3, 2001, pp. 369-399

[54]   Raul Hilberg, *The Destruction of the European Jews,* (3 volumes), New York: Homles & Meirer, 1985,   p. 1219

[55]   For petting zoos, see: Ernst Klee, Willi Dressen, Volker Ries, 'Schöne Zeiten': Judenmord aus des Sicht der Täter und Gaffer, translated to English 'Those Were the Days': The Holocaust As Seen by the Perpetrators and Bystanders, London:  Hamish Hamilton, 1993, pp. 226; For swimming pool with high diving board, see: Jean-Claude Pressac, *Auschwitz:Technique and operation of the gas chambers,* The Beate Klarsfeld Foundation, 1989,  p. 509 [online: http://www.mazal.org/Pressac/Pressac0509.htm ]

[56]   R.P. Brittain, "The Sadistic Murderer", *Medicine, Science and the Law,* (1970), Vol. 10, pp. 198-207;  R. Langevin, M. H. Ben-Aron, P. Wright, V. Marchese, L. Handy, "The Sex Killer", *Annals of Sex Research,* Clark Institute of Psychiatry, Toronto, 1988, Volume 1, Issue 2, pp 263-301.

[57]   P. E. Dietz, B. Harry, R. R. Hazelwood, "Detective Magazines: Pornography for the Sexual Sadist?" *Journal of Forensic Sciences,* Vol. 31, Issue 1, January 1986, pp. 197-211.

[58]   For example see:  Adam Parfrey, *It's A Man's World:  Men's Adventure Magazines, the Postwar Pulps,* Los Angeles:  Feral House, 2003;  Tom Brinkman, *Bad Mags 2,* London: Headpress, 2009; David Saunders, *Norman Saunders,* St. Louis, MO: The Illustrated Press, 2008 or Google Images: "pulp adventure detective magazines"

[59]   P. E. Dietz, B. Harry, R. R. Hazelwood.

[60]   Tom Brinkman, pp. 501-537

[61]

http://en.wikipedia.org/wiki/American_mutilation_of_Japanese_war_dead

[62]   Simon Harrison, "Skull Trophies of the Pacific War: Transgressive Objects of Remembrance," *Journal of the Royal Anthropological Institute,* Vol. 12, Issue 4 (2006), pp. 817-836.

63  J. Robert Lilly, *Taken by Force: Rape and American GIs in Europe,* New York: Palgrave Macmillan, 2007.

64  See Anthony Bianco, *Ghosts of 42nd Street: A History of America's Most Famous Block,* New York: HarperCollins, 2004 and Robert Stone, *Prime Green: Remembering the Sixties,* New York: HarperCollins, 2007, for their descriptions of New York's 'tenderloin' on 42nd Street and the Bowery during the 1960s and 1970s.

65  Tom Brinkman, *Bad Mags 2,* pp. 538-557

66  The master account of Harvey Glatman is by Michael Newton, *Rope: The Twisted Life and Crimes of Harvey Glatman,* New York: Pocket Books, 1998.

67  The photographs can be viewed at: http://www.murderpedia.org/male.G/g/glatman-harvey-photos-2.htm

68  http://www.silviapettem.com/books.html

69  Jeff Bahr, Troy Taylor, Loren Coleman, Mark Sceurman, Mark Moran, *Weird Virginia,* New York: Sterling Publishing Company, 2007. p. 104.

70  Peter Vronsky, *Serial Killers,* p. 281

71  Catherine Purcell and Bruce A. Arrigo, *The Psychology of Lust Murder: Paraphilia, Sexual Killing, and Serial Homicide,* New York: Elsevier, 2006, p. 26. Kindle Edition

72  Steven A. Egger, *The Killers among Us: An Examination of Serial Murder and Its Investigation,* Upper Saddle River, N.J.: Prentice-Hall, 1998, pp. 74–75.

73  Vronsky, *Serial Killers,* p. 41

74  Ginger Strand, *Killer on the Road: Violence and the American Interstate,* Austin, TX: University of Texas Press, 2012. [Kindle Edition]

75  Hickey (2013), p. 237

76  Strand, (Kindle Locations 892-894).